What does it mean when the person you are talking to points his feet away from you?

Where is the best place to stand in a room if you want people to notice you?

What are the most common signs of female/male sexual interest?

What are the five strategies for seeming interested in a boring business meeting?

When is smiling an attractor—and when is it a turnoff?

Could an innocent head tilt send the message that you're easily manipulated?

THE POWER OF BODY LANGUAGE

America's body language expert

TONYA REIMAN

shows you how to get the power to send and receive the messages you want—and never be left in the dark again.

Body language expert **Tonya Reiman** is a weekly Fox News Channel contributor. A motivational speaker, consultant, and corporate trainer, she has also appeared on *The O'Reilly Factor,* the *Today* show, *Access Hollywood, Extra, Fast Money,* and other television shows. She has been heard on ESPN radio and has contributed to national publications including *The New York Times, The Wall Street Journal,* and *Time.* She lives in Long Island with her husband and three children. Visit her website: www.ThePowerofBodyLanguage.com.

This title is also available as an eBook

TONYA REIMAN

THE POWER OF BODY LANGUAGE

HOW TO SUCCEED IN EVERY BUSINESS AND SOCIAL ENCOUNTER

POCKET BOOKS
New York London Toronto Sydney

Pocket Books
A Division of Simon & Schuster, Inc.
1230 Avenue of the Americas
New York, NY 10020

First Pocket Books trade paperback edition January 2009

Designed by Jan Pisciotta

Manufactured in the United States of America

10 9 8 7 6

ISBN-13: 978-1-4165-6109-5 (pbk)
ISBN-10: 1-4165-6109-9 (pbk)

To Kenny, my love, best friend, and husband.
You keep me centered and nurtured as only
a soul mate can. I carry you in my heart.

To my three hunnybunns, Stephanie, Christian, and
Jaidan, you are my sunshine. You are each
made up of unconditional compassion,
love, goodness, honesty, determination,
and beauty. I am grateful you
are a part of my life.

Acknowledgments

I would like to thank:

My mother, Denise, who loves me for two and never let me believe there was anything I couldn't do. My stepfather, Joe, for his unending encouragement and love. My mother- and father-in-law, Carol and Ken, who have given me love and support from the moment I became a part of their family. My sister- and brother-in-law, Lisa and Michael, who have been there at every crucial moment with me, holding my hand when I needed it. My Nana, who, I hope, knew she was my hero. Gram, for keeping in touch with me even when I couldn't keep in touch with her. All of my aunts and uncles who have sometimes been more like sisters and brothers—especially my Uncle Billy, whom I love dearly and who has taught me the meaning of courage during difficult times. My best girlfriend, Cari Rocher, hello from the pumpkin patch . . . we have shared so much of our lives together, and I am grateful for you every day. My friend, Skylr Monaghan, who has helped to push me to new limits and new learning. And my lifelong girlfriends, Donna Mascale and Aida Potata O'Leary, always a part of me. Janine Driver, I am so glad I have come to know you.

Of course, thank you to the crew on Eagle who helped me whenever I needed it.

A special thanks to Bill O'Reilly for great conversations and the opportunity to bring body language to the masses. Thanks also to Jessie Watters for traveling with me along this exciting learning curve; David Huppert for the opportunity; and Sarah Haley for taking such great care of me.

To my buddies, Darianne Bramberg, Danielle Vignjevich, Frank Veronsky, Rhea Landig, BJ Gillian, Trevor Bowden—thank you for being the special people you are.

This book has been a team effort. I don't know where I would have been without my literary agent, Laura Dail, who was always by my side when I needed her, teaching me the ropes and being my greatest cheerleader. To my writing buddy, Mariska Van Aalst—I feel like we have been friends forever—thank you for your "me"ness.

Thanks to the wonderful people at Simon & Schuster, who have been superb leaders as well as caring listeners: Maggie Crawford, Anthony Ziccardi, Jean Anne Rose, Louise Burke, and Lisa Litwack.

Finally, I would also like to thank my past bosses who gave me such a hard time about short skirts, high heels, and long hair. You taught me more than you can imagine.

Contents

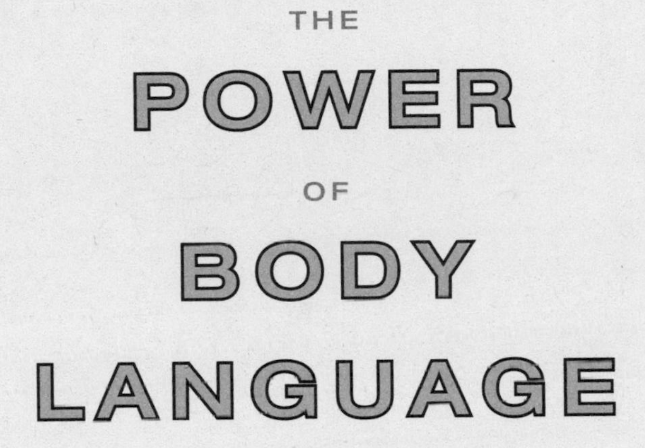
THE
POWER
OF
BODY
LANGUAGE

Introduction

What I hide by language, my body utters.

—John Barthes

As a body language expert, I'm in the business of helping people understand each other better. I teach people how to study movements, gestures, and facial expressions so they can decode other people's thoughts and feelings. The media often asks me to comment on the body language of famous or infamous people such as politicians, Hollywood celebrities, and criminals. Judging from the amount of media coverage they receive, nothing fascinates us more than the private lives of celebrities.

While individual celebrities may fascinate us, when two celebrities come together in love, we are transfixed. We create cute names for them, like "TomKat" and "Brangelina." We track their dinner dates, their holiday plans, their "baby bumps."

That's why, when a celebrity manages to maintain some distance from the media and keep her private life somewhat private, we're that much more curious. Few A-list celebrities have been as successful at holding the paparazzi at arm's length as actor Renée Zellweger—even after her ill-fated marriage to Kenny Chesney.

Zellweger met Chesney, a quadruple-platinum country performing artist, in January of 2005 at a concert benefiting the victims of the tsunami. After a brief, intense courtship, they married in a small, romantic ceremony on the beach.

Then their whirlwind romance came to a crashing halt. A mere 128 days later, Zellweger filed for an annulment.

The gossip media was abuzz with wild speculation about the fast demise of the marriage. She had checked the box marked "fraud" on the annulment application—what did that mean? Reporters, bloggers, and fans couldn't help but wonder, What kind of fraud? Was Chesney gay? Did Zellweger just discover it? Was she crushed?

Through it all, Zellweger maintained her dignity and stiff upper lip while under the constant watch of the public eye. She probably thought the story had gone away and that she was home free by December 2006, a full year after the annulment was finalized, when she appeared on *Late Show with David Letterman* to promote her new film, *Miss Potter.*

A frequent guest on the show, Zellweger had always enjoyed an easy, joking rapport with Letterman, who had customarily been warm, welcoming, and respectful to her.

That may have been why she was caught off guard when, after a cordial welcome, Letterman abruptly changed the subject and attempted to pin her down with a question about her marriage to Chesney. A week later, I had the opportunity to analyze Zellweger's body language on *The O'Reilly Factor,* and I was astonished by what I saw:

At first, Zellweger's signals telegraph a strong connection with Letterman—her body is turned toward him, her posture straight and tall, her shoulders back, her chest out. She's maintaining eye contact with him, with her back to the cameras. Her legs are crossed in a pose universally seen as the sexiest sitting position for women, the leg twine, which highlights the muscle tone of her legs. She preens a bit, touching her hair and tossing her head, standard female signals of self-confidence, attraction, and interest. She's playfully flirting with him and clearly anticipates that this encounter will be as pleasant as their earlier interviews.

The moment Letterman asks the question about Chesney, all of those rapport signals start to fall apart. Even as she's forcing a smile, teasing Letterman for having the temerity to ask, trying to keep the moment light, this Oscar-winning actor's body language betrays how deeply hurt she is by the invasion. She completely stops making eye contact with him. She leans directly away from him, exposing her neck in a submissive gesture that shows how vulnerable she feels about the issue. As she sits up again, at the same moment, she shifts her body so her knees and feet point away from Letterman, and she orients her chest and shoulders toward the audience.

Having introduced the topic, Letterman continues with the line of questioning, although he, too, starts to change his body language. He averts his gaze and stares down, seeming to ask the desk his remaining questions.

Their rapport has disappeared. Both parties have stopped looking at each other. While Letterman and Zellweger both continue to speak to each other verbally and show outward social signs of "making nice," their bodies relate an entirely different conversation. Her body language is saying, "I'm so angry and frustrated that you brought this up"; his body is saying, "I'm sorry that I had to do this—let's just get through it."

Zellweger begins to rock her body back and forth in increasingly larger movements and responds to his comments with big, forced, barking laughs. Her fingers twist in her lap. Yet all the while she has a big smile on her face.

As Letterman makes a joke about having been disappointed when she got married because he had wanted to marry her, she turns completely away from him and drops her head down, still smiling. Then, the most telling moment: for just the briefest instant, a flash of true anger covers her face. She scowls, narrows her eyes, purses her lips, and all traces of even fake smiling leave her face. There's no doubt—it might seem like she's joking, but she is just plain livid.

As quickly as her anger appears, it disappears. That "microexpression" lasts only for a fraction of a second, not nearly long enough for the untrained eye to catch it. In fact, I had to slow down the clip for Bill O'Reilly during my analysis on the show. But once you've seen this signal, you know what to look for. You can't miss it.

Zellweger's flash of anger evaporates and she smiles brightly again, swings her head around, and looks directly at Letterman. For the first time in the twenty seconds since he asked the initial question, she looks him in the eye—and a bit forcefully. She even subtly moves her head around to draw him back into direct eye contact. Perhaps not coincidentally, soon thereafter he straightens his tie in his trademark gesture of discomfort and says, "Probably none of my business, is it?" and she says, "Well, now that you mention it—no!" with a big barking laugh.

We all have aspects of our private lives that we like to keep private. When we need to interact with the world, we put on our public face and try to conduct our business without letting anyone see behind the veil.

While we intend to maintain our privacy, very few of us are successful at completely obscuring our true feelings. Even the most accomplished actors can unintentionally betray their genuine emotions with body language signals.

Once you have studied and mastered body language, you will be astounded to discover how much a person can unwittingly reveal about himself without saying a word. While most people never pick up on these signals, once you learn to recognize them, you will detect them everywhere—and even be able to control them more easily in yourself.

I'll never forget the first time I learned the power of body language.

I was in a psychology class at Pace University, an eager-to-impress student. I sat in the front row of the class, taking copious notes as I listened to Professor Mitchell deliver his lecture to a packed auditorium.

This particular day, Professor Mitchell was talking about proxemics, the study of how humans interact with each other within physical space. He described the zones of personal space, telling us one of his trademark great stories, walking back and forth in front of the classroom.

Gradually, as he spoke, he moved closer and closer to me. Naive little old me continued to take notes, somewhat oblivious to what Professor Mitchell was doing, but subconsciously starting to feel increasingly uneasy.

In the middle of a sentence, he abruptly stopped talking. His tone changed, and he said loudly, "OK, I want everyone to look at this young lady."

Every head in the classroom turned in my direction, and the class drew an audible gasp. Professor Mitchell was leaning over my desk, nearly nose to nose with me. Although my hands were still on my desk, the rest of my body was stretched as far back as it could go.

My professor had moved in so subtly, I'd no idea what was happening. Until he had concluded this little "experiment" and called attention to my posture, I hadn't even realized I had contorted my body to try to get away from him. My body had automatically responded to his sly, but very aggressive, takeover of my personal space. He had used his body to communicate messages of power, dominance, and total control. And his skilled use of body language coupled with my total lack of awareness gave this man the complete upper hand.

I was dumbfounded, awestruck, and immediately hooked. I had to learn these secrets for myself. And so my passion for body language was born.

Research has found that as much as 93 percent of our interpersonal communication is nonverbal. How your body moves, what expression your face makes, how fast you speak—even where you stand or sit, how much perfume you have on, what type of jewelry you wear, or whether your hair is long or short—all of these elements send messages far more convincingly than any words spoken. An estimated one thousand different nonverbal factors contribute to the message you send in every interaction. Cumulatively, these nonverbal elements have much greater power than the paltry 7 percent impact of the words coming out of your mouth.

Every flick of your wrist or change in your vocal tone reflects something about how you are feeling or what you are thinking to the person with whom you're speaking. Do you trust this person? Do you truly believe in the product you're selling? Do you want to turn and run for the hills? The languages of the body don't just supplement what we say—they usually dominate our conversation.

Our conscious brains might be focused on decoding the spoken words in the conversation, but the subconscious does the really heavy lifting, "reading" the body's many languages for nonverbal cues that tell us about the other person's true intentions. Emerging science in the fields of psychology, anthropology, linguistics, and sociology shows that nonverbal signals are the most honest and reliable sources of communication. Our primate ancestors developed a keen insight and understanding of the nonverbal languages of the body, and we've inherited that "sixth sense" from them. In fact, a single class of brain cells—the "mirror neuron"—has evolved from one that aided primates' survival into one that helps humans share knowledge, teach fine arts, learn how to fight or show compassion, possibly even how to speak—all based on the act of reading one another's body language. Exciting new neuroscience research has revealed that from birth a certain part of our brains is constantly wired and rewired based on our nonverbal interactions with others. The brain's ever-more-sophisticated communication system reacts and changes with every interaction, constantly learning more and telling us nearly everything we need to know about the people around us.

The problem is that many people have conditioned themselves not to listen to these signals. We deny our "gut reactions" because we think they're not as reliable as our rational evaluations of other people. As a result, we end up getting duped, swindled, jilted, misled.

Take Jim for example.

Jim was a copywriter at an ad agency. His high-pressure job was becoming more like a snake pit every day. He was glad to have a friend in Tom, a younger colleague whom Jim had mentored. Tom and Jim shared all the available office gossip, analyzing corporate politics to figure out when the next restructuring might happen. They both knew their jobs depended on coming up with new ideas that sold products.

One of the most anxiety-producing parts of their jobs was to pitch ideas to a room full of colleagues and senior creative executives. To prepare, Jim and Tom would often practice on each other. One day, when Jim was pitching his new idea to Tom—his first "real" idea in a long time—he felt something had changed in their relationship. He started to feel unsettled. Was it the new idea? Was it Tom?

Tom wasn't doing anything different—he was just sitting there, watching Jim's pitch, just as he always did, perhaps even a bit more intently than usual. As Jim detailed his idea for the tagline and advertising strategy for a new brand of diet soda, Tom's arms were crossed, his brow was furrowed in concentration, his eyes were focused on Jim's presentation. Just as Jim got to the best part, Tom's eyebrows rose and he crossed his legs.

"Yeah, I guess it's a good idea, Jim," Tom said when Jim had finished. Immediately, Jim felt crushed—that wasn't the kind of response he was hoping for. Tom looked at the floor, scrunching his lips together. "You might want to work on the end of your—oh!" he looked at his watch. "Conference call at two! We'll talk more later." Tom got up and walked quickly out of Jim's office.

Jim sat there feeling deflated. *I bet he's just humoring me*, Jim thought. *My idea probably really sucks.*

For the rest of the day, and the next morning, Jim had an unsettled feeling. *I wish I could shake this*, he thought. He looked for Tom to go for coffee, but was oddly relieved when Tom wasn't at his desk.

Later, during the pitch meeting, Jim took his regular chair at the table and was surprised to see Tom on the other side. Usually they sat together. Tom flashed a tight grin at Jim, and again Jim had that unsettled feeling. What was going on?

The managing director bounded into the meeting, and everyone snapped to attention. "Excellent, great to see everybody," she said, looking around the table. "We're going to do things differently today. This morning, I heard an amazing pitch, one that's going to sell a heck of a lot of diet soda, and I want to share it first thing so we can all work on it for the remainder of the meeting." Jim's stomach flipped over, and he shot a look at Tom, who kept his eyes on the paper in front of him. "Tom here was standing in the elevator this morning, when I happened to get on . . ." The managing director proceeded to detail Jim's idea, which Tom had claimed as his own.

Now, wouldn't it have been useful for Jim to know *before* he shared the best idea of his career that Tom was not his real friend? Wouldn't it have been much easier and less gut-wrenching to realize that fact weeks earlier, when Tom had started to slowly pull back from their friendship and give off cues—such as less eye contact, more arm folding, and less nodding when Jim spoke—that he couldn't be trusted?

In this book, I will teach you to consciously read these nonverbal signals, so you can know what the people around you really think, not just what they say. When you learn the techniques I share in these pages, you'll begin to notice who your true friends are, and who is out to deceive you. You'll learn to recognize whether someone is falling in love with you or simply trying to mislead you. You'll learn to tune in to your instincts and to trust them, so you'll know not to disregard your gut when it screams, "I don't care what he's saying—don't trust him!"

When we lose touch with our natural body language ability, we can also unintentionally send the wrong signals and end up turning people off or pushing them away. In this book, you'll learn how to control your own nonverbal signals and communicate only the messages you want to send—and none of the messages you don't. Just by learning a few key tricks and principles, you can tap into the miracles of your brain's natural communication system to greatly enhance your ability to read other peoples' body language as well as control your own. Ultimately, armed with some useful information and a bit of practice, you will become what I call a Master Communicator—someone who understands the body language of all players and can manipulate the playing field to his or her advantage.

Does *manipulate* strike you as a negative word? It shouldn't. One of the primary definitions of the verb *manipulate* is "to manage or utilize skillfully." In this book, you will learn to skillfully manage and utilize your own natural awareness of body language, both to read other people correctly and to transmit only the messages that help you achieve your goals.

It's that simple.

Several years after I was introduced to the power of body language in my psychology class, I learned how useful it was to be a Master Communicator. As an analyst and staffing specialist for a Fortune 500 financial firm, I interacted with new employees every week. While I was surrounded by people who were trading in financial resources, I traded in human resources. Like those other traders, I had to quickly evaluate the potential of scores of prospects, pluck out the ones whose stock was on the rise, and carefully avoid those who might not perform at the level we'd expect. When someone met my eyes and spoke in confident, strong tones, I would take another look. When someone continually shifted in her chair, crossed and uncrossed her legs, or refused to make eye contact, I knew she would never last. I made these decisions based almost entirely on my gut, and my first impressions frequently became my final judgments.

Sound harsh? Superficial? A bit heartless? Perhaps. But it is a fact of life we all have to face: people judge you on the first impression you make.

Recent research from Princeton University shows that when we meet someone for the first time, we make our initial judgments about a person's attractiveness, likability, trustworthiness, competence, and aggressiveness within 100 milliseconds—one-tenth of one second—of meeting them. And once those impressions are formed, they tend to stick and become even more entrenched. Only by carefully managing any future interactions can you ever hope to revise a bad first impression.

Over time, those people who are looking to hire, award new contracts, or even fall in love have been exposed to many of these first impressions. The results are collected into their own mental databases, each powered by a personal logarithm that determines precisely which characteristics are going to make a person a "yes" or a "no" to fulfill that particular need in their lives.

We all want to be a "yes" far more often than we want to be a "no" when we apply for jobs or try to win over people in social and business situations. And that's why it is important to master that all-important first impression, in all areas of our lives. Master Communicators know how to ace that first one-tenth of a second. In this book, you'll learn all you need to know to turn every first impression into a "yes."

One of the trickiest things about first impressions is that they work on a subconscious level. This applies no matter how smart you are—even intellectual giants cannot form a fully conscious thought in one-tenth of one second. But just because some thoughts are subconscious, that doesn't mean we can't learn to control them in ourselves—and in others.

As a certified hypnotist, I know that our subconscious can be trained to help us send more powerful nonverbal messages. If you want to appear happy, or confident, or commanding, you can train yourself to exude those traits, even if you don't feel them at first. On the flip side, by learning to control your own body language, you'll automatically learn to control the subconscious thoughts and impressions others will have about you.

A few years after I left the financial world, I reentered the realm of body language at the behest of a good friend and mentor. Thereafter, in my practice and in seminars throughout the United States and around the world, I helped scores of people to overcome their anxieties about work, dating, parties, and presentations and showed them how to feel comfortable in all kinds of settings and situations in which body language plays a huge role. As I've worked with people, I've found that one of the most effective tools in overcoming stumbling blocks in social situations is a particular kind of mental practice—to visualize yourself doing certain actions in a specific sequence.

One of my clients, Jenny,* was afraid to enter a room full of people by herself. She especially had trouble at parties, approaching groups of people to join in conversations. Together, she and I developed a mental script that she could use to remind herself of the correct body language to use when entering a group:

> *I approach the party, I stand tall, my spine straight as steel. I walk with confident steps, making eye contact and smiling at one individual after another. I look for either people standing alone or groups of three or more to join in order to strike up conversation. I approach a gathering of people, I look for the person whose foot is pointed away from the center of the group—that is my opening. I smile, nod, and wait to be acknowledged and invited into the group. I focus first on listening, and I do not worry about what I will say. When I have something to say, it comes out naturally and as part of the fabric of the conversation. I am strong, confident, happy, and serene.*

Here again, the emerging research on the brain's communication system holds the key to strengthening your subconscious mind. The same methods that elite athletes and classical musicians use to perfect their craft can help you master the most effective opening line in a speech or at a nightclub. With this book, you will learn how to tap this

* In order to protect their identities, I've changed the names and certain identifying details about Jenny and all of the clients I mention throughout the book. In some cases, I combined details about several clients to create composite profiles.

neurological system to feel more mentally and physically confident and authoritative as you also project those traits to the outside world. I'll help you just as I've helped so many of my clients—I'll give you the exact directions on how to move your body, adjust your posture, and change your facial expressions, so you can exude attractiveness, likability, and self-control while you also enjoy the same vitalizing sensations in your body.

Over the years, I've been consulted by people and organizations, from Fox News anchor Bill O'Reilly and *Access Hollywood* to the *New York Times* and *Psychology Today,* to help uncover the hidden messages in body language. I've helped government employees understand where the lines fall in appropriate workplace behavior. I've helped men and women learn the signs of trustworthiness and deceit in order to determine if their spouses are cheating or if their friends are true. I've advised fleets of salespeople from fields as diverse as construction and magazine advertising on how to read their clients effectively, make the right pitches at the right time, and ensure closed sales and happy repeat customers.

But body language isn't just about reading signals. I've helped managers learn to use their own body language to work effectively with staff, staff to work effectively with customers, and CEOs to negotiate with other CEOs. I've even helped politicians minimize the effects of damaging press just by coaching them on certain facial signals and hand gestures. I'm very gratified to have helped to empower thousands of people by teaching them body language.

While you and I may never have the opportunity to work together directly, this book will teach you much more than I could ever impart in one or two sessions with you as a client. You'll hear stories of people who are just like you whose lives have been changed forever because they made just a few small adjustments to their body language. You'll learn how a real estate agent made one critical change in the way he stood with clients during his sales calls—and increased his sales dramatically. You'll learn how one dateless young woman developed a signature flirting move that had gorgeous, successful guys lining up to talk to her. You'll hear about people like Cindy—confident, ambitious, and successful, yet somehow spinning their wheels, all because of a few missteps in their ability to read body language signals and respond appropriately.

Cindy first called me to book a session to learn some hypnosis techniques for relaxation. As an overworked manager recently promoted to oversee sixteen of her former peers—all men—she needed to unwind a bit. The stress was really piling on, primarily because her staff wasn't listening to her, and her team wasn't meeting its sales goals.

Cindy's phone voice was very attractive—confident, dominant, lower in pitch, but nicely varied in tone. Overall, an excellent voice, by nonverbal standards. I wondered what could be happening in that office to hold her back.

The day she walked through my door for a consultation, the mystery was over. Cindy had come directly from the office, and when I looked at her outfit, I was amazed that her team was getting any work done. Her tight suit was cut perfectly to show her every curve. Her striking pale skin was offset by dramatic red lipstick, and her short, spiky hair and four-inch heels completed her extremely sexy but highly unprofessional look.

After we had settled in, I asked her if she'd like a body language analysis at the same time. She eagerly agreed. I took a moment and then leaned toward her. "Cindy, how do men look at you in the office?"

"What do you mean?" she asked, a bit taken aback. "The normal way, I guess."

"Do they ever do this?" I mimicked the once-over, an up-and-down glance.

"Well, sure, of course," she said, and smiled. "Because I dress to kill."

Obviously, Cindy was very proud of her body and her sense of style, and deservedly so. But while her outfit would have "killed" in a nightclub, it was slowly murdering her managerial career. "Cindy," I said, "it's time to make some changes."

When it comes to dressing for business, there is an unspoken line in the office, and Cindy had long since crossed it. As a telephone salesperson, she'd performed 90 percent of her job over the phone, and her very attractive voice had helped her to do quite well. But once she'd made the transition to management, her tight suits and stilettos had become a distraction in the office.

Although Cindy was dubious at first, she agreed to slowly introduce changes into her usual appearance, one week at a time, on a trial basis. First, we changed her makeup. Cindy and I went to a makeup specialist, and together we found "her" colors—lipstick in a more neutral tone and eyes that were now muted and not ringed with black liner. At the end of week one, the blinding red lipstick was gone—and you could finally see the warmth and intelligence in Cindy's eyes.

Week two, we worked on outfits. "I'm going to swim in these," Cindy protested, as she took her one-size-bigger suits, with their two-inches-lower hemlines, into the dressing room. Trying them on with her new, slightly lower heels, she had to admit they were more comfortable—and didn't her staff seem just the slightest bit less defiant that next morning during the daily meeting?

Finally, we headed to the hair salon to soften out her spiky look with something a bit less confrontational, and more sophisticated. When Cindy emerged from the salon, she looked like a new woman. With just a few slight adjustments to her appearance, she'd gone from overdone office floozy to striking young professional.

Two months later, Cindy returned to my office for a refresher session on relaxation hypnosis. "Now I have the kind of 'problems' I always wanted," she told me. She described how the sales team's productivity had shot up, and she was adding staff and juggling expanding responsibilities. "The funny thing is, I didn't change a single thing besides the way I look," she told me, her eyes shining. "I give the same kinds of talks, set the same goals for the team—but now, instead of not listening or rolling their eyes in meetings, the guys actually raise their hands to speak. They truly want to impress me.

"I haven't changed the way I manage people—but I can't believe how much of a difference my new look has made in the body language of the people I manage."

Now I'm going to show you how to harness the power of body language so you can experience the life-changing effects of becoming a Master Communicator. You're about to learn that you're already an amazingly astute "speaker" of body language. All you have to do is tune in to your natural ability to read others and to transmit the messages you want to send. You'll do that by first becoming self-aware, then by becoming more aware of the messages around you, and finally by making slight tweaks to your own signals—and I'll guide you every step of the way.

To start, I'll give you full descriptions of all the body language signals and tools at your disposal and explain how they work. Then, I'll show you how to use them in specific situations so you can succeed in every encounter by perceiving other peoples' true intentions and by using body language to achieve your goals. Finally, I'll teach you the Reiman Rapport Method, a ten-step process to master universally pleasing body language. The Reiman Rapport Method puts all the signals together in a quick and easy process that will enable you to build rapport with anyone in any situation.

While all of my advice is on the up-and-up, in certain situations, I am going to teach you how to manipulate the playing field to your advantage because—let's be honest—sometimes we have to do that. I'm not suggesting that you do anything devious—sometimes you simply have to consciously change your body language in order to be *more* honest. As you'll discover, some body language can be an obstacle that obscures the truth! But it doesn't have to be.

So if you're ready to learn the power of body language, and become a Master Communicator who can succeed in every encounter with other people, turn the page and let's begin. If you have any questions as you go through the book, please feel free to contact me at Tonya@BodyLanguageUniversity.com.

CHAPTER 1

The Power Behind Body Language

We respond to gestures with an extreme alertness and, one might almost say, in accordance with an elaborate and secret code that is written nowhere, known by none, and understood by all.

—Edward Sapir

Over a million years of children asking mothers for more food, hunters collaborating on a big kill, even the first guy showing his friend how to make a fire—all of that happened without a single word being shared. Some experts believe spoken language appeared on the scene only 160,000 to 350,000 years ago. Given that humans of some kind have walked the earth for about two million years, that's a long time to depend upon gestures and grunts to get your point across. But clearly, it worked!

Body language has remained just as useful ever since. Right now, if you were dropped in the middle of the African plains, or in the deepest jungles of South America, or on an ice floe in the far North Atlantic, you could successfully ask the native people for help—food, clothing, shelter, directions—without using a single word. That universal meeting of the minds is only possible because body language is our original shared language. Far pre-dating speech, this highly effective means of communication connects us not only with other humans but with other primates and even other mammals such as dogs and horses.

Made up of your facial expressions, the way you hold your hands and body, your movements and mannerisms, even your pitch and vocal tone, body language is literally everything you can do with your body to say whatever it is you're trying to say, without words. Or, interestingly enough, sometimes what you're trying *not* to say.

Body language signals—both truthful and those that attempt to hide the truth—can have a profound effect on our lives. A wrong signal during an interview could cost you the job. A mixed signal on a first date can kill a budding romance. A fumbled cultural signal could blow a big international deal. But a shared rapport signal can set the stage for a satisfying lifelong relationship.

Almost everyone is born with the ability to "speak" the body's many languages—in fact, it's the only way we communicate as babies, before we learn how to talk. However, once we learn words, we tend to rely on them to get our points across. Admittedly, words are indispensable when we need to convey specific information efficiently or discuss complex ideas. But words can also be a distraction, and even a trap.

Reclaiming Our Lost "Intuition"

At some point, we got fooled into thinking that speech must be the highest form of communication because we are the only life-form that has the ability to speak. Evolved beings that we are, we don't always remember our roots as preverbal grunters and gesticulators. And so we spend the years between childhood and adulthood unlearning the nonverbal skill we mastered as babies—and end up being frustrated, rejected, and often deceived in the process.

We might spend hours picking apart conversations—"What did he *mean* by saying, 'It's not you, it's me'?"—when we really got the message the first second it was delivered. Our bodies always "have a hunch" or "get a sense" of whether someone is lying to us or loves us. But do we always listen? Sadly, no.

That's about to change.

His Signals/Her Signals

Nothing Escapes Her

Women have more complex connections between both hemispheres of their brain, allowing them to take in more information more quickly. In contrast, men tend to use only one side of their brain at a time. In a social situation, this would allow a woman to absorb many messages from a man's body language and the surrounding environment simultaneously, whereas a man takes those messages in one at a time.

Some body language is conscious—we know we should stand up straight and smile, give hugs to some people and handshakes to others. When we rediscover how to read more subtle body language signals, however, a whole other world is revealed to us. When we understand other people's thoughts, we know how other people *really* feel. We can plainly see when what a person says doesn't necessarily jive with what she feels. And we know that, in turn, others can see the same discrepancy in us, which is why it's so important to send the right signals at the right time. This two-way channel, this intricate, delicate dance that we do almost entirely subconsciously, is communication at its most honest—and most revealing.

As you walk down the street, you constantly and unknowingly flash your eyebrows at total strangers. They do the same thing back. Neither one of you is likely to realize what's going on. But you've just exchanged an unspoken sign of interest and acknowledgment—and you will probably do it forty or fifty more times today. Or perhaps you put on your most innocent face to plead ignorance—"Officer, I had no idea I was going eighty-five!"—while your eyes blink furiously and shoot looks over the officer's left shoulder. No matter how innocent you're trying to look, your nervous blinking and shifty eyes give you away.

Here's the thing: while we all have the capability to read and exhibit the right body language, doing so reliably and consistently is a skill. Just like some of us can barely make toast and others have perfected crème brûlée, there is a vast continuum of knowledge and mastery over body language.

Let's find out where you stand. Take this quiz for a quick snapshot of your place on the body language continuum.

1. **Whenever you go into a party, the first thing you tend to do is:**
   a. Charge straight over to the bar and loudly order a drink, laughing with the bartender.
   b. Walk toward the nearest corner and stake out a post from which to view the room.
   c. Take a moment to look around the room and determine in which direction you would like to go.

2. **In the ten minutes before you're scheduled to give a presentation, you spend most of your time:**
   a. Doing a three-minute breathing exercise to calm yourself down.
   b. Reviewing your notes to make sure you remember everything you want to say.
   c. Pacing the floor and sneaking peeks at the audience as they arrive.

3. **[For women] When you flirt with a guy, you do these three things:**
   a. Smile quickly, look down, and walk in the opposite direction.
   b. Make eye contact, look down briefly, and repeat eye contact with a sidelong smile.
   c. Make direct and prolonged eye contact, smile, and start a conversation.

4. [For men] When you flirt with a woman, you do these things:

a. Smile.

b. Smile, turn in her direction, and hope she notices you.

c. Smile, walk toward the object of your affection, and offer to buy her a drink.

5. When you enter a room for a meeting, but the meeting has not yet begun, you immediately and instinctively:

a. Walk right over and talk to the person in charge of the meeting.

b. Put your materials down at the prominent position at the table so your seat is saved.

c. Take a seat in the corner and wait for the meeting to begin.

6. You're single and open to dating. You've agreed to meet up with your friends. When you are at the bar, you:

a. Strike up a conversation with the bartender.

b. Go to the dance floor and start dirty dancing.

c. Sit at the bar and position your body toward others you find intriguing.

7. You're giving a talk and you notice people in the audience are looking at their watches and showing signs of boredom, but you still have ten minutes to go in your presentation. You:

a. Look at those individuals and ask, "I get the impression you have an issue with what I'm saying—is there a way I can explain it better?"

b. Try to avoid eye contact with those who are bored; you don't want to antagonize them.

c. Speak louder and faster.

8. Sitting on a crowded airplane before a long flight, you don't want to strike up a conversation. Suddenly, the woman next to you asks you the time in a friendly tone of voice. You:

a. Close your eyes and inform her you do not know the time.

b. Check your watch, look at the woman, smile, tell her the time, and then maintain eye contact as she launches into a story—you don't want to be rude.

c. Look down at your watch and inform her of the time with brief eye contact and a quick smile.

9. You're about to meet a potential client for the first time at a restaurant. You need his full attention to make the sale. You:

a. Sit at the bar with the baseball game for background noise—you want him to feel comfortable and casual.

b. Sit at a table and take the chair against the wall—he'll have no other view but your smiling face.

c. Sit in the middle of the restaurant—you don't want him to feel claustrophobic.

10. You are in the middle of your performance review, and it's not going the way you had hoped. Your boss is unfairly criticizing your work. You:

a. Maintain composure and eye contact with open body language. Allow your manager to finish and, with arms open, address each issue point by point.

b. Fold your arms, break in, and dispute each point as she raises it.

c. Allow your manager to finish, excuse yourself, and walk out of the room with your head held high.

Determine your score by using this key. Add the numbers attributed to each response to get your total score, which is interpreted below.

1. a, 1; b, 3; c, 2
2. a, 2; b, 1; c, 3
3. a, 3; b, 2; c, 1
4. a, 2; b, 3; c, 1
5. a, 1; b, 2; c, 3
6. a, 3; b, 1; c, 2
7. a, 2; b, 3; c, 1

8. a, 1; b, 3; c, 2
9. a, 1; b, 2; c, 3
10. a, 2; b, 1; c, 3

If you scored 10–16: You're the life of the party, right? Well, you may need to slow down just a bit. Without intending to do so, you may be scaring people off. You could probably learn a lot about what other people want, and how you might be able to give it to them, by listening to them more closely and by making a greater effort to mirror their body language.

If you scored 17–23: You have a balanced approach that likely serves you well. You're in tune with how to use your body language to serve both your needs and the needs of people around you. You're able to establish rapport quite easily and you may be ready for some advanced techniques.

If you scored 24–30: Your intentions are good, but you might need to step it up a bit. Right now, you're in danger of disappearing into the wallpaper. Practice being more assertive in your body language, and people will respond with increased respect and deference.

Becoming more aware of your own body language, and more in tune with other people's, can help you in every area of your life. *We will never increase our knowledge of other people or how we ourselves are perceived until we learn the power of body language.*

So, how can we do this? First, we have to learn where body language signals come from in order to learn which ones we can control and which are more difficult, if not impossible, to control.

The Origins of Body Language

Deep in the hidden recesses of our brain, we have a hair-trigger sensor that instantly tells us if the person standing in front of us is a friend or a foe. Will she help me gather food, or will she steal it? Will he help protect me from the wolves, or toss me to them?

Body language is the sum total of the signs we give off that help others make those decisions. For example, when others seem genuinely happy to see us, those positive signals make us feel safe. That safety feels good, so we want to spend more time around those people. When people project anger signals, whether intentionally or unintentionally, we feel threatened and we want to avoid them—they do not feel safe.

Every interaction presents a choice between safe or unsafe, yes or no. Sounds simple, right? But the factors that go into making that distinction are fascinatingly complex. When we first meet someone, our brains scan him for hundreds of signs that will tell us more about that person and how he might help or hurt us. Some of those signals are hardwired into our nervous systems; some are passed on by our parents; some are culturally specific. We're alert to how close people come as they approach our personal space, to their facial expressions, to the smoothness of their body movements. We check off their sex, age, race, grooming. We look for clues to social status. We look at the dimensions of their face—how far apart are their eyes set? How low is their forehead? What gestures are they making, and how should I react? We do all of this evaluating, and much more, in the span of seconds.

I'm asked all the time if the body language assessments I make are based on science or if they're just my opinion. The answer is—both! The interpretation of body language is a subjective undertaking, sometimes open to more than one opinion. But like other scientific fields that examine human behavior, the study of these signals—what we do on a daily basis, the way we are perceived by others—is actually the subject of a field of research that stretches back hundreds of years.

The Universal Aspects of Body Language

The study of body language has fascinated researchers for centuries. The biggest debate has centered on the origin of body language—does our nature or our nurture dictate how we speak without words?

In his book *The Expression of the Emotions in Man and Animals,* published in 1872, Darwin spelled out his belief that primates are born with specific emotions, and these emotions are visible on the body and the face. The book was a best seller in its day. But despite this initial flurry of interest, for most of the century thereafter, almost every researcher, anthropologist, and psychologist believed that body language was solely the result of external influences—nurture, not nature. Experts from Sigmund Freud to Margaret Mead forcefully argued that child rearing and culture defined body language—period.

This view held firm until the mid-twentieth century, right about the time when the supremacy of Freud's "blame the mother for everything—including body language" theory started to fall apart. In the mid-1960s, psychologist and researcher Paul Ekman undertook an ambitious cross-cultural study, collaborating with other researchers in twenty-one countries to determine if emotions were, indeed, universal. Ekman found that the facial expressions of six emotions—surprise, fear, anger, sadness, disgust, and happiness—were judged the same in every country studied. (Later, Ekman added a seventh—contempt—to this list.) Unimpressed, his critics angrily shot back their usual argument, that these similar expressions must be the result of cultural influences like movies and television. Basically, it was believed that the reason everyone scowled in anger was because we had all seen John Wayne movies!

In order to settle the argument once and for all, Ekman went to a place where people had never even heard of John Wayne, let alone seen one of his movies. In his landmark study of the South Fore people of Papua, New Guinea, a civilization that until that time had had only limited contact with the outside world, Ekman found the same results—these people could very clearly identify and portray anger, as well as five other emotions, in the same way as the people studied in twenty-one other countries.

The results blew the nurture theory out of the water. Finally, many experts begrudgingly accepted what Darwin had asserted a hundred years earlier—that we share many of our emotions with the apes from which we descended.

Now, granted, this assertion remains controversial in certain circles, and many in the scientific community would argue. But I believe the proof is written all over our faces—and our bodies.

Both primates and humans from all cultures show surprise with the same facial expressions.

True to its name, body language is not just about the face. In fact, some experts believe that except in moments of extreme emotion, the face is not always a reliable indicator of our true feelings. Why? Because the face is the easiest part of the body to manipulate. Our bodies tend to tell a more truthful tale than our faces.

If we're trying to disguise our true feelings, the upper half of our bodies can more easily remain static while the lower half of our bodies betrays us. We may smile and nod during a conversation with someone we disrespect, but if our feet are pointed at the door, our body language says we can't wait to get away. We call this unintentional betrayal of our inner thoughts and feelings "leakage." Your emotions and true feelings are "leaking" out of you.

His Signals/Her Signals

Body Language Babes

Studies from around the world have repeatedly noted that women are far better than men at decoding the nonverbal cues of others. It doesn't matter if the person expressing the emotion is a man or a woman—a woman will be able to label nonverbal cues more accurately.

An equally important aspect of body language is the nonverbal information the voice sends—dozens of messages lurk in the pitch, tone, speed, and volume of our voices. In fact, research shows that while people try to control their voices when they lie, the voice is actually a great source of leakage. Researchers estimate that as much as 38 percent of all communication comes through vocal cues *other than* speech.

While we now know that a significant portion of body language is universal, we've also seen by traveling to different countries or even different cities and states that certain aspects of body language vary from culture to culture. Family traits, culture, environment, and education all produce differences in how people express themselves. What if the root of body language can't be explained by nature *versus* nurture, but instead, as the late David Lykken, a behavioral geneticist, termed it, nature *via* nurture?

The Neurological Aspects of Body Language

One recent breakthrough in neuroscience may form the missing link between nature and nurture that explains not only why primates share emotional expressions but also how our environment can radically change our body language. In 1996, in a finding often hailed as the neurological discovery of the decade, Italian researchers Giacomo Rizzolatti and Vittorio Gallese at the University of Parma identified a previously undiscovered class of brain cell called "mirror neurons." First found in monkeys and more recently in humans, mirror neurons are a type of motor neuron, a nerve cell that controls muscles and, as a result, how the body moves. But the mirror neuron controls so many interpersonal functions, you might think of this versatile cell as the Swiss Army knife of body language.

Sometimes called "monkey-see/monkey-do" neurons, these sensitive brain cells not only fire when we perform an action but even when we just see, hear, or even suspect that someone is about to perform an action—and they make us literally "feel" that action in our body. If you've ever felt your arm lurch while you watched a tennis match on TV, or flinched and covered your groin when you saw a buddy get nailed with a football, you've experienced your mirror neurons at work. These brain cells, theorized to be the biological root of empathy, are activated whether you feel a sensation directly—if, say, you were the person nailed with the football—or when you observe it, or even if you just *hear* it happening.

For decades, sports psychologists have used the power of mirror neurons to improve athletes' performance. When a basketball coach shows his team films of last Friday's game, the players' eyes follow the action on the court, and their mirror neurons fire in response, causing the corresponding muscles in their bodies to contract. Just because they're watching the film, their muscles "practice" the plays and their brains feel as if they are back in the game.

Mirror neurons are found in several areas of the brain, and each area has its own particular specialty. The mirror neurons in the right parietal operculum are the ones that trace other people's actions and help us get in tune with other people's movements. You experience the activity of mirror neurons every day—you yawn in a meeting because your boss yawns, or you blush when your colleague flubs a presentation. Even the television networks are in on it—they use laugh tracks on sitcoms to stimulate our mirror neurons so we laugh more easily. In effect, laughing—like yawning or blushing or crying—is contagious. Mirror neuron research suggests we are biologically empathetic creatures, which may be why we're so attracted to people who exude happiness and confidence: they automatically make us feel happy and confident, too.

His Signals/Her Signals

Mirror Neurons ❤ Porn

The action of mirror neurons, brain cells that allow us to experience empathy, may help to explain the addictive nature of pornography. When a person watches other people having sex, even on a television (or computer) screen, a part of his brain actually feels like he's getting some action, too. (And who can blame a guy for liking that?)

As we grow up and interact with lots of different people, we gradually fill our experience database with memories of our own and other people's emotions. Then, as we navigate through future social situations, we tap in to this vast database of experience for clues on how to interpret other people's actions, anticipate what they'll do next, and react accordingly.

Some people may have a natural, instinctive ability to read and respond to these social cues. Let's say that you're at the company cocktail party. You introduce yourself to a new colleague and ask her about her last job. You heard she left Company A—what was it like to work there? She bristles just the slightest bit, smiles widely, and says, "I really loved it, but it was time for a change." Because your mirror system is highly active, you pick up on the subtle nonverbal cues—her quickly averted eyes, her fake social smile, the crispness of her words, and her suddenly straighter posture—that mean she doesn't want to discuss her old job. You let the matter drop and instead introduce her to another colleague standing nearby. You can see that the new employee seems visibly relieved—genuine smile, relaxed eyes, restored eye contact—and grateful for your graciousness. Because your mirror system is very active, you're naturally more empathetic, able to intuit the new employee's feelings simply from watching her subtle nonverbal reactions.

But what if you're not able to read these social cues? Perhaps this is your first company mixer, you're nervous, and you don't know how to handle these brief interpersonal moments in a professional way. When you meet the new colleague, you ask, "Why did you leave Company A? I heard that place is incredible." She stiffens, she demurs, but still you don't pick up on those nonverbal hints. Instead, you dig deeper. "A change? Really? What did you do there? What didn't you like about your old job?" The new colleague looks startled at your forwardness, and another colleague, a friend, shoots you a "shut up!" look. You feel your cheeks flush with embarrassment. If you have a fully functioning mirror system, after you bank that humiliating experience in your database, you'll be less likely to ask prying or personal questions in a work setting.

It's not always that simple, though. Researchers are starting to uncover evidence that some people might have disruptions in their mirror system that hinder their ability to navigate social situations smoothly. For example, recent research indicates that the mirror systems of autistic children and adults show virtually no activity when they try to identify with the emotions of others. While research is still at an early stage, some specialists are hopeful that these findings could lead to a therapy for autistic kids that improves their ability to empathize and read body language. They think that perhaps coaching them on the use of imitation and mimicry might help increase activity in the mirror system and strengthen the neural connections associated with greater empathy.

People who are blessed with normally functioning mirror systems, but who just might need a bit of a tune-up, could use similar strategies to strengthen their body language abilities. We know the brain continues to develop and change throughout our lifespan. Increasing the number and variety of our social experiences can strengthen our neural connections and allow us to fully tap in to this innate ability to connect. If you've had trouble socializing in the past, the worst thing you can do is hide in the corner. Get out there, stand up straight, smile, and look people in the eye. Listen to their stories; put yourself in their shoes. Practice empathizing with them, and give them the positive vibes that they'll want to mirror back to you. Your mirror neurons can help you become a Master Communicator, as long as you practice, practice, practice!

His Signals/Her Signals

I'll Tend, You Fight

Many women respond to stress by nurturing and seeking social support—the "tend and befriend" cycle. Most men respond to stress with a more confrontational "fight or flight" response. For years, researchers believed men and women both experienced only fight or flight, but now they know the hormone oxytocin, important for breastfeeding and childbirth, is part of the reason that women sometimes seek out the help of others and try to build alliances that will help protect themselves and their offspring. The "tend and befriend" response may be part of the reason why women are much better at reading social cues.

Obviously, mirror neurons are not the only part of the brain involved in our social interactions. Many other parts of our nervous system are recruited to interpret even the most basic emotions. For example, when we see someone else experience fear, our amygdala, another part of the brain that stores memories of emotion, is activated. But the place where the "nature via nurture" effect really takes hold is right at home, with Mom and Dad.

The Familial Aspects of Body Language

Our body language is not solely the product of our brain chemistry and our primate past. The signals we receive from those around us, starting from the day we're born, continually shape our body language.

When babies are born, they enter into an emotional house of mirrors. Some researchers postulate that as a baby sees his parents' happy smiles, he absorbs those positive expressions, and he can feel them in his body. His mirror neurons cause his muscles to reflect them, first with interested eye contact, then with a smile. Then his parents show delight, reinforcing the reflection. The baby feels his parents' joy in his body and automatically seeks to repeat the experience.

As early as a few days—perhaps even hours—after they're born, babies start to imitate the gestures and mannerisms of their caretakers. Not having ever seen their own faces, these newborn babies have an innate ability to mimic expressions. In fact, babies are much more interested in adults who mirror their own activity than those who intentionally mismatch it—they'll watch the mirroring adults longer and smile at them more than the ones who mismatch their activity.

Andrew Meltzoff, a developmental psychologist at the University of Washington, has termed this tendency the "like me" theory of child development. He says that babies are constantly evaluating other people's actions to validate their belief that others are "like me," and they start to do this way before they're able to use language. The ability to see others as "like me" is part of what helps babies bond to their parents as well as hone their ability to read and respond to other people's body language. That's one reason why it's so important to smile at babies and use tender body language with them—you're priming them to respond to others in the same empathetic, bonding way.

As children grow, their mirror neurons constantly accumulate experiences—what it feels like to crawl, walk, ride a bike, what to expect from other people, how they will make us feel. The body language that a parent shows a child will invariably be the body language the child will use when he grows up—as well as the body language he will seek out in others. Show kids love, trust, and affection, and chances are they'll find friends and partners who show them those same qualities.

His Signals/Her Signals

Girls Body Language Champs from an Early Age

Girl and boy babies start out equal in their ability to read body language. But once girls pass infancy, they're better at recognizing faces than boys. And starting at age eight, most American girls are able to label nonverbal actions more accurately than boys. This advantage carries through to adulthood.

As we grow up and leave the nest, we never stop using the "like me" method of evaluating others. This approach carries on as we choose schoolyard buddies, employees, dance partners, and mates. Whether we share a love of the same music or worship the same god, human beings prefer to be with those who are similar to ourselves. This large-scale version of the parent-child house of mirrors expands ever outward, causing groups of like-minded people to clus-

People from the same family tend to mirror one another so often it becomes an unconscious habit. In this photo, you see my children, Christian, Jaidan, and Stephanie, mirroring one another for the camera.

ter together and, in turn, mimic each other. Over centuries, one tight-knit group starts to develop certain behaviors that will perhaps be very different from the group two towns over—which is where you might find the cultural origins of body language.

The Cultural Aspects of Body Language

So much of body language is defined by our culture. Whether we meet each other with a handshake, a kiss on the cheek, a forehead touch, or a bowed head, each greeting is completely dependent on culture.

These cultural expressions are dictated by what are called "display rules," the specific expectations every group has about body language behavior. For example, you only have to stand on line for a bus in San Francisco to see an interesting difference in cultural display rules about personal space. If you queue up for a bus on Market Street in the business district at rush hour, you'll stand in a very orderly line, with a three-foot bubble of personal space, your fellow commuters busily tapping their BlackBerries without so much as a glance at you. But if you board the bus a few blocks farther up the hill, in Chinatown, you might find yourself a part of a crush of people, stomachs pressed against backs, each person simultaneously vying for a seat on that same bus.

His Signals/Her Signals

Empathy Starts in the Crib

Female babies cry more in response to other babies' cries than male babies do.

Cultural display rules vary from country to country, state to state, even city to city. For example, in the United States as well as in most other countries, nodding your head up and down is a signal interpreted as "yes." We use it to emphasize a point when we say yes, or we simply use it nonverbally to indicate agreement. In Bulgaria, however, shaking your head from side to side means "yes," and nodding your head up and down means "no." That would be an important difference to be aware of if you were stuck at a Bulgarian train station in the middle of the night.

When you begin to see the vast spectrum of differences in body language throughout the world, it makes sense that display rules are based on culture, not on biology. The reason couples in Puerto Rico touch each other 180 times more often than couples in England has nothing to do with biology and everything to do with how often their parents touched them, and their grandparents touched their parents, and so on and so on . . . back to the time of Stonehenge.

As we become a global society, divergent cultural norms inch closer and closer to each other with each generation. The more exposure kids have to people of different cultures, the more likely they are to recognize a variety of people as "like me" as well. Studies show that the people who have the most contact with other cultures have the least bigoted views about others. We see a person first, then a Bulgarian. We realize that their head nod isn't "wrong" or "backward," it's just different. And we can show a great deal of respect (and score major points!) by learning those different display rules *before* we do business with people in other cultures. (For example, a hand signal that means A-OK for Americans might just get you beaten up in Turkey or Greece.) Knowing each others' display rules, and respecting them, is a huge step toward bridging cultural gaps with body language.

The Individual Aspects of Body Language

While cultural norms might have some influence on our body language, our individual temperaments usually have a greater impact on how we conduct ourselves. Some traits can be genetic, such as the tendency to be assertive, empathetic, or aggressive. Other temperament traits, such as being shy or extroverted, may not be genetic, but they definitely have an impact on how we communicate. The more extroverted you are, the more emphatic your gestures are likely to be, and the more you are likely to use your entire body when you communicate. In contrast, introverts use smaller gestures, and fewer of them.

Another individual difference is our sex. Men and women have different ways of transmitting and receiving body language signals—a quick stop at any "happy hour" could tell you that. And like the rest of body language, some of these differences are due to innate hormonal and biological differences; others are due to cultural influences. (We'll take a look at some of the most intriguing of these differences in sidebars throughout the book, entitled "His Signals/Her Signals.")

Thankfully, any of these individual body language tendencies can be accommodated and, if necessary, improved upon with self-awareness and practice, practice, practice. And as long as we give ourselves plenty of high-quality models to learn from—upbeat friends, positive relationships, confidence-building successes—we'll continually become more insightful, more empathetic, and more skilled at body language.

Now it's time for you to put the power of body language to work for you. In order to start deciphering body language on a second-by-second level, you first need to learn the five basic truths of all body language.

The Five Immutable Truths of Body Language

Remind yourself of these five truths when you're out in the world, interpreting body language signals. They will help you to think clearly about what you're seeing, make smart judgments, and trust your instincts. Once you know these truths, you'll be ready to start applying the specific lessons in the following chapters.

Truth #1: Body language is a constant. You always communicate. No matter what, your body's stance, your facial expressions, the cut of your clothes, always say something. Even if you're just trying to communicate that you don't want to communicate, you are communicating—in that case, it would be a look of indifference.

You can't get out of it. Face it, own it, know that you're being "read" every time you set foot in public. You even communicate when you sleep, whether flat on your back or in the fetal position.

Truth #2: Body language is always determined by context. What's acceptable at your local bar on margarita night is not going to fly at the company's formal holiday party. The context—the social rules, the cultural implications, the group's expectations—plays a huge role in what types of body language will work for you and what will work against you in certain situations.

Instinctively we know this, but I'm constantly surprised by clients who say, "Well, that [perma-scowl; yellow teeth; constant jittering] is just *me*—I can't be someone I'm not."

Trust me: You will always be you, no matter where you are. But why not use the unspoken rules of the situation to help you, rather than hurt you? You can wink at your daughter during her dance recital, but you wouldn't wink at the queen of England, would you? (I mean, unless you were the president of the United States.)

Truth #3: Body language can never be judged based on one single signal. As you make your way through the book, you will learn many details about specific body language signals. Please resist the temptation to "diagnose" people based on one signal. For example, you may have heard that covering your mouth with your hand can be a sign of deception. A body language novice might say, "Look, she's covering her mouth—she's lying!" But maybe she's politely covering her mouth because she's chewing.

Sometimes a cigar is just a cigar. You need to read several signals that suggest the same thought or emotion before you can safely assume that signal to be "true." In later chapters, I'll teach you to look for groups of gestures and to study these groups until you recognize patterns, a process called "baselining" or "norming" someone.

Truth #4: Body language reveals the discrepancies between what a person says and what a person truly believes. In order to fully "listen" to a person's true message, you have to tune in to both the verbal and nonverbal aspects of their message, watching their body language and listening for the pitch, rate, tone, volume, and rhythm of their words. When a person is being truthful, their body language is what's called "congruent"—their movements, facial expressions, and vocal tone will match the words they're saying verbally. These people are usually perceived as trustworthy, because all of the messages they're sending are the same.

However, when someone's spoken language and body language do not match up, there is a disconnect, and their message becomes "incongruent." Incongruence is one of the most powerful aspects of body language because it alerts us to the fact that the verbal message is not the whole picture.

Now, it's not as if everyone whose body language is incongruent is a crook or an untrustworthy person. Sometimes you'll see this incongruence in people who are telling social white lies. ("Oh, Grandma, this is delicious," as you're slowly shaking your head; or "I'm delighted to be here!" as you cross your arms and legs.)

Experienced liars are sometimes able to mask their incongruence—but only to a certain degree. For most people, even when they can control the signs on their face, more telling signs of their true feelings will "leak" out of other areas of their body language. Psychologist Robert Rosenthal of Harvard University ranked five kinds of nonverbal cues in terms of their "leakiness":

1. Incongruent cues—these are most telling because they indicate internal conflict, feelings of hesitation, signs of deception, and so on.
2. Brief cues from face and body—signs leaked and quickly corrected.
3. The voice—surprisingly, more likely to betray concealed emotions than your face.
4. The body—somewhat easy to control if you know what you're doing.
5. The face—the least "leaky" because it is the most controllable.

Throughout the book, you'll get tips on how to detect, decode, and interpret messages of leakage or incongruence.

Truth #5: Body language mastery allows you to tune in to "microexpressions," the brief flashes or gestures that betray inner feelings. These flashes of intense facial expression—which some experts refer to as "hot spots"—might only rest on the face for less than one-quarter of a second. Those slight slips, leakages, and things that we try to cover up are nearly impossible for us to control. As such, microexpressions are where the true communication takes place. But they happen so quickly that you might never register them on a conscious level. Experts spend hours rewinding videotapes to decode particular moments of microexpressions to deduce their meanings, but in a typical conversation, we don't get that chance. I'll give you the tools to rev up your own innate signal decoder, so you'll be able to tune in more accurately to these signals. When you become a Master Communicator, you'll start to automatically detect and decode the microexpressions that slip right by your conscious mind. You'll know right away if someone is trying to lie to you or otherwise mislead you—and you'll be able to adjust your body language accordingly.

Your Plan to Become a Master Communicator

As you read this book, you will gain knowledge and power as you master each of the body's secret languages. You will learn how to read other people's signals and know which signals to use and how to use them. As you progress, you might realize you have a specific body language issue you want to address. If so, focus on that area of body language for three weeks. Set daily goals for yourself. For example, when I work with people who aren't good at making eye contact, I tell them, "Smile and meet the eyes of four people each day for twenty-one days. Once you've done that, come back and I'll give you another assignment." By the end of those three weeks, people will normally say to me, "I don't even think about making eye contact anymore—I just do it automatically." They're usually already feeling better about themselves, which they've noticed makes other people like them more. Then they're ready to take on their next signal, and so on, always working toward becoming a Master Communicator. At the end of the book, you'll learn how to put all these steps together with the Reiman Rapport Method, a universally effective method of increasing rapport with anyone in your life.

Throughout the process of developing your body language skills, try to seek out others whom you admire. Watch them carefully, and your mirror neurons will absorb lots of useful information about the body language you want to emulate. Then, mimic it. Try to walk their walk, hold your head the same way, smile just as often and as broadly as they do. Eventually, you'll train yourself to the point where it will be natural and you won't have to fake being bolder, feeling more confident, or having a more magnetic personality—these states of mind will be your reality. You may start as an actor, but soon you'll embody the role.

The face is the first place we look for information about other people's emotions. Let's look at some of the most commonly used facial expressions and what they can tell you—as well as what they might be hiding.

CHAPTER 2

The Language of the Face

An eye can threaten like a loaded and levelled gun,
or it can insult like hissing or kicking; or,
in its altered mood, by beams of kindness,
it can make the heart dance for joy.
—Ralph Waldo Emerson

In the days after 9/11, no place was more shell-shocked with disbelief and grief than New York City. In an article entitled "New York Drops Its Game Face," written five days after the attacks, *New York Times* reporter Alex Kuczynski noted how normally stoic Manhattanites now wandered around in a state of "emotional nudity." Whereas they would sometimes completely ignore each other on the street and stare blankly across the subway car, traumatized survivors had begun to look into one anothers' faces and to maintain eye contact with strangers, seeking connection and offering empathy in exchange. One expert noted that a frequently traded expression during those days was "lip compression," seen when a person contracts his lips together into a horizontal line across his face. He said this particular facial expression not only communicates shared grief, it also stimulates the brain to help counteract the feeling internally. The expression itself became a self-soothing mechanism and a mechanism for soothing others, all made possible by the mirror system.

Within a few weeks, once the immediate threat had lifted, New Yorkers gradually worked their way back to their more emotionally private selves. But their experience is a telling example of how we use facial expressions to help us hide our emotions and reveal them—and even help heal them.

The Billboard to the Soul

Our conscious facial expressions help us share our feelings of love and connection, agreement and collaboration, disgust and dismay. They can also be used as a mask to hide those feelings—but they can't make the true underlying feelings go away.

As much as we'd all like to believe we have complete control over our feelings and can choose whether or not to share them, that's not the case. Whatever emotions we manage to consciously conceal from our faces will eventually leak out—often through our body movements, but sometimes through "microexpressions."

As I mentioned earlier, microexpressions are fleeting expressions of emotion that flash across our faces in as little as 1/25th of a second. These tiny muscular movements sometimes go undetected by our conscious minds, but are eagerly absorbed by our mirror neurons and are just as eagerly reflected. In a 2000 study, Swedish researchers used subliminal techniques to show pictures of happy or angry faces to subjects without their knowledge. Just 30 milliseconds—3/100th of a second—of exposure was all it took for the subjects' corresponding facial muscles to imitate the emotion, without their having a clue about what they'd seen.

Our mirror system seems to act like an internal polygraph, reacting more strongly to displays of actual emotion than to pretend emotion, just by picking up on incredibly subtle facial clues. For example, let's say a guy grins at his date when she compliments his haircut. "Thanks," he says, but he doesn't really care all that much about his hair, so his smile might be convincingly polite, but fake. Later, she compliments his watch, which he really loves. Now he's genuinely flattered, and his cheek and eye muscles contract more symmetrically—he flashes her a "real" smile. Her brain will automatically pick up on this difference.

Now, we may not always be quick enough to catch those microexpressions as they happen. But I believe we can strengthen our own internal polygraphs by training ourselves to recognize certain facial expressions and emotions. Paul Ekman and his colleagues have determined that forty-three finely tuned muscles in the human face can be combined and reorganized into 10,000 possible combinations of expressions; they've even linked 3,000 of these expressions to specific feelings in the body. Once we have a handle on how to spot the more overt expressions, we become more intuitive about those underlying, subconscious microexpressions. Remember, almost all of us are naturally able to "read" these expressions—sometimes we just need a bit of practice to tune in to that native ability that we've lost somewhere along the way.

The Seven Universal Emotions

We are born with the facial expressions of seven universal emotions—surprise, fear, anger, sadness, disgust, happiness, and contempt—hardwired into our bodies. Like preloaded software for the body language database, these seven emotions are effortlessly recognized by our mirror systems in every human interaction we experience.

Ekman's research showed that these seven emotions were shared by people from all walks of life, all over the globe. But although we all have these emotions, we don't always show them. We might disguise a feeling of anger with a forced smile, or try to hide sadness or fear from our children. While the face is the primary medium for communicating emotion, it is also the most easily disguised.

When we openly express our emotions on our faces, those emotions are unmistakable. You can't miss them. They might only appear on the face for 1/25 of a second to 4 seconds, but our brains can gather quite a bit of information from that fast glimpse.

Capturing naked emotion on film is a challenge—especially in our feelings-phobic world, where most people won't walk out of their front door without their game face on. Let's take a look at each of these emotions and their most distinctive characteristics. As you look at each picture, try to mimic the expression and see if you feel the corresponding emotion in your body.

Sadness

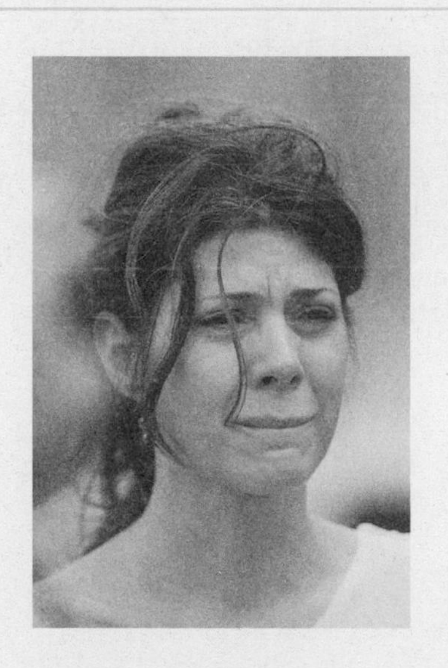

Actress Marisa Tomei's face exhibits sadness during a mass at Union Square on the first anniversary of the World Trade Center attacks.

Sadness is one of the most longlasting emotions. In typical sadness, you see somewhat of a clown face. The chin drops down, the eyelids tend to droop, the skin gets flaccid. Everything just starts to hang down, as if your features are melting off your face. The corners of your mouth go down, and sometimes you can see trembling. At the same time, the inside corner of the eyebrows rise up and a vertical line forms along the forehead's corrugator supercilli muscle, almost creating an upside-down V. Here are some of the most common signs of sadness:

Raised inner eyelids—an inverted V
Horizontal lines across the forehead
Eyelids droop
Mouth pulled downward
Raised lower eyelids

Surprise

Surprise is one of the fastest emotions. Let's say you walk in your front door and someone jumps out at you and yells, "Surprise! Happy Birthday!" What's going to happen? Your mouth is going to hang open first. Then your eyebrows rise, your eyes widen, and you'll likely see the whites on the top and bottom of the eye. The mouth opens wide into a circle O. All of this happens very quickly. Then, if it was a pleasant surprise, your face might settle into a smile; or if it was a scary surprise, your next expression will likely be fear. Let's review some of the facial signals you'll see in surprise:

President Dwight D. Eisenhower's face shows all the hallmark signs of surprise.

Eyebrows curve and rise up
Whites of the eyes can be seen above and sometimes below the iris
Upper eyelids go up
Lower eyelids stay round
Wrinkles appear across forehead
Mouth opens—lips part, width depending upon level of surprise
Whites of the eyes seen above and sometimes below the iris

Fear

Fear can sometimes follow surprise. In fear, the eyebrows are drawn together, centered toward the middle, and you see two little lines that appear directly next to the end of the eyebrow. The mouth draws together and the lips get very tight. The upper and lower eyelids become very tense, the pupils dilate, and the eyeballs bulge outward—usually the whites of the eyes are visible above and below the iris. You'll know someone is truly afraid when you see these signals:

President George W. Bush's face shows fear as he regains his footing after stumbling on the steps of Air Force One.

Eyebrows are raised and drawn together
Upper eyelid rises up
Whites of the eyes can be seen above the iris
Lower eyelids are tensed
Lips are parted, pulled down, and tense

His Signals/Her Signals

Written All Over Her

Emotions are easier to read on a woman's face than on a man's.

Anger

Studies have found that we can pick an angry face out of a crowd faster and more accurately than we can pick out a happy face. In anger, the eyebrows will lower and come together almost into a V shape. (Most comic-strip villains share this facial feature.) Little lines form between the brows. The eyes either widen and glare without blinking, or they narrow into little piercing slits, the lower eyelids tensing up. These are the most prominent facial signals for anger:

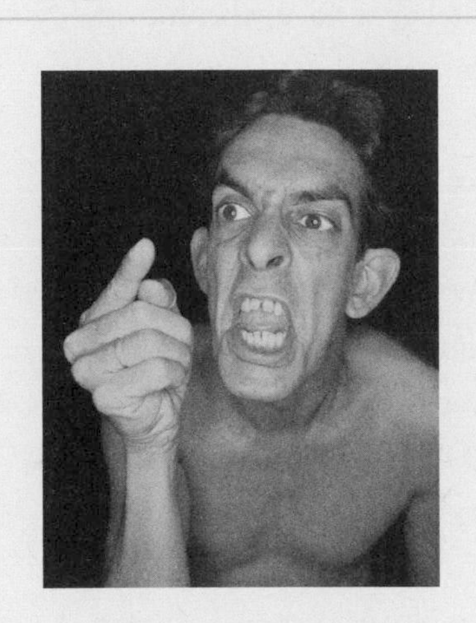

A man pointing his finger displays anger.

- Brows are furrowed
- Brows get lower
- Upper eyelid lowers
- Gaze becomes intense
- Lower eyelid tenses
- Nostril flaring
- Open square mouth
- Lip tension
- Lower lip bulge

Disgust

When you feel disgust, your nose will crinkle, almost as if you just smelled rotten milk and you're about to throw up. The upper lip pulls in as the

The nose crinkle is one of the most distinctive features of a disgusted face.

outer edges of the mouth turn down. This expression has a powerful effect on our mirror system. One recent study showed that whether we feel disgusted or witness someone else's disgust, both experiences activate the same parts of the brain, the anterior insula and the adjacent frontal operculum. We may not have seen or smelled anything gross, but if we just look at the other person's expression, we feel like we have. Some of the most distinctive signs of disgust are:

Forehead usually relaxed

Eyebrows are lowered

Wrinkling in the upper nose area

Tense lower lid

Pursed lips

Raised upper lip, leaving mouth slightly open

Happiness

Happiness is seen in our favorite expression—the real smile. If you look at the picture here, you can see how a happy smile is actually quite different from a social smile—your gums show a little bit more, your eyes turn into half moons, your crow's-feet show up. Perhaps most pronounced is the clearly drawn nasolabial fold, the "puppet" line from the outer edge of your nose to the corner of your mouth. We all love to look at these smiles, and we find it nearly

Former New York City mayor Rudolph Giuliani's face shows the characteristic signs of a "real" smile.

impossible not to smile when we see them. Here are some of the facial signals that denote happiness:

Relaxed forehead

Outer ends of eyebrows slightly pulled down

Narrow eyes

Crow's-feet

Lines under eyes

Raised cheeks

Lines in the nasolabial fold

Mouth corners turned up

Lips slightly parted—top teeth showing

Contempt

Contempt is similar to disgust, but does not seem to reflect a physical revulsion, the way that disgust does. Instead, contempt is seen when people feel superior to others or when they disapprove of their actions or demeanor. Contempt can blend with anger, disgust, or happiness to form several different expressions. While some experts would not agree, Paul Ekman believes that contempt is an emotion exhibited with the same facial expression throughout the world. The facial signals that indicate contempt include:

U.S. Vice President Dick Cheney's face shows contempt as he speaks about the Iranian government at a gathering hosted by the Council of Foreign Relations in Washington, DC.

Wrinkles on the nose

One lip often raised in a sneer

Lips sometimes pushed forward

Tight mouth with slightly raised corners (could be confused with a small smile)

Reading Individual Facial Expressions

You will rarely see any one facial expression at a time. Most often, you'll see a cluster—one or two of these facial gestures combined with other body language signals, such as tone of voice, or hand gestures. Like peeling an onion, we'll start with the outer layer—the overt facial expressions people use consciously—and gradually work our way down to the facial expressions that people display unconsciously. Let's take a look at some of the most common expressions. You can see demonstrations of many of these expressions and other body language videos at www.BodyLanguageUniversity.com.

Eye and Eyebrow Signals

When we look at other people's faces, we first focus on the eyes, then the lips. Some eye signals we can control; others happen entirely automatically. Let's look at the expressions that make eyes the "windows to the soul."

Facial Signal: Eye Contact

We tend to make more eye contact with people we like and agree with and less with those we dislike, disagree with, or are intimidated by. When you look another person in the eyes, you're saying that you feel good about yourself—you're confident, you're trustworthy, and you know what you're talking about. Most of all, it tells a person that you listen, an increasingly rare thing in our society. An attentive listener will hold eye contact roughly 70 percent of the time, but often we spend our "listening" time just trying to collect our own thoughts. Our conversations become like cafeteria food fights—we duck out of the way while they're talking and then hurl our words at them as soon as they've finished. Increase your level of eye contact, and you tell a person, "I'm listening to you and am not thinking about anything else."

His Signals/Her Signals

Gaze into Her Eyes

Women love eye contact. They gaze into anyone's eyes—women or men—especially one-on-one, and they tend to like it much more than men do. Men will tolerate it with women, but they don't like it as much, and they definitely don't do it as often with other men.

When we're actually speaking, we don't maintain eye contact the entire time. We might use it as a way of directing turn-taking. For example, you might look down, gather your thoughts, then look up and finish the thought. If it's your turn to talk, but you're still collecting your thoughts, keep your eyes down or to the side—anywhere but on the person's face. This break in eye contact will tell the listener that it's still your turn to talk. When you're ready to relinquish the floor, turn your eyes back to the other person and briefly pause—that's an authoritative way to say, "OK, it's your turn now."

What to watch for: Too much eye contact. We typically believe people who look us in the eye, and we tend to distrust those who don't. But extreme eye contact can also be an indication that someone might be lying. Experienced liars will purposely maintain eye contact just to come across as honest and trustworthy. You won't know their typical patterns until you "norm" them, or assess their normal level of eye contact. (See chapter 7 for more on this deception-detection technique.)

What you should work on: Using eye contact often, if not always. If you have trouble maintaining eye contact, you *must* work on this critical skill. Studies have found that employers view prospective hires who don't make eye contact as unattractive, detached, passive, incompetent, and lacking composure and social skills.

When you're getting started, just do a little at a time. Begin by making eye contact while you listen to someone else speak; work up to eye contact while you speak. Studies show that people who maintain eye contact while they speak are seen as more persuasive. Do this with five people a day, adding a few more people each week. You'll gradually feel more comfortable, and you'll notice people responding to you more positively.

Facial Signal: Stalker Stare

You feel the stalker stare when you're having a conversation with someone and they're just staring at your eyeballs and blinking only twice or three times a minute. You might feel like you're being stared down. But often when people give the stalker stare, they are concentrating intensely.

When I work with clients who are perfecting their public speaking, some tell me they get spooked when they're faced with a sea of blank, staring eyes in the audience. I tell them that this might be the way some people pay attention, but it's more likely the way some *pretend* to pay attention. This can be a dangerous signal. Depending upon your topic, you might need to step up the energy level in your presentation.

What to watch for: When people are trying to intimidate you. Whether or not someone is doing this deliberately to throw you off balance, you don't have to let it change your own reaction. You can either stare right back, if that doesn't bother you too much, or you can refuse to meet their eyes. After all, they're your eyes! You don't have to give in to their eyeball intimidation. This is the facial equivalent of dropping your hand out of a dominant handshake—it's always your option to just say, "No, thank you. I won't be needing your bullying today."

What you should work on: Look in the eye-nose triangle. Sometimes we do a stalker stare without being aware of it. If you're talking to someone, and you sense that they're starting to squirm and not meeting your eyes, take note of your own eye contact. You might be the person who never blinks. That's why it's always important to look in the eye/nose triangle, the area of the face between the two eyes and the nose. By giving the other person's eyeballs a break, you will avoid staring them down.

Several years ago, while lecturing to a singles group on how to meet other singles, I encountered a man in the audience who did everything he was supposed to do to build rapport—he smiled appropriately, he tilted his head to demonstrate interest, he nodded often to indicate agreement, he even leaned forward in his seat to show me he was captivated by the seminar. The only mistake he made was maintaining eye contact the entire time.

What? You might be thinking, "Isn't that what he was supposed to do?" Yes, but his problem was that he didn't blink. His eye contact was so intense it was eerie. Every time I looked his way he was looking into my eyes—no blinks, no lowering his gaze to the eye/nose triangle, no eye aversion—just pure stalker stare.

After the lecture this man came over to me and introduced himself. Roger was a nice-looking guy with a good build, and after speaking to him for a few minutes, I realized he was quite affable with a good sense of humor. "Tonya, here's the thing," he said, lowering his voice and leaning closer to me, speaking almost in a whisper. "I really don't have any trouble getting women to talk to me initially. The problem is, after a few minutes, they all seem to make excuses and walk away. I can't figure it out."

"Roger, to be honest, I think I already know why—and from personal experience," I said. I related how his stalker stare was unsettling, and I told him that if he was doing the same thing to women in social settings, it was likely the root of his problem.

The idea that he might routinely stare people down came as quite a surprise to Roger. Once he became aware of his issue, he realized people did squirm when they were around him. He had thought he came across as powerful, when in fact he came across as peculiar. As we talked some more, I could see that Roger had a slower-than-average blink rate, which was probably the primary reason for his stalker stare.

I gave him some simple advice: Don't force yourself to blink. Instead, force yourself to move your eyes around when you are speaking to people. Move your gaze from left eye to right eye to nose. This little change in his eye contact made a big difference in Roger's "hit rate" with women—as well as how he felt about himself.

His Signals/Her Signals

Quit Staring

Women are more likely to break eye contact with men because they don't want to lead them on. Men often misread prolonged eye contact as a sign of attraction.

Facial Signal: Pupil Dilation and Constriction

The most common reason for our pupils to dilate is to allow our eyes to take in more light. When we move from a sunny place to a shady one, the pupil dilates from 2 millimeters wide to almost 8 millimeters wide. However, a landmark discovery made by Eckhard Hess at the University of Chicago in the 1960s found that our pupils also dilate when we see something that excites us. As a result, we instinctively view individuals with enlarged pupils as attractive, warm, friendly, and conscientious people.

Models on magazine covers sometimes have their pupils doctored to give them larger pupils because publishers know this cue for sexual arousal sells more magazines. Researchers found that in heterosexuals, both men's and women's pupils dilate the most when they look at images of naked members of the opposite sex. Women's pupils will dilate when they see pictures of children, whether or not they have had kids of their own, but only men who are fathers will experience pupil dilation under the same circumstances. Additional research discovered that our pupils will also dilate when we are terrified or when we are lying.

What to watch for: Changes they don't know about. The fun part about this nonverbal signal is you are able to tell what someone is interested in just by watching his eyes. On a person with light-colored eyes, you might be able to see this reaction at a distance of three to five feet; with darker colored eyes, perhaps two feet. Chinese jade dealers used to purposely wear glasses when evaluating stones for purchase, because dilated pupils revealed their interest, a clue that would harm their negotiating power.

A few things to remember: Of course, light will have a great impact on the size of someone's pupils, so this sign is hugely dependent upon context. (You can't make an assumption your friend suddenly hates you if his pupils constrict in broad daylight.) Also, some people have larger or smaller pupils by nature, so you have to see them in several settings before you can draw any conclusions.

What you should work on: Pay attention to the lighting. If you're hoping to seduce someone over dinner, look for a darkened corner of the restaurant; the dim lights will encourage your pupils to dilate, making you more attractive to your date. Guys, take note—one study found this is especially effective with women who have a preference for "bad boys," because large pupils in men hearken back to signs of prehistoric man's aggressive sexual interest.

His Signs/Her Signs

Beauty Is Pain. . . . and Sometimes, Even Worse

The link between pupil dilation and female beauty has been known and exploited for centuries. Courtesans in Italy used an eyedrop drug called *belladonna*, or "beautiful woman," to dilate their pupils in order to make themselves more desirable to men. One problem: this drug was made from a poisonous plant called deadly nightshade. True to this ominous name, the beauty treatment caused tremendous eye pain and ultimately, with prolonged use, death.

Facial Signal: Blinking

Most of us need to blink at least six to ten times a minute in order to coat our eyeballs and keep our eyelids from sticking, but that frequency can increase to upward of a hundred times a minute when we're under stress. One researcher found that when President Clinton was asked about his teenage drug use during a presidential debate, his blink rate went from an earlier debate average of 43 blinks per minute to 117 per minute.

You often see an increased blink rate when a person is lying or overly anxious. The person feels pressure to answer a question, which speeds up the thought process and, consequently, the blink rate. When you are in deep thought or concentration, or if you're staring, the blink rate can slow down to two or three times per minute.

What to watch for: A deviation from a normal rate. You have to get a feel for how often a person blinks in order to use this sign as a reliable indicator. Once you're attuned to this signal, you'll notice how people's averages differ—there's really a wide range. Some people have a medical condition called blepharospasm, an uncontrolled muscle spasm in the eyelid that causes them to blink excessively, for example. In general, if someone is blinking two to three times more frequently than they usually do, something is going on.

What you should work on: Using it to flirt. Although we might want to control blinking during times of high stress, trying to do so consciously will just make it worse. It's much better to learn to relax your whole body during stressful times. When you stay more relaxed, your body won't trigger the automatic processes that speed up blink rate.

One way to use blinking consciously would be to flirt: flutter your eyelashes briefly while you tilt your chin down, perhaps while you're taking a sip from a straw. (Yes, it might seem a bit old-fashioned, but people still drop napkins, and how old is that?)

5 Strategies to . . .

seem interested during a boring meeting

Meeting going long? When you want to look interested while you zone out, try these tips. You won't get a promotion for your convincing performance, but at least you'll stay awake.

1. *Tilt your head to the right.* Think like your dog—when you talk to him, he tilts his head. That's a submissive gesture that tells you, "I'm interested in what you're saying. I'm listening to you." One recent study found that when you tilt your head to the right, people see you as more trustworthy, and when you tilt your head to the left you are seen as more attractive.

2. *Occasionally smile at the person speaking.* Listen, I know it's tough to do, but otherwise you'll get a glazed look on your face, even when you're maintaining eye contact.

3. *Keep blinking.* Further to the glazing issue, when we get bored we often stop blinking and just stare to make it look like we're interested. Blink about fifteen times a minute, the average non-bored rate. (Bored blinkers average around five to ten.)

4. *Nod in agreement, not slumber.* But make sure you know what you're nodding about. Don't get caught nodding when your boss is saying, "Oh yeah, I'm probably going to get sued for this."

5. *Shift your body.* If you've tried all of the above and you're still falling asleep, pick your whole body up and shift into a different position. That move will jolt your body awake and help you to pay better attention. And the momentary disruption in the meeting is nothing compared to what would happen if you let out a big snore.

Facial Signal: Winking

A wink is a bonding mechanism that can be used by friends or prospective lovers. Picture a crowded room of people, and a woman looks up and sees this attractive, extroverted guy who winks at her. He makes her feel sexual, as if only the two of them are connected in this vast room of strangers. A wink says, "I'm not noticing anybody else at this particular moment." If you're attracted to or otherwise agree with the winker, you might find it flattering or fun; otherwise, it will probably be a bit of a turnoff.

You might get a wink from a coworker during a boring meeting or from your spouse during a particularly unappetizing dinner with the in-laws. This wink says, "You and me, we're in this together." In a business-type situation, winking at someone who's in a superior position could be a bit risky. Make sure your relationship is sufficiently secure before you try it.

One of the best examples of an ill-advised wink was President Bush's wink at the queen of England during her visit to the United States in spring 2007. During a speech to honor her, Bush made a slip of the tongue that suggested she was over two hundred years old. He covered up that faux pas with another one, a wink to say, "Sorry about that—but let's pretend that was just a joke between us."

President George Bush used a wink to apologize to Queen Elizabeth for a slip of the tongue—adding insult to injury.

What to watch for: When someone uses it to bond against you. If you catch a wink between two other people, it can feel very exclusionary—with good reason. They may have shared the wink about something completely unrelated to you, but it still makes you feel as if you're on the outside. If someone winks at you but you have no interest in bonding with this person, just turn your head immediately and do not acknowledge the wink. He'll get the message.

What you should work on: Practice makes perfect. The wink is one of those signals that are only good when they seem completely casual and unrehearsed. You blink with your nondominant side—if you're a lefty, you blink with your right eye, and vice versa. Some people are natural winkers; others have to work to develop the skill. If you open up your mouth when you wink, you're not a natural winker—you need practice. Wink at yourself in the mirror five times whenever you walk in to the bathroom. Eventually it'll become second nature and you can use it to bond with anyone—friends at parties, colleagues in meetings, or the supermarket checkout clerk.

Facial Signal: Eyebrow Flash

The eyebrow flash is a universal, instinctive response of recognition, a natural greeting sign that also can indicate interest and liking. You see it when someone's eyebrows lift up very fleetingly, for about ⅕ of a second. Every day, when you walk by people in the street, you flash your eyebrows without even realizing it—your faces are saying hello to each other without your conscious participation.

What to watch for: How common it is. Depending on how many people you encounter in a day, you could do this forty or fifty times a day and not even realize it—and 80 percent of the people you've "flashed" will do it back and won't realize it either.

What you should work on: Looking at strangers. The eyebrow flash is unconscious—you do it automatically—so you can't train for it. But depending on where you live and the cultural display rules in your area, you should try to stay as open as possible to strangers and allow your face to greet them. Remember: Your mirror neurons are constantly collecting memories that help you become a better communicator. Plus, when you remain open and look at strangers' faces, especially in the workplace, you'll automatically be regarded as a friendlier person. You never know when that "stranger" from another division whom you've been eyebrow-flashing for a few months could turn out to be your new boss.

Facial Signal: Eyebrow Lift

The eyebrow lift stretches out the skin underneath the eyebrow, sending the brows high and round in little semi-curved arches. The eyebrow-lift expression most often indicates disbelief. Depending on how long it stays on the face, it could also be a quizzical look.

The eyebrow lift is a very versatile tool to transmit intense emotions. It can make you appear more dominant, submissive, surprised, or even energetic. David Givens of the Center for Nonverbal Studies says we often use the eyebrow lift to make demands on others or punctuate our opinions in conversation.

What to watch for: How long it stays on the face. Depending how long the expression stays on my face, it might indicate (a) I'm truly shocked by what you're saying ("No way!"); (b) I'm horrified ("Oh, my goodness, I can't believe that happened to you!"); or (c) I'm showing mock surprise to indicate skepticism ("Oh, *really*?"). Any overexaggeration with the eyebrow lift runs the risk of coming across as patronizing to the other person.

What you should work on: Be careful not to overuse it. Often we don't even realize we're lifting our brows. Some might use this signal deliberately and exaggeratedly, thinking it's a good way to indicate interest. But because it is a universal sign of disbelief, if you overuse it, you might be seen as chronically skeptical. Concentrate on keeping your eyebrows down when others voice their opinions.

Facial Signal: Skeptic's Eyebrow

This signal was made famous by John Belushi and Jack Nicholson. If someone raises one eyebrow while you're talking to them, and perhaps smiles slightly, you can easily assume they do not take you seriously, think you exaggerate, or do not believe a single word of what you're saying. Used in humor, an arched eyebrow can be a flirty move, but at its core, it indicates deep skepticism. This sign is most often seen among friends who are joking with each other, but you might also see a flash of it during a sales pitch. If that's the case, you have some serious work to do to make the sale.

John Belushi raised the "skeptic's eyebrow" to an art form.

What to watch for: When you're not in on it. Let's say you're in a meeting, giving a presentation, and you see one of your less-than-collegial colleagues flash someone else a skeptic's eyebrow. Don't ignore it. He's trying to make other people doubt you, and you have to nip that doubt in the bud. Call him on it—say, "So, Bob, this is a good time to ask you—do you have any questions? Is there anything you want to talk about? Anything you're unclear about? Anything you feel I haven't explained properly?" Calling attention to the skeptic makes him articulate his doubts—and it also puts him on the spot.

What you should work on: Using it to instill doubt. Just as your colleague tried to use this against you, you can return the favor. If you want to quietly sow a seed of doubt about what another person is saying, or show that you doubt their sincerity, just toss off a quick skeptic's eyebrow at the third party. As long as the speaker doesn't catch on, that sign is going to linger and fester and create a quiet discord in the conversation.

Facial Signal: Widened Eyes (Surprised, Afraid, or Innocent)

As I mentioned earlier, when we are truly surprised or afraid, our eyes will widen in response. In fear, the mouth pulls back and down; in surprise, the eyes will be more round and the mouth may be open, too. If you don't see the mouth opening, the person is probably just trying to look innocent.

While it might be a controversial mating strategy, this signal is often used by women to indicate vulnerability—"I need your big strong arms to keep me safe!" Marilyn Monroe's signature eyebrows were

Before: Norma Jeane Mortenson had naturally dark hair and eyebrows.

After: Marilyn Monroe's trademark bedroom eyes included an eyebrow makeover.

consciously crafted to give her this wide-eyed, innocent look to provoke a paternal, and ultimately sexual, reaction in men.

What to watch for: When someone is trying to interrupt. If you're talking, and someone widens their eyes and combines it with a head tilt, they might be trying to tell you you're yammering on a bit long. The eyes are saying, "Really! That's fascinating! Now can I make a comment?"

What you should work on: Don't overuse it at work. Overusing this signal can make you seem like you're in a constant state of wonderment. Keep it out of your business relationships. You'll either be pegged as dumb or as someone who's trying to fake innocence and naïveté—neither of which will help you.

Facial Signal: Widened Eyes (Enraged)

The eyes-widened signal could also mean rage. You'll see the difference in the mouth, which becomes taut, drawn together in a little circle, and the eyebrows, which seem to come down instead of lifting. That look of staring someone down with eyes wide open and no brow lift at all is a look of intense anger.

Normally we try to mask our feelings of anger—it's part of the social contract to pretend that things just don't affect us that much. So when you see this signal, it's a sign that your safety might be in question—or, at the very least, that something unpleasant is about to happen.

What to watch for: Stay away from this in a stranger. If you see someone you don't know with this look on his face, why subject yourself to it? Don't take the chance that you'll be caught up in something terrible, just get away from him. This type of anger rarely can be reasoned with.

What you should work on: Smile to mask your rage. Sometimes you might find yourself on the angry side of this signal. Let's say your coworker betrayed you, and you are furious. You see her at the annual holiday party, you both know she stabbed you in the back, but you don't want her to know she got to you. Add a nice fake smile to this wide-eyed look, and look her right in the eyes. Overtly, she'll see, "What you did doesn't bother me a bit," but inside, her gut is going to hear, "Watch your back."

Normally I wouldn't recommend that you mask your emotions. After all, the best way to have congruent body language is to say what you mean and mean what you say. But the world can be cold and cruel, and sometimes it helps to have a body language trick or two up your sleeve to counter the manipulative tactics of others.

Facial Signal: Droopy Lids (aka "Bedroom Eyes")

This signal was the second part of Marilyn Monroe's signature eye look. Usually, you see droopy lids when someone is tired, depressed, or lazy. But among adults in the mating scene, droopy lids have other connotations.

Many women use this sexy signal in combination with an over-the-shoulder turn. If someone gives you the droopy lids look, as long as their lower eyelids aren't tensed, it's all about seduction. If you do see the lower eyelids tense, that's a more contentious, angry, or "I-don't-have-my-glasses-on" kind of look.

What to watch for: Guys can do it, too. Clark Gable made this look famous in the 1930s, and it's currently enjoying a resurgence among current male sex symbols, such as the entire male cast of *Grey's Anatomy.*

What you should work on: Make sure not to overuse it. While this is a sign for seduction—as in "bedroom eyes"—don't forget what else goes on in the bedroom. You don't want someone to confuse "sexy" with "sleepy."

Facial Signal: Sideways Glances

When you use this signal, you tilt your head down and away from the person you're looking at, and then look back at him. In doing so, you'll leave that same side of your neck exposed.

This flirting gesture is a naked appeal to a man's protective side. The eyes looking upward make them appear innocent, larger, and are meant to suggest a "Hold me, big boy" kind of a plea, but the sideways glance turns it into a sexual look. (See the picture of Christina Aguilera under "Lip Lick" on page 82 for a great example of a sexy sideways glance.)

What to watch for: Can also be used for sarcasm. Especially when paired with a raised eyebrow, à la Jack Nicholson, the sideways glance can be used by men in a flirtatious, skeptical way. If you're a woman and want to use it for this connotation as well, take care not to tilt your head down. (I use it occasionally—I look over my shoulder and do the glance, "Come *on*!")

What you should work on: Use it sparingly. This eye signal is among the most contrived because it doesn't happen naturally. The sideways glance can be very effective with the right guy, but just know that this gesture sends tremendous signals of vulnerability.

His Signals/Her Signals

She Has a Knack for Faces

Studies have found that women are significantly better at putting names to faces, starting in preschool.

Facial Signal: Furrowed Brow

When both eyebrows are drawn together, a person's forehead will form horizontal lines, and you will also see a line down the glabella, the region right between the two eyebrows.

This signal could show acute anxiety, fear, or anger, or a combination of these feelings. In anger, although the inner corners of the brows are brought together, the brow is also lowered, giving an intense look to the eyes. In fear and anxiety, you might notice horizontal lines in the forehead and additional white in the eyes.

What to watch for: If a person is concentrating. If you see this expression in a business meeting, presume that the person is simply focusing intently on a thought or on your face, not that they're angry or anxious about your ideas.

What you should work on: Relaxing your face. If your face makes this expression too often, by the time you're forty, you will start to retain those lines in your forehead all the time. I am constantly reminding my kids not to furrow their brows and to consciously relax their foreheads. Habits start early, so prevention is important. Once you have these wrinkles, even if they are from concentrating, there is a chance people will perceive you as angry or fearful.

Smiles

Scientists believe the smile originated from the primates' fear grimace and then evolved into a submissive gesture: "I'm not aggressive. I'm not here to hurt you." Today, that is still one of the functions of a smile—to tell total strangers that you're unthreatening—but the endless variations on a smile enable it to say so much more. Whether you're sharing your pleasure, happiness, optimism, or simply being polite, a smile is by far your most versatile and personally beneficial facial expression. You'll learn about some of the many varieties of smiles here, then later I'll show you how to put each one to good use in building rapport with the Reiman Rapport Method (see chapter 9).

His Signals/Her Signals

The Smiles Have It

According to the book *Smile!* by Jonathan Levine, DMD, the average baby smiles 200 times a day; the average woman smiles 62 times a day; the average man smiles 8 times a day.

Facial Signal: The "Real" Smile

The face reflects our positive emotions more accurately than our negative emotions, primarily because of the unmistakable genuine smile. Also called the Duchenne smile (for Guillaume Duchenne, who "discovered" the muscles involved by prodding subjects with live electrical wires!), the "real" smile is seen when the corners of the lips turn up, the eyes turn into half-moons, and those telltale crow's-feet crinkle up at the outer corners of the eyes.

It's tough to fake this kind of smile, and you'll know it when you see it. A genuine smile is more symmetrical than a fake, or "social," smile, and it doesn't last as long. But a genuine smile is the gift that keeps on giving: genuine smiles can trigger the release of endorphins, serotonin, and dopamine, all neurotransmitters associated with pleasure and happiness. And few things delight your brain more than seeing a genuine smile on someone else's face.

What to watch for: The eyebrow scrunch/crow's-feet crinkle. Very few people can fake a real smile because you have to engage a very specific muscle—the orbicularis oculi, pars alteralis, which makes both the eyebrows and the skin between the upper eyelid and the eyebrow come down. Some people can fake the mouth curl, but not many people can do the full eyebrow scrunch/crow's-feet crinkle.

What you should work on: Surround yourself with happy people. The only way you can flash more of these genuine smiles is to be truly happy, and of course you should do everything in your power to have a happy life. One bankable way to do that is to pick positive friends who are more likely to give you great smiles to mirror. Consider the possible effects of *not* having those smiles to mirror.

Several years ago I was introduced to my friend Gina's husband, Jack. As I put out my hand to shake, Jack nodded at me with a very serious look and solemnly said, "Nice to meet you."

Of course, I didn't feel as if he was pleased to meet me. I instantly felt uncomfortable. After that, whenever we would see each other socially Jack always gave me the same cold, serious look. During our light conversations I would inevitably find myself babbling because I was so uncomfortable talking to him.

Now, I pride myself on being a very friendly, outgoing person. I like everyone unless they give me a reason not to. But this guy made me squirm. His stiff walk, the coolness of his voice, his rigid facial expression, never wavered. When I was with him, I noticed that I felt disliked, self-conscious, and insecure.

I continued to feel this way for several years until one evening, while Gina and I were sitting on her couch having a few drinks, Jack came home and sat down to have a drink with us. A few hours later, we'd all had several, and I realized that Jack had started smiling. He wasn't acting any differently; his voice, movements, posture, everything else, was exactly the same. But that smile immediately changed the way I felt about him, and just like that, my opinion of him permanently shifted. I was now able to see him as someone who could be outgoing and fun to be around.

Granted, we had all had a few, and the alcohol may have loosened Jack up a bit. But that's not what made the difference in our relationship. I've seen him many times since that evening, and he has reverted to that same cool look of indifference that put me off the first time. What truly changed my opinion of him was seeing him smile, even if only briefly. I was able to see him as a nice guy, and that impression remains with me even when his expression is just naturally somewhat cold and distant. That experience really helped me to understand, on a personal level, what a powerful difference one smile can make.

Facial Signal: The Social Smile

In the social smile, the risorius muscles pull the sides of the lips out, but not up, as they do in the genuine smile. You also don't see a very pronounced nasolabial fold, the line that goes from the outer edge of your nose to the corner of your mouth. But while you may not see many genuine smiles during the day, these pleasant social smiles keep interactions with acquaintances happy and light.

Happy people used to get a bad rap as boring and one-dimensional, an attitude epitomized by Tolstoy's famous line, "All happy families resemble one another, but each unhappy family is unhappy in its own way." But studies show that people believe social smilers are not only less domineering and more fun to be around but also more intelligent.

What to watch for: How frequently they're returned. One recent study found that a passing stranger is nine times more likely to smile at you when you smile at them. That's why I say the easiest way to improve your own mood is to smile at someone else. When they immediately smile back at you, the two of you will step right into a very positive emotional hall of mirrors.

What you should work on: Perfect your own social smile. A good social smile is a tool that expands all of your possibilities, both socially and in the business world. Numerous studies have found that people who smile are believed to be more warm, honest, polite, kind, sociable, happy, flirtatious, successful, and attractive. That's quite a bang for your body language buck! If you're not a fan of your own social smile, you can easily create a new one. See "Flash Your Social Smile" on page 282 for more help.

Facial Signal: Fast and Slow Smiles

Being "quick to grin" isn't necessarily a good thing. New research has revealed that fast smiles, the ones that—poof!—flash across your face in 1/10 of a second, are seen as much less sincere than slow smiles, especially by women. In contrast, both men and women judge a slow smile—one that takes an *eternal* half second to appear—as both more sincere and more flirtatious.

People are sometimes much quicker to smile when they've done something wrong. When I ask my son for his homework and he flashes me a big nervous grin, I know he left it at school. Busted! His smile acts as a defense mechanism. ("I'm just a little kid, Mom, take pity on me!")

What to watch for: Faux fast smiles. Sometimes a fast smile is just a social obligation that someone wants to get out of the way.

What you should work on: Faux slow smiles. The same study cited above also found that slow smiles make you seem more attractive and more trustworthy. Guys should absolutely take this research into account when they're meeting a woman for the first time. Done well, a slow smile appears to reveal your thought process more gradually, which gives the person you are smiling at the feeling she's being comprehensively evaluated—and ultimately deemed one hot mama. ("You like me, you really like me!")

Facial Signal: Perma-Grin

Several studies have shown that while men's smiles are typically seen as genuine and flirtatious, women's smiles are more likely to be seen as insincere, even downright fake. Researchers believe this bias exists because people basically expect women to smile all the time—that a smile should be our default setting. So, ladies, we're in a bit of a catch-22: Smile too little, and risk being seen as a downer. Smile too much and . . . you're in danger of becoming what I call a Perma-Grinner.

When a person smiles constantly, he or she is perceived as silly or dumb. Which is not fair—you could be genuinely happy all the time. But there's a difference between smiling at appropriate times, smiling to demonstrate you're happy, and smiling all the time.

What to watch for: Your own bias against the Perma-Grinner. We sometimes find it unsettling to be around people who smile all the time because we have no way of judging their sincerity. If you want to test the veracity of that smile, bring up a god-awful subject and see how the person fields it. If she can grin through a discussion about Darfur, she may actually have a dissociative disorder that keeps her separated from her true feelings. Sunny though her smile may be, hers is not the kind of "happy" you should aspire to.

What you should work on: Your serious social face. If you stand accused of being a Perma-Grinner, you need to develop a serious face that you can break out in appropriate moments. You can develop one the same way you can develop a social smile. (See "Flash Your Social Smile" on page 282.) When you're in public and feel yourself slipping into a Perma-Grin, bite your lip—that jolt will help you change your expression to a neutral one.

Facial Signal: The Smirk

The smirk can take on a few forms. Usually it's tight-lipped with one side slightly raised. If one corner of the mouth is raised, it might be an endearingly sarcastic smirk. If the top lip is raised, it's probably a "sneer smirk," more dismissive and judgmental. The smirk is considered a type of smile, but I consider it more of an evil grin.

U.S. senator Joe Biden smirks during a Senate Foreign Relations Committee hearing on Capitol Hill in Washington, DC.

At first blush, the smirk might look like an average smile—the corners of the mouth are turned up, after all. But honestly, if the person wanted to show he was happy, he would smile. A smirk conveys something extra—a hint of smugness, cockiness, or superiority, a bit of condescension, a note of doubt or dismissal.

What to watch for: When someone uses it to denigrate you. Similar to the skeptic's brow, the smirk shows others in the group that this person doesn't really buy your argument and can be used to try to persuade others to his way of thinking. George W. Bush used the smirk quite often during his 2000 and 2004 presidential debates to tell the audience, "I don't believe a word my opponent is saying."

What you should work on: Using it to flirt. The smirk is sarcastic, it's bold, it can be somewhat sexy. The smirk says, "I'm secure in myself." Definitely steer clear of the "sneer smirk." But whether you're a man or a woman, feel free to use the one-sided grin version as your come-hither glance and you'll let your crush know that you have a good sense of humor before you even start talking.

Scowls and Frowns

A negative facial expression can do tremendous damage to your best intentions in a business or social situation. But, in the right setting, a scowl or a frown can also be an extremely effective communication tool. Let's look at the differences between these negative expressions.

Facial Signal: The Active Scowl

One study found that just seeing a flash of an angry face for 4 milliseconds—1⁄25 of a second—was enough to make people dislike the very next thing they were shown. Psychologists call this effect "priming"—when a person subconsciously absorbs a certain feeling from one expression and transfers that feeling onto another person or object. Do you see where I'm going with this? If you're trying to pitch an idea or make a friend or generally not alienate your fellow man, it's best to keep the scowls to a minimum.

A scowl is actually an all-purpose negative face. It's not just about anger—scowls can also indicate annoyance, disgust, dislike, even frustration: "I didn't get my way."

What to watch for: When a mouth moves from neutral to negative. When someone's lip line goes from being straight across to turning down somewhat, you've just seen them tip into anger. Usually, any time a person is angry but not masking it with some other emotion, you'll likely see a scowl.

What you should work on: Using it only when you have to. I could easily tell you never to scowl. But that's just masking your true emotions. A good scowl can show someone you're angry and be a healthy release of your anger. Just be careful not to overuse it, or it might become a "static scowl."

Facial Signal: The Static Scowl

Whether due to disposition or facial bone structure, some of us show a static scowl as our neutral face. Unfortunately, while you may be happy as a clam, the neutral face you show the world might make others think you are a sourpuss.

If you see someone with a scowl, don't immediately assume they're angry—they could just have a particular bone structure that makes them look as if they are. For example, I know several people who have overbites, and when they keep their lips closed, their mouths draw down into what looks like an angry scowl. One of my clients, Peter, found that his scowl was costing him business.

I'll never forget when I first met Peter. I was at a wedding, one of those fun family weddings with a lot of food and a lot of dancing. Peter was the DJ, and he was fantastic—he set just the right tone, read the crowd perfectly, and knew just how to settle them down for a serious moment and get them pumped up and dancing again. In other words, he did his job, and did it well—so why was his business not taking off?

I ran into Peter at the bar during one of his breaks, and I was struck by how different his face looked when he wasn't "on." During his set, he'd looked animated, alive, his features full of good humor. But as we struck up a conversation, his face fell into an angry, depressed expression that looked far older than his youthful forty-two years.

"I just don't get it," he said, shaking his head. "They really like me when I do my gigs. And I get lots of referrals that way. But for some reason, I can't get any new clients."

I asked him to mimic the face he got from his clients. He made a sour grimace.

I said, "Pete, I think I know your problem. But we have to track down the photographer so I can show you."

We found the wedding photographer, and I asked him if he could take a quick digital photo of Peter's face. Pete was incredibly dubious.

"Why are you taking my picture?" he asked. "I guess I'm just ugly—is that it?"

"Trust me," I said. "This will all make sense in a second." I instructed him to pose in a completely neutral face, with no emotion, positive or negative.

The photographer snapped the photo, and the three of us huddled around to see the camera's digital screen. Pete's sourpuss mug showed up, loud and clear. "My god," he said. "I look like *that*? No wonder they hate me!"

Pete and I worked together for a few weeks after that, developing his social smile. First, he made huge, fake smiles, smiling so broadly that his face almost hurt. Then he scaled it back from there, finally settling on a smile that felt right for his face. I also advised him to keep his mouth slightly open, to allow his overbite a bit of space—that, too, had an impact on his smile. I told him to practice in front of the mirror five times a day and use his social smile with everyone he met, from prospective clients to the checkout clerk, for the next three weeks.

Three weeks later, a changed man walked into my office. "Tonya, it's unbelievable," he said. "Things are really taking off for me suddenly. And do you know something? I truly feel happier. I feel like, for the first time in my life, when I look at other people, they see me. I never knew how angry-looking I was before. I can't believe how this one thing has changed my life so much."

If you think you might display this facial signal, ask a friend to take a photo of you in a neutral face so you can see if you are scowling. If you are, practice a new neutral face, just as you would practice a serious face or a social smile. (See "Flash Your Social Smile" on page 282 for the process.)

What to watch for: How much the face changes. While all static scowls tend to look alike while they're at rest, you can see a major difference between them once any emotion is introduced. The people who have a static scowl due to their facial structure will tend to brighten immediately when exposed to something pleasant. The people who are static scowlers because of their dispositions are unlikely to brighten in response to anything.

What you should work on: Getting rid of it! Cosmetic surgery is a $10-billion-a-year industry, growing by estimates of 10 percent per year. Much of those revenues come from people dealing with the aftermath of static scowls. If you have to get wrinkles, make them those adorable crow's-feet you get from laughing too much instead of those vertical hatchet lines between the eyebrows that you get from scowling. Also, try to keep your lips just slightly parted so as to avoid an "angry-looking" mouth. George Orwell said it best: "At 50, everyone has the face he deserves."

Facial Signal: Pursed Lips

Pursed lips draw together in a tight circle at the center of the mouth and are frequently paired with narrowed eyes. According to David Givens, pursed lips are what he calls a "gestural fossil" from our primate brain that automatically appears whenever we disagree. In today's world, pursed lips are also a sarcastic gesture—"Yeah, buddy? Try another one on me."

Because this gesture is so instinctive to humans, when you see it, take it seriously—it's no joke. The person you're looking at is very likely not going to believe a word you're saying. That means if you're in a sales situation and your client shoots you that look, stop right then and there and change tactics. Start from scratch by applying the basic techniques for building a rapport. (See "Building Rapport" on page 235.)

What to watch for: The dark cloud. If a person purses their lips during your time to speak, don't let it go. Immediately stop and ask, "Are there any questions I haven't answered?"

What you should work on: Using it when you negotiate. Pursed lips can be incredibly useful if you're trying to drive a hard bargain. Your lips are saying, "I'm not buying any—at least not yet. Keep working on it."

But, whatever you do, don't overuse it—you'll give people the impression that you're impossible to please.

Prozac or Botox?

Dermatologist Turns That Frown Upside Down

Research has shown that just by drawing your forehead into a sad expression, you can start to feel sad. With that mechanism in mind, one dermatologist wondered if interrupting that muscle-emotion connection could improve mood. His preliminary study found that injecting Botox into the corrugator supercilli, the muscle that forms the line down the middle of the forehead, of patients with major depression relieved signs of major depression in nine out of ten women treated, for up to two months after treatment. These results are very preliminary and controversial—but the two-way connection between facial expression and emotion is very real.

Facial Signal: Frown

When we frown, we get a sad clown face. Everything on our face falls—our lips bend all the way down, our eyes tilt down, the cheeks feel like they're tugging down. The only thing going up is that little bubble underneath the lower lip, giving your face that "poor me" look. A frown is the definition of a sad sight. You'll frequently see it when someone is sad, confused, or doesn't approve of you and/or your actions. (See "Sadness" on page 45 for more information on the frown.)

What to watch for: When a friend frowns a lot. She could be going through a temporary rough patch, or she might be a negative person. Or she might just really trust you: one Japanese study found that women were more likely to frown while watching a troubling movie with a friend than a stranger. The researchers believe their relationship made it possible for the women to be more honest with each other.

What you should work on: Avoiding it. For a million reasons. If you let your face sit in a frown for a while, that sag is going to stay, pulling your cheeks down in a droopy dog look. And even Botox can't help you on your cheeks or your chin. Counteract the effects of the frown's gravity with more conscious smiling or do facial exercises that help you develop more pronounced cheek muscles that can diminish the signs of saggy clown-frown cheeks.

Beat the Blush

If you're one of those people who finds yourself blushing in embarrassing or stressful situations, relax. No, really—relax. That's the only way you'll learn to beat it. Most people who blush also experience heart pounding and shortness of breath. When you feel yourself in a situation that might cause you to blush, focus on keeping your breathing deep. Breathe in through your nose, expanding your belly on the inhale, and then out through your mouth. Your objective is to short-circuit your stress-induced fight-or-flight response, the activation of your sympathetic nervous system that also causes your blood vessels (including the ones in your cheeks!) to dilate.

Lip Gestures

Lips are an incredibly expressive facial feature, with twelve separate muscles moving them into different expressions. Because they have fewer layers of skin than our regular epidermis, the blood vessels are closer to the surface and create that rosy look. With their high concentration of nerve endings, lips are so intricately linked with sensuality that lip gestures are often flirtatious and sexy. Let's take a look at a few here.

Facial Signal: Biting Lips

People who bite their lips are usually viewed as embarrassed or shy. It's a childlike gesture, a universal vulnerability signal that tells the world you are innocent or that you don't have much self-confidence. Some people add insult to injury with their nervous habit of raking their bottom teeth over their top lip too often, which can make their skin raw and chapped. Not a good look.

The lip nibble can also be a flirting technique. This works especially well when you have full, pouty lips,

What to watch for: The lip-biting liar. While you can never tell a liar from one cue alone, an inexperienced liar may bite his lower lip after he's told a lie, almost as if he wanted to scoop the lie back into his mouth.

What you should work on: Flirt with the lower lip bite. And steer clear of the upper lip bite. The upper lip bite is almost always seen as nervous because the bottom teeth are not sexy and actually resemble the teeth of a wild animal. The bottom lip bite, however, can be very flirtatious because it emphasizes how plump and juicy that lip is. (For more fun with this, add it to the simple flirt technique on page 269.)

Facial Signal: The Lip Lick

Lip licks are often seen as a sign of anxiety. When your nervous system is activated, that arousal causes you to lick your lips. In the nervous lick lip, the tongue quickly darts out of the mouth, swipes at the top lip on the way out, and then curls under to swipe at the bottom lip on the way back in. Alternately, the person might just lick their top lip in the same anxious, unconscious way. You might see this repeated several times over a few minutes while the person remains nervous.

Christina Aguilera simultaneously does a "lip lick" and a "sideways glance," two body language signals that indicate sexual interest.

What to watch for: When someone thinks you're yummy. For that other type of arousal, we see a different lip lick. The seductive lip lick is done very slowly, licking both lips, usually the top one and then the bottom one. It's almost as if you're saying, man, you probably taste really good!

What you should work on: Don't overdo it. The seductive lip lick can be a real turn-on. But beware: do not use it with a stranger without expecting an immediate, intense reaction. There's a reason this gesture is a favorite among porn stars.

While conducting an interactive "meet your mate" seminar, I was discussing flirting techniques and how men and women can seduce one another with just a look. When we got to the lip lick section for women, Barbara offered to demonstrate. She was very beautiful, and I expected with just a few practiced moves she would be a pro.

Barbara faced the audience and began what was supposed to be a seductive lip lick. However, as she finished, most of the room was laughing. I was positioned behind Barbara, so I didn't understand what had happened.

Barbara turned to me, her confidence shattered, almost in tears. I couldn't understand what could have possibly made the room laugh at her until she began to speak. Apparently, when she had licked her lips, she had licked off her bright red lipstick, which her tongue had then smeared across her front teeth. While my heart went out to Barbara, I have to admit that it was quite amusing, and I had a hard time maintaining my composure. Bottom line, ladies: Make sure that after you lick your lips, you don't drag your tongue over your teeth.

Facial Signal: Lip Roll

The lip roll is seen when a person puts her lips together and then rolls them between her upper and lower teeth. Her lips literally disappear into her mouth. Sometimes people do this in a semi-unconscious attempt to prevent themselves from speaking. As a result, this gesture can sometimes make it look like you have a secret that you're trying not to reveal.

What to watch for: A look of anger. Sometimes the lip roll is seen in an aggressive stance. Usually when someone uses it in that situation, it shows that the person thinks the current confrontation is about to escalate to a higher level.

What you should work on: Not doing it. Some people do a lip roll when they concentrate. But know that in those situations, the lip roll comes off as very indecisive, nervous, and even somewhat deceptive. Your lips are one of your face's greatest assets—don't swallow them.

Nose and Chin Expressions

The nose is one of the least expressive parts of your face, but it does factor into a few emotional expressions, most often not positive ones. The chin is more of a backdrop of facial expressions—it's really just along for the ride most of the time. But a few nose and chin gestures communicate a great deal about what you think of yourself, as well as the person you're looking at.

Facial Signal: Flared Nostrils

You would normally see a nostril flare in someone who's out of breath or intensely angry. Nostril flaring usually happens when we need to draw in extra oxygen—perhaps we're recovering from a quick sprint, or stress has turned on our fight-or-flight response.

You might see this signal in anger, in exertion, or in jest. In the course of a normal day, we don't have a huge need to suck in a big lungful of air unless we are exercising or pretending to be angry. My kids will do this when they're pretending to be quite steamed at me, but I have to admit, it's such a cartoonish gesture that it makes me laugh.

What to watch for: Someone who is very angry. The most basic reason for flaring one's nostrils is to draw in more oxygen to prepare to attack. When you see that signal combined with other signals for anger, steer clear.

What you should work on: Avoiding it at all costs. Could there be a less attractive or more ridiculous-looking thing to do with your nose?

I can't imagine wanting to flare my nostrils in any way other than in jest, unless I was getting ready to outrun a bull. I'm a runner, so I know it's sometimes unavoidable to flare your nostrils to get enough air, but for the most part, in everyday life, you really don't want to do it.

Facial Signal: Nose Crinkle

You see this gesture when the skin gathers on the bridge of your nose, your nostrils flare, and the outer edges of your lips lift. You'll see this signal when something is physically repulsive and you feel disgust. If you walk into a room and smell something horrible, your nose will automatically wrinkle in disgust, unconsciously. But you'll also see it when a person is trying to communicate their contempt or figurative disgust, such as a fashionista responding to a person wearing very tacky clothing.

What to watch for: Clique formation. Groups can use this signal very consciously and to devastating effect, especially among young people. Barring any rotting food or otherwise putrid odors, the nose crinkle tells you that the person standing in front of you is disgusted by something else in the environment, and it's probably you. When a group gathers to communicate this message, it can be devastating.

What you should work on: Tread lightly. Sometimes when you're in a heated discussion and someone makes a comment that you find off-putting, your face might want to make this expression. Resist. It's hard not to take this kind of editorial comment personally. Be very aware that you're not just communicating disapproval—you're conveying stomach-turning disgust.

Facial Signal: Chin Lift and Chin Tuck

When you lift up your chin, the end of your nose automatically rises into the air. That makes it impossible to glance at someone without looking down your nose at them, a very clear signal for superiority. Traditionally thought of as an aristocratic gesture, the chin lift has become very popular in street culture and among rappers such as Ludacris and Snoop Dogg.

The person who uses a chin lift is trying to communicate that they have the upper hand in the situation. Let's say you and I are having a debate; I get the final word, and I'm completely convinced I'm right, even if I'm wrong. I might punctuate the end of my point by lifting up my chin—"Hmm, I win." The chin lift is the ultimate smug gesture.

On the opposite end of the spectrum, when you tuck your chin in sadness, you end up looking smaller and more vulnerable; it's a nonverbal plea for pity. When a person points her chin toward her chest but keeps her eyes on you, it's an instinctive movement to help her protect her throat. You'll start to see the rest of her sag down as well—the face falls into a frown, the shoulders drop, and the body might even hunch over a bit. The whole body starts to droop.

What to watch for: When it's used as a defense mechanism. If you've said something insulting to someone, some people hang their head in a chin tuck, a nonverbal signal for, "Boy, you really got me where it hurts." Others, rather than hang their heads, might choose to do a chin lift that says, "You didn't hurt me. I'm walking away with my head held high." People often use this gesture to hide a feeling of insecurity or to exhibit a sense of pride.

Be warned: if someone tucks his chin, squints eyes, and/or broadens his shoulders, it could be a sign of anger. Think of a bull getting ready to charge.

What you should work on: Keeping your chin parallel to the floor. When we get upset or depressed, we tend to pull our chin close to our body because we want to appear smaller than we are. We turn into these tiny, depressed, downtrodden little balls. A chin tuck is, by definition, a defensive posture. You're telling the other person that you're either on the attack or feeling attacked. In either case, it doesn't reflect well on you—you're either seen as a bully or a victim. To be seen as an equal, keep your chin parallel to the ground.

The classic mother's exhortation, "Chin up!" is actually very sound advice. Not only will lifting your chin increase your feelings of self-confidence, it will automatically allow more oxygen to enter your lungs, elongate your neck, and improve your posture—all of which will help you cheer up.

The face is an endlessly fascinating canvas on which we express our emotions. But for the most part, we can control what gets painted there. In contrast, our ability to control what the rest of the body reveals about our thoughts and feelings is much more limited. Let's look at our body gestures next.

CHAPTER 3

The Language of the Body

I feel you.

—American slang saying

Anyone who lives with a dog knows that dogs can't lie. Excitement, guilt, boredom, love, jealousy, greed—their emotions are always in plain sight, written all over their bodies.

As good as dogs are at transmitting their body language signals, they're even better at reading them. Not coincidentally, dogs are also believed to have a rudimentary mirror system, similar to the one in the human brain. Dogs have been proven to mirror yawns back to their owners, and vice versa. And after 100,000 years of hanging out with humans, dogs have developed the ability to read our body language—and they know incongruence when they see it.

In a *New Yorker* article about Cesar Millan, the famous Dog Whisperer, Malcolm Gladwell credits Cesar's skillfully congruent body language for his ability to instantly control the most wild and violent dogs. Gladwell describes how Cesar managed to tame one particularly recalcitrant dog in just five minutes by combining his steady, symmetrical posture with a quick, definitive touch on the shoulder and brief "sh-h-h" when the dog got too close to a forbidden object. Gladwell believes that dogs trust Cesar because his body movements match his message, with absolutely no ambiguity. Dogs calm down because they know where they stand. They don't initiate a power struggle with him, as they often do with their owners, because there is no question of who is in charge.

Now, I'm not suggesting you become the alpha dog with every person you meet. After all, it's not just Cesar's dominance that makes dogs trust him—it's the way his body reflects that power, in every step and every movement. He meets the dogs on their home turf and takes a moment to understand their nonverbal signals, and his confident, response to them puts them at ease. Grateful to know that someone is in charge, the dogs follow his lead.

The same principle can and does work in any encounter between two human beings. First, you take an accurate read of the other person's thoughts and feelings by decoding her body language, then you respond with physical signals that both acknowledge her unspoken messages and accurately reflect your own.

When your body language and your spoken words don't match, people can detect dissonance, unease, and deception. But when they do match—when they are "congruent"—you send signals of trustworthiness. Your new acquaintance's inner sensor says, "He means what he says. I can believe him. He is safe." And, with that, you become a "yes."

The Real Source of Information

You've learned how to read people's faces, to see the signals that communicate their thoughts and emotions, and to become aware of microexpressions that fly across the face. But many people have trouble believing that the most honest emotional expression comes from the body, because body movements, gestures, and postures seem like such a *primitive* way to communicate. We have this glorious ability to communicate with speech—of course it must be superior to hand gestures and slouches! Both speech and gesture are controlled in the Broca's area of the brain, which is very close to where mirror neurons are believed to reside. Interestingly, studies have shown that people who have been blind since birth use hand gestures to communicate, even when they speak with other blind people, and this effect is seen across the lifespan, from toddlers to adults. Gestures don't just help the listener understand your messages, they also help you articulate them.

How do some people learn to integrate these two channels of communication so well, while others have so much trouble? Why are some people able to read others' signals intuitively and exhibit the charisma and body language prowess of a Cesar Millan, while others remain absolutely clueless and invisible?

Many people would say that charisma stems from a strong sense of self, an inherent belief in your own worth, the knowledge that you're one hot tamale. While I think that's partially true, I believe that charisma is developed by integrating that faith in yourself into the way you trust your intuitive sense of others' body language and respond with confident, steady messages that build rapport. You become so fluid in your movements that you don't even think "Chin up, shoulders back, hands at sides," you just think, "Wait till they see me coming."

As with all aspects of body language, developing your gestural ability starts with learning how to accurately read other people's signals. Confidence and natural gestures go hand in hand because insecurity and nervousness can lead to jerky movements. One of the best ways to quiet your own anxiety is to learn as much as possible about whatever situation you're about to enter. When you know how to read people's body language, you have a great source of inside information constantly available to you. The body is a much better indicator of true emotions and feelings, simply because most people don't try to mask their body's revealing signals—they don't even realize those signals are happening. This allows you to more easily understand people's true feelings and respond in a way that makes people feel really good, so they want to please you in return—which is another way of saying, you'll have some serious charisma.

The next step on your way to becoming a Master Communicator is to learn to read people's body language signals so closely, and so thoroughly, that you'll open up that wealth of inside information. You'll be able to see what they need, decide how you want to respond, and react with body language that's congruent to your thinking and your goals—you'll begin to develop the building blocks of charisma.

Throughout this chapter, we'll carefully examine dozens of different body language signals. We'll talk about where you'll normally see them, what might surprise you about them, and how you can use these signals to your advantage.

Head Gestures

The head is capable of a whole range of gestures that are independent of the face. Several of them, including the head nod and the head tilt, have been scientifically proven to increase rapport. Others are downright sexy. Let's take a look.

Facial Signal: Head Nod

The head nod, the movement of the top of the head down toward your conversational partner, is an (almost) universal signal for acknowledgment and approval. Some experts believe the head nod is derived from the submissive bow; others think it stems from our reptilian ancestors' head bob. Either way, it's a positive sign that indicates comprehension and accord.

You typically see the head nod when someone is paying close attention to what you're saying. They needn't be agreeing; they might just be listening and, with the nod, encouraging you to continue. The

The Secret Signal Decoder

Your Cheat Sheet to Their Hidden Thoughts

"Yes" Gestures

Open palms

Forward lean

Smile

Direct body orientation

Enhanced eye contact

Head nodding

"No" Gestures

Folded arms

Tapping

Hand holding up the chin

Feet and trunk pointed in different directions

Hands on the knees

Hand over the mouth

Increased fidgeting

Constant eye movement

Shaking head

Scowl

Eye squinting

"Maybe" Gestures

Taking a sip of a drink

Biting the tip of an eyeglass

Cleaning glasses

Scratching head

Chin stroking

head nod is a great barometer of general interest in the conversation. However, when someone nods excessively and becomes almost like a human bobble-head doll, it indicates meek compliance—"Yes, absolutely, you bet, you're right."

What to watch for: The impatient head nod. Another time you might see the continual nod is when someone is trying to hurry you along—"Yes, sure, I knew that, c'mon, let's get on to the next point." Sometimes a chronic nodder will purse his lips, or put a finger to his mouth, and start to nod even faster, as if to say, "I get your point. Wrap it up—my turn to talk."

What you should work on: Nodding often, even when you're alone. Imagine what a person would think if you didn't nod at all during a conversation, but instead, just kept your head stock-still. They'd think you were not interested or, disagreed, or were bored, right? The head nod is a natural rapport-building technique, because it gives people an immediate sense that the two of you are of like minds on the subject at hand. Indeed, when you nod as someone else speaks, you're priming yourself to agree with what's being said. The same effect happens even when you're alone—one series of studies revealed that nodding to yourself will reinforce your faith and confidence in your current thought, whether or not the thought itself is positive. (Beware: if you think, "I *never* do well in front of a crowd" or "Man, I'm not going to be able to finish my project," and you nod at the same time, you're subconsciously reinforcing that negative, and you're doomed.) These same studies found that the act of nodding alone can put you in a better mood.

Body Signal: Head Shake

When a baby doesn't want to eat his strained peas, you see him shake his head from side to side, almost as if he's twisting away from the spoon. Believed to be a hardwired gesture, the head shake is a universal negation seen when one does not agree with what's being said or done (such as having yucky food stuffed in one's mouth).

You might see this when someone doesn't agree with you, but usually people are too polite to resort to this kind of overt sign—they might tilt their head and squint instead, for example. But when someone hears horrible news or sees something that is shocking and terrible, they will shake their heads as if to make it go away—"I can't believe what I'm seeing/hearing."

His Signals/Her Signals

Nod If You Can Hear Me

Men and women treat the nod very differently. Women tend to nod a lot more than men, as a means of encouragement and an indication of their attention to the speaker, but not always because they're totally on board with what's being said. On the other hand, men tend to nod when they agree with something.

What to watch for: When someone does it unconsciously. This cue is a frequent sign of leakage, seen when people don't honestly believe what they're saying. I can't tell you how many clips of politicians I've analyzed in which they emphatically state their agreement verbally while unconsciously shaking their heads. When you see this type of incongruence, it means the person is either covering his backside or experiencing interior conflict—he might not fully know what he believes at that point.

What you should work on: Using it sparingly, and then only with other people. Sometimes an emphatic "no-way-no-how" head shake is an assertive, definitive way of responding to someone who's stepped over the line. Or if a colleague proposes a plan that you know will be a huge waste of time for minimal rewards, you could casually shake your head while you voice your concerns; combining the two signals will strengthen your argument in the minds of the others at the table. But don't try a head shake on yourself. One study found that shaking your head actually decreases your self-confidence in your own opinions.

After reading all the studies on the significance of head movement during conversation, I decided to perform a little experiment on a friend. We were just talking, as we normally do, about an upcoming social event. I kept my head very still and didn't move it in any direction. Instead, I only looked directly into her eyes as she spoke. After only a minute or two, she started to move her head—tilting it, nodding—much more than usual, probably unconsciously to coerce me to mirror her movements. Eventually, she could not hold out and started directly asking me if I agreed with her: "Come on—you're not saying anything—what do you think?" Try this experiment with a close friend—you'll notice that it won't take long for them to react very strongly to your lack of responsive body language signals.

His Signals/Her Signals

It's Not the Size of the Cerebellum . . .

Men's overall brain size is 10 percent bigger than women's. But women are better at processing language because they have more brain cells in their left brain, the seat of language. They also use both sides of their brain for speech; men use only one.

Body Signal: Head Tilt

The head tilt is primarily a sign of vulnerability. When you tilt your head to one side, you've exposed your neck on the opposite side, as animals do when they want to appear submissive. This signal can increase trust because it shows a willingness to be open and receptive. One recent study suggested that people who tilted their heads toward their partners were judged friendly, kind, and honest.

What to watch for: When someone is manipulating you. Because the head tilt is such a strong cue for trustworthiness, this simple move is one of the most powerful manipulation tools in body language. Let's say a guy looking for some action goes into a bar and starts chatting up an unsuspecting woman. He might not be interested in anything more than her body, but if he tilts his head while she's talking, she'll think he's fascinated by her. The resulting boost to her ego will make her more inclined to trust him and respond to him.

What you should work on: Using this to your advantage. The guy mentioned above has a much better chance of scoring the woman's phone number if he tilts his head to the right as opposed to the left. A fascinating recent study suggests that people who tilt their heads just eight degrees to the right are seen as more trustworthy than those who keep their heads upright or tilted to the left. Women specifically noted that the left tilt seemed "flirtier" than the right tilt. On the other hand, a left tilt might work better for the woman who's trying to attract a man because, in the study, people who tilted their heads to the left were seen as more attractive.

These study results might also help you during the interview process. Going for a job in accounting, law, medicine, or another field bound by a strict code of ethics? Tilt to the right. Trying to become America's next top model? Tilt to the left.

Body Signal: Hair Toss

A hair toss involves a swing of the head that allows the hair to flutter around the shoulders. Women with all kinds of hairstyles and lengths do it. You don't need long, Rapunzel-like tresses to do a hair toss—you can use this move even if you have a short, cropped hairdo. Some men who have long hair do it, too, and as long hair comes back into style among male teens, I'm sure we'll start seeing this more and more.

Many animals have a way of signaling to other creatures with their plumage—dogs get their backs up, peacocks fan their feathers, lions shake their long manes. We're no different. Our hair served many evolutionary purposes—it kept us warm, hid us from our enemies in the wild, even shielded our heads from the sun. Today, the hair toss remains a very strong signal to the world that says, "I am here and I feel good about myself."

What to watch for: A woman showing you she's hot stuff. Essentially, the hair toss is a "preening" gesture, a way to signal to another party that we're putting our best attributes on display for him. Some women do it when they feel confident in the situation; others do it as more of a nervous gesture. A woman might not even be interested in you—but that doesn't stop her from wanting you to be interested in her. But mostly this is done as an attention-getter.

What you should work on: Developing one of your own. The hair toss says, "I feel good about myself. I feel positive and confident." This dominant signal can be very useful in flirting but also can be a way of asserting your power. Just be careful to do this subtly—you don't want to become a caricature of a drama queen, throwing your head around willy-nilly.

Body Signal: The Once-Over

Some zookeepers describe the differences between predator and prey to children by using this rhyme: "Eyes in front, I like to hunt/Eyes on the side, I like to hide." This rhyme also describes a key difference between the way men and women look at each other.

When men look at women, they tend to use hunt-vision, most pronounced in the up-and-down glance known as the once-over. In contrast, due to different brain wiring, women can more covertly take in a guy's entire body in one quick glance. Women can hide their once-overs by not moving their heads at all, and they're still able to take in all the pertinent details.

You might not actually *see* the once-over, but it's happening. Once-overs are not always sexual, but we constantly take these snapshots of other people to help us form impressions and determine if someone is a "yes" or "no."

His Signals/Her Signals

Weighing the Evidence

Women tend to believe that men desire women to be thinner than they really do. On the flip side, men tend to believe women desire men who are heavier than women really do.

What to watch for: When you see a woman do it. When you see a woman do a once-over, she's either being flirtatious or a trouble-maker—she *wants* you to see her do it. Women can easily take in everything they want to know about you in a quick glance. If a woman gives a guy the overt once-over—provided it's not followed with a mean laugh—she's most certainly expressing interest. If she gives another woman the overt once-over, it's sometimes a calculated sign of disdain for the woman, or perhaps what she is wearing.

What you should work on: Master both varieties. The obvious once-over can be useful for both sexes in a flirting situation. Just look at each body part slow and easy, letting the person know that, yes, you are most certainly taking it all in. The covert once-over is just as handy—you just need to be more discreet so the person thinks your eyes are perhaps misdirected instead of feasting on her.

Hand to Head Gestures

Several gestures in this group fall into the deception triad of "See no evil / speak no evil / hear no evil" signals. After reading a few of these, you might think it wise to never bring your hand near your head again.

The reason hand-to-mouth gestures indicate deception is actually because almost all of them reflect anxiety. Years ago I worked with a high-level manager who picked his lip at the first sign of trouble at work. His direct staff knew there was a problem if Bob was going to town on his upper lip. We never thought much about it until a senior manager from another division called one day to ask if Bob had come out of a meeting picking his lip or smiling. That day we found out that this little bit of body language was keeping entire departments abreast of what was happening during critical business meetings. Bob's one unconscious gestural tic had become a widely known gauge that indicated whether a meeting had gone well or fallen apart.

Body Signal: Hands to Mouth

When hands touch the mouth, it may indicate one of several things. This gesture could be a sensuous signal, evoking thoughts of intense desire. Or it may also be an indication of surprise, nervousness, shame, embarrassment, or anticipation. Often, it can be a strong signal of deception. The context and the execution of the gesture will tell you the intention.

Just as some of us sucked our thumbs when we were young to help manage our own anxiety, we now use any manner of hand-to-mouth gestures to self-soothe. Nail-biting or lip-picking is probably a sign of more intense anxiety, but some people also like to touch and rub their lips when they're in deep concentration. That extra bit of self-comforting helps them focus better. Some people touch the notch right between their upper lip and the bottom of their nose; other people will pinch their upper or lower lip together.

Also, any time a person's hand comes to his mouth, there's a chance he might be fibbing. Be careful to look for other cues as well, of course. But in general, we don't like the fact that we might be lying, so we tend to put our hands in our mouth. That, too, is a gesture that dates back to childhood.

What to watch for: When someone is using it to flirt with you. Self-touch can also be a sign of seduction. Rubbing your finger along your lips or sucking on a finger is obviously very sexual. Aside from when you eat in earnest, anytime you lift something to your mouth, it could be sexual—women sucking on ice cream cones, biting bananas, drinking from a beer bottle, licking a spoon. Anything that gets the mouth involved can imply a sexual interest.

What you should work on: Learning to do it more seductively. A general rule of thumb: your hands should not be in or near your mouth unless you are trying to seduce someone. Most women know when they're trying to use this signal for seduction, but they might not be doing it overtly and seductively enough. Just as when you lick your lips seductively, you want to do one of these moves nice and slow—you don't want it to look like you're trying to get a piece of food off your lip. When you're licking ice cream, keep your tongue out a half second longer than it needs to be. Or when you brush your finger along your lips, give the indication that you're in deep thought when, in fact, you're trying to be innocently sexual.

Also, ladies, look for one of those over-the-counter lip enhancement glosses or creams. Among their ingredients are capsicum, also known as red pepper, which stimulates blood flow and makes the lips look plumper and rosier. (Lip enhancers work because plump, juicy lips remind men of sexually stimulated vaginal lips—that's why they go batty for women with bulbous lips like Angelina Jolie's.) If you're applying a lip balm in front of a guy, always go for the pot versus the stick—while you're making them glossier and more sexy looking, you'll get the added bonus of touching your lips.

Body Signal: Hand on Nose

Whether it's a pick or a rub, touching your nose with your hand is generally not a very flattering gesture. It's also one of the gestures most commonly associated with deception.

When we experience a bout of sudden anxiety, our blood pressure increases, causing our soft tissue to swell, including the soft tissue in our nose. This swelling makes our skin tingle, so we're often unconsciously compelled to touch or scratch our nose. This "Pinocchio effect" happens whether you're waiting to be interviewed or waiting to be interrogated—it's a nervous system response as opposed to a direct signal for lying.

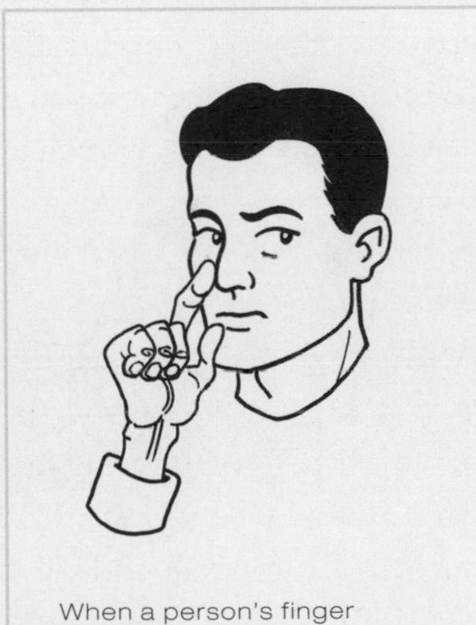

When a person's finger touches his nose, it indicates nervousness or possibly deception.

What to watch for: When it's combined with other signals. As with all body language signals, you must take care not to jump to conclusions too quickly. If you see someone touching or rubbing their nose, look at their other signals—are they giving you no eye contact, or too much? Are they angling their body away from you? Are they stuttering and not speaking fluently? Look for a combination of signals for deception before you jump to conclusions. Typically, when somebody has a nose itch, they scratch, but if someone is feeling anxious, they swipe.

What you should work on: Trying not to do it. Either it looks like you're lying, or like you're picking your nose—what's worse? Steer clear.

Body Signal: Hand on Ear

A hand on the ear could be anything from a tug on the earlobe to a serious excavation project. I think our mothers would all agree that drilling into your ear in mixed company is not a good idea. Aside from being an off-putting grooming behavior, an ear touch can send other signals about you.

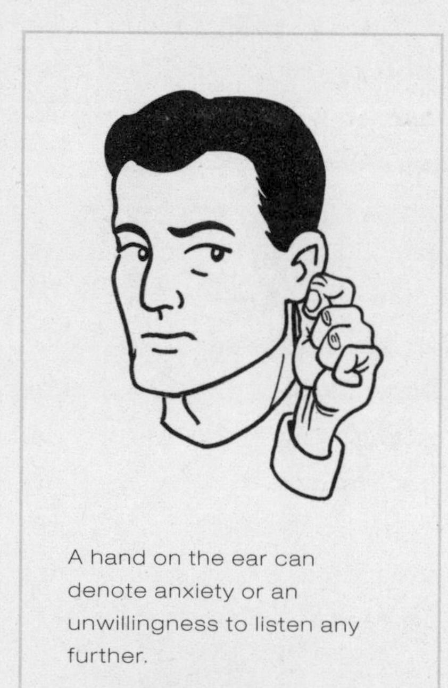

A hand on the ear can denote anxiety or an unwillingness to listen any further.

If you're rambling on and on, you might see someone reach up and rub their ear. They don't mean to do it—it's an unconscious gesture that basically says, "I don't want to listen to this anymore. You're hurting my ear." Normally they'll also show other signs of growing disinterest at the same time, such as turning away or lowering their eyes.

What to watch for: As a sign of deception. When a person touches his ear during a conversation, it can signify "hear no evil"; in other words, my subconscious is uncomfortable with this lie and I really don't want to hear the lie come out.

What you should work on: Not doing it. As with all touches to the face and head, you're giving off signs that you're less trustworthy—even if that is not the case. Follow George Washington's lead. He was reportedly very conscious of body language and used to practice the maxim, "When in Company, put not your Hands to any Part of the Body." Wise words.

Body Signal: Hand on Chin

Hmmmm. I am considering what you are saying. A hand placed beneath the mouth, cheek or chin is a spontaneous and comfortable position when an individual is evaluating, considering, and analyzing—but it can also indicate fatigue and boredom.

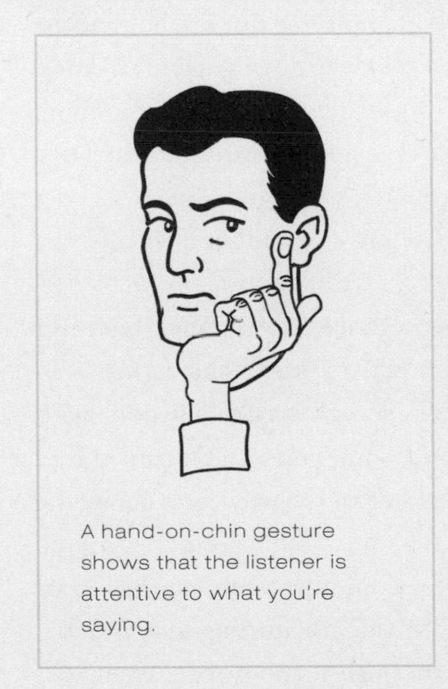

A hand-on-chin gesture shows that the listener is attentive to what you're saying.

If a person points the index finger up toward the ear and keeps the thumb touching the bottom of the chin, there is some kind of assessment going on.. And if the index finger then moves to rest on the top lip, the stance has suddenly become a bit more skeptical; it reflects a suspicion of deception. (See "Hands to Mouth" on page 99.)

What to watch for: When they feel bored. Often when we listen to others speak, we might telegraph our interest by gently resting our head on our fist. Sometimes, we drop our faces into our whole open hand as if to say, "You go ahead—I'm just going to sit here and listen." Especially when the entire palm is open, fingers together, the hand can provide a nice little nest for the chin. But that nest can get awfully comfortable, and if the talk is the least bit dull, this signal can rapidly become one of boredom and fatigue. If you see someone slipping away from you like that, you might try to engage them a little bit more so they're a more active participant in the conversation.

What you should work on: Go for the spread-finger version. Given a choice between the two varieties of hand on chin, go for the more evaluative thumb on chin and index finger pointing upward. This signal shows others that you're interested and you're thinking critically about what's being said. Take care not to obscure your mouth with your index or middle finger, as that sends signs of distrust—either you are skeptical about the situation, or you're about to lie yourself.

Body Signal: Head or Neck Scratch

A scratch to the head or neck can have a variety of meanings, but most indicate some measure of disbelief. A person might scratch her head with a crooked finger or two. The neck scratch is normally done with the index finger of the dominant hand, sometimes accompanied by a head tilt as the finger scratches on the side of the neck, just below the earlobe.

A head scratch is a classic way of communicating confusion or puzzlement: "I'm not sure I follow." Most of the times these days, the head scratch takes on an almost cartoonish flamboyancy, a sarcastic gesture that says, "Huh! You don't say!"

What to watch for: When they don't believe you. The skeptical neck scratch starts with the head tilted to one side, the pointer finger scratching down the side of the neck around the area of the earlobe, showing uncertainty and disbelief: "Really? Are you sure about that?"

However, the neck scratch might also indicate deception—the person may be consciously trying to draw attention away from her mouth, but because it's with a neck scratch, she's also communicating disbelief in her own statement: "I don't really know what I'm saying to you."

What you should work on: Using the neck scratch to flirt. A powerful way to tap in to the erogenous power of the neck is to delicately stroke the suprasternal notch, the neck dimple in the middle of the front of your neck, between the collar bones. It's a disarming gesture that says, "I'm open," while also showing that you are certainly hot stuff.

Body Signal: Head or Neck Rub

The suprasternal notch is also known as the "neck dimple." Joan Allen shows how a woman can accentuate this very attractive area of the body.

Massage is a natural stress reliever, and you might rub the back of your neck simply to relax your muscles in a tense situation. When someone directs this signal toward you, you can use that information to learn more about how curious they are or how intensely they feel about a situation.

Sometimes people will rub their head with two straight fingers in a gesture that says, "I'm in deep thought." The gesture can indicate that they are confused by the last thing you said and might need a bit more clarification.

What to watch for: When someone is stressed or annoyed. The neck rub is also a symbolic gesture that says, "You are a pain in my neck." You can sometimes use it to decipher the core sticking point in a conversation. Watch when a person first begins to rub his neck—the issue that he's talking about at that particular moment is the crux of the problem for him.

What you should work on: Try to minimize it. The neck rub gesture can be seen as very negative and dismissive, and is indicative of a high level of tension. Try not to do it during negotiations, as it screams to the other person that you feel the pressure.

Torso Signals

Our torso signals are all about power—either giving ours up or trying to get more. As the housing for all of our internal organs, our torso is an area that can feel vulnerable to attack, and our signals all reflect our perceptions of that vulnerability.

Body Signal: Shoulder Shrug

In the shoulder shrug, the whole body shrinks down and the palms go out in an open, submissive gesture. Most of the messages of this signal center on uncertainty, whether for someone else's messages or your own.

The shoulder shrug is often paired with another gesture. For example, when you apologize, you raise your shoulders and tuck your neck down while opening your hands wide, palms facing upward. This is an unconscious attempt to make yourself appear smaller and vulnerable and therefore more likely to be forgiven.

What to watch for: Total acquiescence. When the shoulder shrug is taken to the extreme, it says, "I give up." It indicates either that the person doesn't really have a strong opinion about what's being discussed, or perhaps they're just not able to complete a task that they've already begun. Occasionally, a person will use this gesture unconsciously while making a very committed verbal statement. When that happens, the incongruence tells you that they are either lying or very uncertain of their answer. If you say, "I was not in that bar!" while you're lifting up your shoulders and exposing your palms, you might want me to believe you, but I probably won't.

His Signals/Her Signals

The Leg Cross

Most men consider this the most delicious sitting position for a woman. This position gives off several signals about a woman's sexuality, and she uses this position to unconsciously invite a man to notice the muscle tone of her legs. The leg cross is done by pressing one leg strongly against the other, giving it a very taut appearance. Sometimes, a woman will place her hand on her thigh, giving a clear invitation for attention.

The "leg twine."

Even though men find this posture delightful, it should not be used at work. The only way for a woman to sit at work is with both feet on the floor. If you must cross something, make it your ankles—but work toward a perfectly symmetrical sitting position.

What you should work on: Use it only when necessary. Unless you are really unsure of something and want to communicate that doubt clearly, you should avoid the shoulder shrug. If you shrug too often, other people will think of you as unsure of yourself and therefore not equipped to make good judgments or decisions.

His Signals/Her Signals

The Figure Four

This type of sitting position is more common among males and is considered a space-occupying position because it not only displays the lower half of a person's body, it takes up a large portion of space. If it is done in conjunction with a backward lean, arm cross, and finger-to-chin evaluative pose, it is usually a negative pose, demonstrating a competitive and confrontational attitude. But if it's combined with an open, easy countenance, the figure four can demonstrate an overly confident and casual attitude—in other words, ladies, watch out.

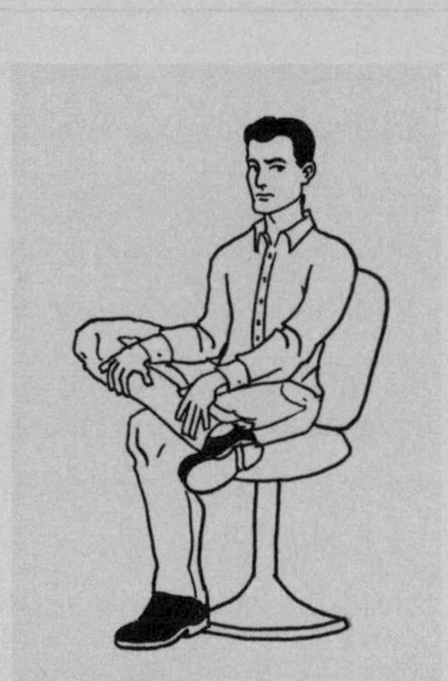

The "figure four."

Body Signal: Hunched Shoulders

This posture is not only a signal but sometimes also a symptom—of too much stress and too much computer time. Similar to dogs whose hackles rise when they are provoked, people tend to hunch their shoulders in response to anger or prolonged anxiety. If we stay in this position too long, it can start to compress our organs and inhibit oxygen flow in the body, making it difficult to speak in a strong and fluent voice.

The standard corporate desk job is probably more responsible for this signal than anything else, but no matter how you get them, hunched shoulders telegraph insecurity and a total absence of authority. If I walk into a room, and I'm looking at twenty people, the last person I'm going to presume is the chairman of the group is the man or woman with the hunched shoulders. This posture denotes depression, low self-esteem, and a lack of confidence.

What to watch for: When you see it in someone who normally has good posture. The shoulder hunch is automatic for many of us in times of stress. You should become aware of this posture and what it indicates, because you might not realize you're doing it. Anytime I am tired or apprehensive, my husband will just walk over and put his palms on my shoulders and push them down. I cannot begin to tell you how that one simple movement sends a wave of relaxation and awareness through the rest of my body.

What you should work on: Not doing it. Make a habit of constantly pointing the outer edges of your shoulders toward the ground. Try it now—feel how your neck elongates automatically? Sometimes when we're under stress, our bodies clench up into hunched shoulders with the head pulling down and back, which just encourages the body to hold on to that stress instead of releasing it. Remember to keep your spine straight, envisioning a stack of dice, one on top of another. Aim for your shoulders to form a straight line; if you can maintain this angle, your posture will improve and you'll be less likely to slip unconsciously into a submissive stance when you don't want to.

Body Signal: Backward Lean

When you lean backward in your chair, your shoulders fall and your chin tucks a little bit into your chest. Feels nice, right? Still, you might want to use this position with close friends only. Otherwise, you might be sending a very disrespectful message that can get you into trouble.

The backward lean is a great way to tell other people that you are arrogant and cocky. Picture a manager sitting with his team, leaning back; maybe he even has his hands tucked behind his head. This "lazy lean" tells everyone around, "What's being discussed is not important enough for me to have to sit up straight."

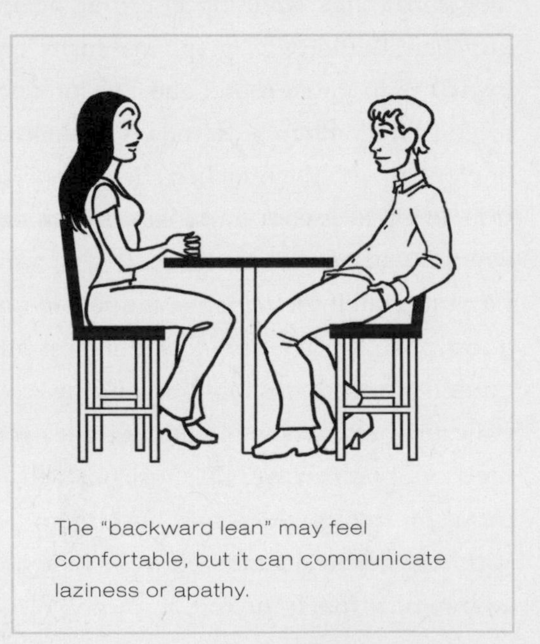

The "backward lean" may feel comfortable, but it can communicate laziness or apathy.

What to watch for: If they're using it to get away. If you tend to be a "close talker," you may see this signal more frequently than others. People may subtly be trying to tell you that you're in their space. The only time you want to see the backward lean in a social setting is when your relationship is so close and well established that you don't have to worry about expressing your utter relaxation. Imagine that you and your friends have just finished a good meal, and you all lean back in your chairs and just settle in to digest.

That kind of backward lean shows intimacy and trust, instead of fear and avoidance. But if someone does the backward lean before your relationship is at that level of trust and comfort, they're likely saying: (a) "You're too close," in which case, you should move back; or (b) "I don't care what you think of me," in which case I hope the feeling is entirely mutual.

What you should work on: Use it for the right reason. If you're trying to tell someone that they're in your space, leaning back is one way to do it. But know that if you're doing it in other situations, you're saying loud and clear, "I feel no need to impress you."

Body Signal: Forward Lean

When you are interested in someone or someone is interested in you, you will notice that one of you will tend to lean forward. A forward lean not only indicates liking, it also translates into sincerity and confidence.

As opposed to the aloof manager who uses the backward lean to show his arrogance and superiority, the manager who wants his team to feel supported and valued will sit forward more often. A forward lean says, "I'm interested—tell me more."

The "forward lean" can make another person feel important, as long as it doesn't invade her space.

What to watch for: When someone shifts position. If someone has been in a forward lean for a while and then suddenly sits back, that's a cue that they disapprove of what was just said. And vice versa—if you've hit positively on a hot button issue for them, they're more likely to sit forward in an unconscious attempt to get closer to more of the same kind of information.

What you should work on: Don't use it in a sales situation. Although this gesture can help build rapport in preexisting relationships, use caution in new relationships. Never go into anyone's personal space uninvited. (Note the illustration on page 111—see how the man leans forward, very interested, but does not enter the woman's personal zone.)

As a bonding gesture, the forward lean is way too familiar for a sales situation because the customer will read it as an aggressive move or, worse, an attack. Also, the forward lean can decrease your leverage with a customer because you may be seen as too desperate for the sale.

Some people find the forward lean such a natural gesture that they have a hard time using it selectively. Recently, at a business banquet, I met Harold, an extremely friendly, chatty, and likable salesman from the South. Harold was sitting to the left of me during dinner, and during the first ten minutes of our conversation, Harold leaned directly into me and touched me approximately seven times. He gazed into my eyes as if I were the only person in the entire room.

As we sat together, he must have asked me twenty questions about how body language impacts sales. Then, after dinner, the woman sitting to the right of me asked me a question that required a lengthy answer, so Harold began speaking to the person on his left. Curious to see if Harold had assimilated any of the information I had imparted about body language, I watched his exchange with the woman.

As I watched him lean in fully toward the women next to him, grabbing the back of her chair, I noticed the woman physically recoil. Clearly, my points about proximity and the forward lean hadn't made an impression on him. At first, I assumed Harold had not noticed the woman's reaction; however, I noted that his hand did not remain on the back of her chair for very long. Instead, he slowly brought it back to his side, all within a matter of seconds.

Moments later, Harold and I were talking again, and he brought up this encounter. "It's such a habit for me to get close to someone—up until now, I never noticed their reaction. I was usually too busy thinking about what made me comfortable," he said. "But did you see that women flinch when I touched the back of her chair? You would have thought I was getting ready to stab her!"

He was shocked, almost angry, at the thought of someone being so startled by his forward lean. We spent several more minutes discussing the do's and dont's of the forward lean, and by the time the night was over, he said he was in awe of all he had learned just chatting over dinner. A few weeks later Harold wrote me an e-mail telling me how he'd started to ease off the forward lean just a bit, and he could already see that his changed approach was making his customers feel more in control—and more willing to do business with him.

Body Signal: Chest Thrusts

Women often do this by accident. They might intend to have good posture but then overdo the natural S curvature of the spine, sticking out their chest and butt simultaneously. When a woman does a chest thrust, instead of achieving the more desirable relaxed alignment of proper posture, she ends up with a little too much of the "lady lumps" on both ends.

A man will puff out his chest to look his best, most impressive self. Women also do chest thrusts to exhibit their goods in the most pronounced way possible. She's either walking by with her breasts thrust forward to say, "Feast your eyes, but don't touch," or "Wow, I'm really interested in you." Either way, it's preening—she's showing off her body. The moment these two people see each other, they might both take deep breaths, straighten their spines, suck in their guts, and stick out their chests—a mutual signal that demonstrates our subconscious desire to appear attractive to the opposite sex.

What to watch for: If someone feels competitive. The chest thrust can also be a form of "broadside display," the act in which an animal tries to make himself seem larger or more intimidating to his enemies. Oddly enough, men are less concerned about their appearance in front of other men unless there is a potential sexual or physical threat. But women will do it to other women on a much more regular basis. Let's say two women used to be gym partners but had a falling-out. If they happened to see each other in the gym, they might both suck in their bellies and start working out a little harder and faster. Again, they're trying to show off, but in this case, they each want to ensure that the other woman cannot find fault in her and that she is seen in her best possible light.

What you should work on: Doing it carefully. Good posture should always feel loose and natural, not forced. Chest thrusts cause you to overextend your back, which is bad for your posture in the long run. Also, be wary of doing the chest thrust in a business setting—it's way too sexual and predatory a signal. And if a woman does this in a bar, she should know that she's almost certain to attract attention, wanted or otherwise.

Arm and Hand Signals

Many scientists believe that it is the gesture that allowed humans to become more social beings. Gestures do much more than help us to communicate with others. Research suggests gestures not only help listeners understand our spoken messages more clearly, but also help speakers "package" thoughts and words more coherently.

Body Signal: Arms Crossed

Crossed arms can be a very comforting gesture—it's as close as you can come to hugging yourself. The problem is it's also an extremely cold, closed off, and defensive posture.

Crossed arms can make a person appear defensive.

When you see this signal in any situation in which you're trying to persuade someone, you have some work to do. Closed arms scream, "I'm defensive and closed to what you are." Folded arms, even when done innocuously, are perceived as a negative stance, and subconsciously, your conversant will presume you are not open to what is being said or that you may even be borderline hostile. Be careful not to do this in a work setting, as it can instantly peg you as closed-minded.

What to watch for: When you use it to bond. For women, crossed arms can be an incredibly warm and comfortable posture, especially if they are doing it to camouflage big breasts—or even tiny breasts. It's a natural, instinctive way for women to self-nurture and, when done in groups, can even serve as a bonding mechanism. If you were to come to my block, you'd see five moms standing on the sidewalk, all of us with our arms crossed. Objectively, you might think that means five closed minds, but because we are mirroring each other, we are actually holding rapport with this supposedly hostile gesture. Of course, this gesture is also used to keep our body heat in and warm us up—always remember to look at the context.

What you should work on: Loosening up, both yourself and the other person. If you see a person with their arms crossed during a talk or a presentation, make eye contact with that person for a few extra seconds, making sure he knows you are focusing on him. Often, I will ask that person to participate in a part of the seminar. For example, who will I ask to demonstrate the proper handshake? The person who has his arms folded. This affords me the opportunity to make this person feel special as well as force him to open his body language. If you're in a one-on-one setting, hand something—a pen, a piece of paper—to the person with crossed arms and say, "Hey, did you see this? Can you take a quick look at this for me?" As he reaches for the paper, instead of just handing it over, hold on to it for a beat longer than usual, so you create a break in his body language. Anything you can do to open up a person's body movements will help cue that person's brain to open up as well.

Body Signal: Arms at Sides

This neutral position feels as solid as a tree trunk. Your feet are planted comfortably apart; your arms hang down at your sides, slightly bent at the elbows to give yourself a relaxed stance.

You see this pose most often when a person feels very confident. When you have your arms at your sides, you telegraph the solidity and symmetry that make people trust you.

What to watch for: How you feel when you're with someone. The beauty of this pose is the power you can have over other people simply by using balanced, symmetrical posture. When someone stands in such a solid yet relaxed way, it can have a calming effect on the entire dynamic of a group.

What you should work on: Developing it. I realize that not everyone is going to feel comfortable with this posture right away. We all have our little standing eccentricities that we use to boost our confidence, whether it's jutting a hip out or crossing our arms. But the arms-at-sides posture is the ideal.

Before you walk into a public setting, shake your arms out a little to relax them. Feel free to hold something in your hand—a pen, a water bottle, a notebook, some kind of prop that gives your hands a purpose—if it will make holding your arms at your sides easier for you. But the ultimate goal is to be able to stand with anyone, anywhere, in perfect symmetry with your arms hanging gracefully by your sides.

Body Signal: Palms Exposed

Any time a palm is held upright, pointing toward the ceiling, it's a universal sign for supplication and openness. Primatologists have found this sign among chimpanzees who use it to beg for food or otherwise enlist support from others. Darwin considered the palm up a part of the shoulder-shrug gesture.

Exposing one's palms makes a person seem more honest.

Palms up tells others, "I'm honest, I'm vulnerable, I'm pleading with you." It's a perfect way to let others know that you're not closed-minded but, instead, open and willing to hear them out. It's a way of offering yourself to the other person.

What to watch for: When someone is using it deliberately to mislead you. Many liars know this gesture is very powerful. You'll see when people are denying that they have lied—they'll expose their palms and say, "Trust me, I didn't do it." They might combine it with a shoulder shrug and a look of indifference, for good measure.

What you should work on: Using it when pleading your case. Open palms say all kinds of good things about you. You're not threatening; you're open to collaboration; you can be trusted to tell the truth. Of course, when you are trying to come across as powerful and dominant, you would want to use this gesture sparingly and rely more on the next gesture, palms down.

Body Signal: Palms Down

Palms down is a dominant gesture that suggests control. Parents often use it to tamp down any errant negative energy among their youngsters. As such, whenever someone does it to us as adults, it can seem patronizing.

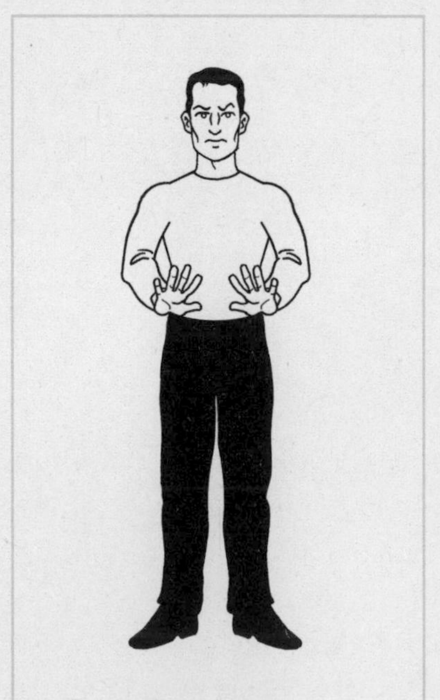

Palms down is an authoritative gesture.

You see palms down when someone wants to assert their authority or demonstrate a level of control over a situation. Think of the dominant handshake—the same principle is at work here. Power players tend to use palms-down gestures in an attempt to influence others, but these can sometimes work against them. You want to use a palms-down sign sparingly with your boss unless you need to drive home a powerful point—in effect, you'd be saying, "You might be the boss, but this is my area of expertise, and in this area, I am the dominant of the two of us." Even subordinates tend to feel unnecessarily strong-armed when their managers use palms-down gestures.

What to watch for: When someone is actively patronizing you. Let's say you were very upset about something, and you were voicing your concerns to your boss or another authority figure at work. If she responded by saying, "Calm down," or "cool your jets" and combined it with a palms-down gesture, it's likely you would feel incredibly insulted. In effect, palms down minimizes any contributions or thoughts the other person is offering at that moment.

What you should work on: Use it strategically to underscore your expertise. The palms-down gesture is really useful when you want to prove your authority in a given situation, such as when you're talking about a product during a sales call, when you're making a presentation, or when you need to drive home your point with emphasis.

Body Signal: Palms Forward (or "Stop Sign")

The "stop sign" tells others not to interrupt.

The palms-forward gesture literally tells people, "Stop." Palms forward is a gesture used to request that your audience give you their complete and utter attention.

Lifting one palm to a crowd of talkative people is an unmistakable sign requesting quiet and order. Most people recall their days in school and will calm down very quickly. This move even works when you're talking to one other person, but this time, it's to prevent them from butting in. Generally the double palm thrust tells people, "Stop and listen to what I have to say."

Another variety is the textbook talk-to-the-hand: If you keep your straight palm at chest level, turned up to the person with whom you're speaking, it usually indicates, "Okay, no talk from you now. It's my turn. We can finish with you after I've said my share of whatever I need to say."

What to watch for: When it's used as a barrier. If you're coming toward me, and I lift my palms up to you, that's a clear sign that I don't want you to touch me or even come close. If I'm just sitting here with my hands closed, I'm giving you more leeway to touch. But by pushing my palms out toward you, I'm putting up a barrier.

What you should work on: Perfecting your use of the "double stop sign." This gesture is very powerful. This is a more emphatic version of the talk-to-the-hand mentioned above. While you're talking, you might sense some resistance from the other party. If you lift up two hands, the message is, "Stop. Hear me out. Don't talk, don't interrupt. It's my turn to speak."

Body Signal: Sweeping Gestures

Gestures help us excite people about our ideas, and they also help us learn. A recent study from the University of Chicago found that students who watched a math teacher make sweeping gestures during class were four times more likely to use the same gestures during a test and, as a result, got significantly more problems correct. Researchers said that linking the gesture and the spoken word lecture served to "cement" learning for the students. This effect can be applied to

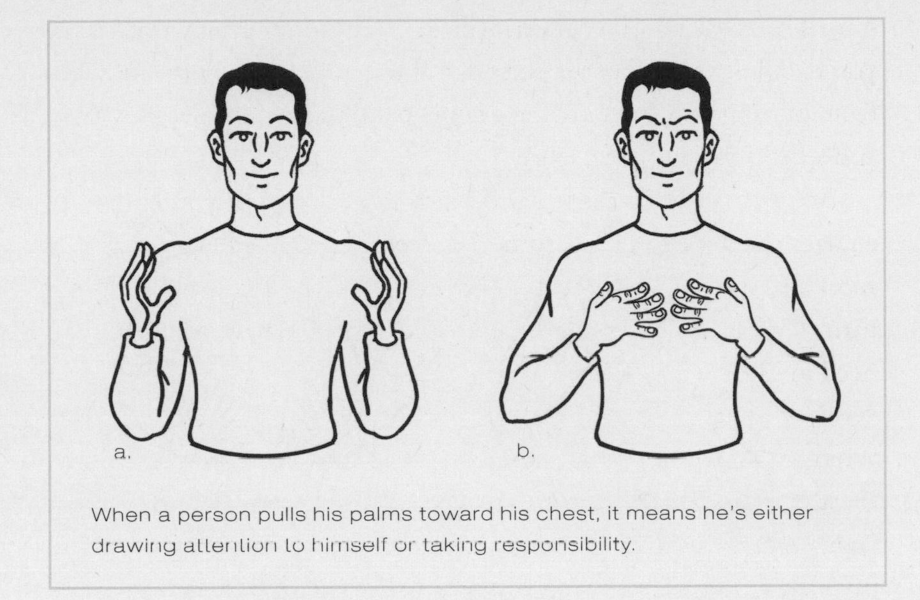

When a person pulls his palms toward his chest, it means he's either drawing attention to himself or taking responsibility.

almost any instructional situation, whether it be teaching your child how to read or explaining your product to a group of potential clients.

Sweeping gestures are most effective when they're used to punctuate certain points and, above all, congruent with one's speech. For example, as in the *a* and *b* illustrations above, you might see someone make a sweeping gesture and then bring their hands in toward themselves. This gesture could mean, "It's all about me," or it could be a very powerful way of saying, "I take responsibility for this." The energy and the emphatic motion of a sweeping gesture underscores the degree of the speaker's passion for the idea and also the magnitude of the event he's discussing. Or, you might see the opposite, as in the *c* and *d* illustrations on page 122, when a person's hands start on his body and then vigorously sweep away, as if he's trying to take the onus off of him.

What to watch for: When the gestures don't match the words. Sometimes gestures can help you determine when someone is not telling the truth. One politician I recently analyzed was talking about

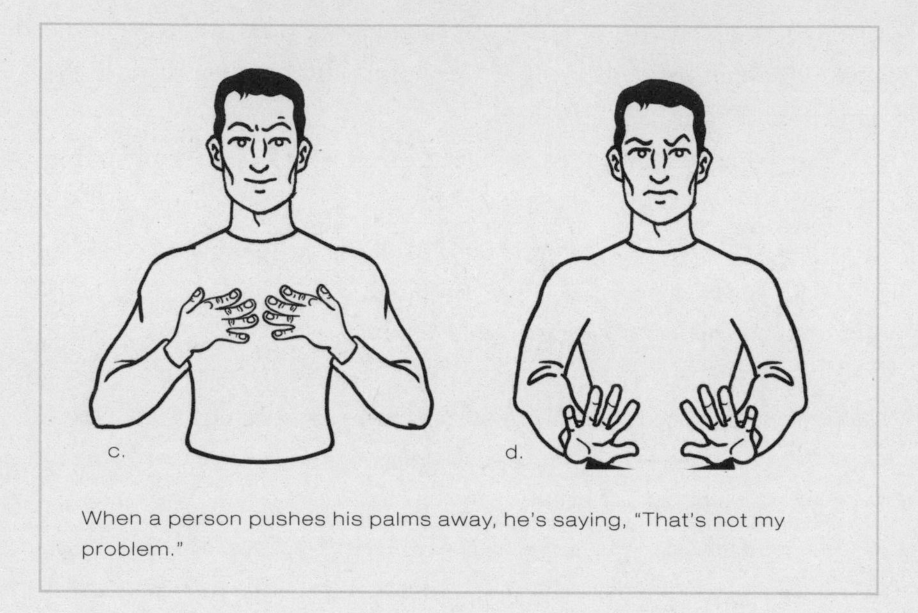

When a person pushes his palms away, he's saying, "That's not my problem."

the cost of the Iraq War and if he believed it was worth it. He started off by saying, "It's very important that we do this," and his hands were somewhat close together, as in *e* below. Then he said, "It's not that big a deal," and his hands swept out openly, as in *f.* So his gestures directly

The distance between a person's palms in a sweeping gesture tells you how he feels about the magnitude of the event he's describing.

contradicted what he was saying, and at the same time the width of the space between his hands told us very distinctly how big or little the issue felt to him.

You might see this incongruence when someone is willfully trying to mislead you: "Oh, yeah, I got a big raise this year" (figure *e*). "But Tom was really screwed over and received much less" (figure *f*). Obviously, the speaker thinks he got the shaft, but he's too proud to talk about it—so he lets his hands do the talking!

What you should work on: Focus on congruent gestures. When we tell lies, we may think we're being very convincing, but we constantly make slips in body language that give us away. While we're focused on covering the facial emotions of how we feel about a certain situation, we don't spend as much energy thinking about the rest of our nonverbals—and as you can see here, they slip out, very naturally and easily.

To prevent this from happening, the first tip is, of course, to be honest! The abstinence plan is the only way to avoid getting busted for lying.

If you can't help yourself, at least work on keeping your gestures somewhat contained, restricting them to the area below your shoulders and above your hip line. That way, if you tell a lie, an incongruent gesture will be more contained and less obvious. This kind of strong, contained gesturing is a big part of the Reiman Rapport Method, which you'll learn in chapter 9.

Body Signal: Chop

A distinct group of dedicated nerve cells in our lower temporal lobe has no other job than to respond to our hand gestures. One gesture sure to provoke a strong brain response is the chop. In the chop, your active hand lifts and falls perpendicular to your opposite palm, lifting and falling, almost as if you are chopping wood. Because it mimics the motion of a weapon, we read the chop as extremely emphatic and a bit of a strong-arm tactic.

The chop is so aggressive, it almost feels like a conversational last resort. Each chop usually hits on a key word: "I [*chop*] did [*chop*] not [*chop*] do [*chop*] that [*chop*]!" You're pushing your point vigorously, driving home that you definitely know more than the other person does about the topic at hand.

What to watch for: The use of the dominant hand. Normally in the chop, the person's dominant hand will be on the top. If her dominant hand isn't on the top, it brings up a serious question—is she really feeling strongly about this, or is she pretending? Bill Clinton is a lefty, so when he used his right hand to emphasize his innocence on national TV, he telegraphed his insincerity. When you're really being truthful, you feel more passionate about an issue, so you'll automatically use your dominant hand when you gesture.

What to work on: Modifying the chop to make it less threatening. One alternate to the traditional chop is the palms-up chop. Try this: Turn both of your palms faceup, and move your dominant hand over the top of the other palm. Now, smack them together, but not as often as with the chop. Place emphasis only on the verbs, say, instead of every word. This gesture will feel less threatening than—but equally emphatic as—the traditional chop.

Body Signal: Politician's Point

With the increase in awareness of body language, some politicians are becoming very savvy about what their gestures and postures say to the public. One of the most recent introductions into the body language lexicon is the politician's point. The thumb and forefinger meet, just like in the A-OK symbol, and then the hand is used to point to others.

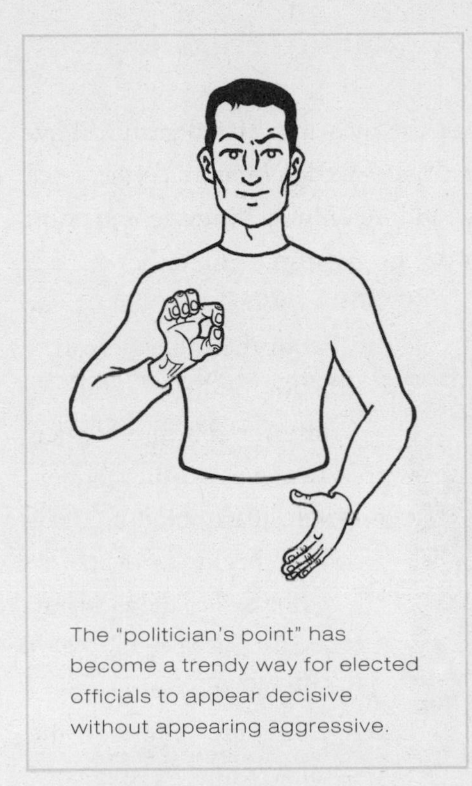

The "politician's point" has become a trendy way for elected officials to appear decisive without appearing aggressive.

You see the politician's point anytime you used to see pointing. A traditional straight finger point has been long decried as symbolic for pointing a weapon at someone. Politicians don't want to come across as violent, but they still want to get their points across. Enter the politician's point. The politician's point drives his or her message home quite succinctly, appearing as though the speaker is saying, "The whole truth is right in between my pointer finger and my thumb, and I am going to share it with you."

What to watch for: Who chooses to use it. This is a fascinating case study in body language—it's not often that you see the introduction and adoption of a symbol on such a broad scale among a certain population. Keep an eye out for politicians who use this—obviously they've been told to tone down their aggressive body language. And while this gesture is new to the political arena, this one was a favorite for Tony Soprano. And as we've seen from Tony, some gestures, even if they're not direct, can feel very threatening.

What to work on: Trying it out for yourself. This gesture can seem somewhat forced—not many of the gestures we use have been so consciously crafted to send a message—but it can be useful. If you tend to be a pointer, give it a try—it certainly can't be any more offensive than poking your finger in someone's direction.

Body Signal: Single or Double-Barrel Point

The pointed index finger is one of the most hardwired gestures, bypassing a lot of the typical neurological middlemen to connect the brain directly with the finger. Depending on how it's done, the point can be a tool for building rapport or destroying it.

Bill O'Reilly often pulls out his double barrels.

When angled away from the other person, a point enlists another's interest and directs their awareness to another person, place, or thing. Babies begin to learn to point before they learn to speak, and once they start talking, they often say a word and point at the same time. Caregivers' use of pointing helps babies to understand that objects have names. The use of pointing is an essential part of the development of language and an excellent teaching tool. Just as when parents respond to babies' emotional cues, when parents respond to babies' pointing, their rapport is enhanced and solidified.

What to watch for: When someone wants to assert power or authority. The other kind of point is aimed directly *at* another person, a universally understood gesture of insinuation, that sometimes conveys aggression. Because the pointed index finger is symbolic of a gun, when you point it at someone, even innocently, it can feel like an accusation or a threat. Bill O'Reilly's most imposing gesture is the one-finger point combined with a head tilt and a smirk or another intimidating facial expression. I had the opportunity to analyze Bill

O'Reilly's on-screen interaction with Geraldo Rivera and did the play-by-play as they exchanged verbal blows. At one point, Bill pointed his finger at Geraldo so forcefully that I thought he might actually spring out of his chair to move farther into Geraldo's personal space.

When you point with two fingers, you can sometimes double the impact of the gesture. The double-barrel point is a favorite of Bill's. I have seen Bill employ the double barrels often enough to know that it is an excellent sign of how strongly he feels about a given issue. If a person has already been using the single point and then moves up to the double point, you've just triggered a very hot topic for them. If you're in an argument with someone, keep an eye out for those moments of transition, as they can tell you a great deal about someone's most strongly held beliefs.

What to work on: Not pointing at anyone. If you point your finger away from someone else, either to direct someone's gaze, to emphasize a point, or to help someone understand a concept, that's fine. But if you're pointing your finger *at* someone, know that it might be interpreted as intimidating and possibly rude. Often it leaves a bad impression on other people. And, by all means, leave the double barrels to the professionals unless you are prepared for the consequences!

Body Signal: Pen Point

You can also use props to point, such as a pen, a laser pointer, or a ruler. Any of these props would be considered an extension of your finger and will likely get you closer to your conversant. While these props can serve the same function as a finger in directing attention, they can also be used to simulate an attack.

Using a prop in order to make a point during a conversation is similar to doing a hair toss—you're using something a little bit extra to capture someone's eye. If you use a pen to direct someone's attention, it also creates a more "we're-working-here" productive feel.

What to watch for: When someone uses it as a conversational weapon. Using the pen closes the distance between you and the other person; it can be read as an invasion of space. A person might intend to use the pen to communicate industry and teamwork, but when used in an accusation, a pen can seem like a sword. Brandishing it, you might be seen as piercing the air between the two of you.

What to work on: Using it to influence their movements. Let's say you were sitting at the signing table with someone. You would point to each clause in the contract with the pen, directing their eye precisely to the areas you want to highlight. They'll be transfixed by the movement of your pen to such a degree that you can lead them like a puppy on a leash! And yet, to them, because of the involvement of the pen, it will feel more collaborative and team-oriented than if you were doing the motion with the more authoritarian index finger.

Body Signal: Steeple

The "steeple" is a powerful, authoritative gesture.

The steeple is formed when the two hands form a prayer gesture, but the fingers meet in direct alignment with their counterparts on the opposite hand—thumb to thumb, pinkie to pinkie, and so on.

David Givens calls the steeple a "precision gesture," one made possible by the same brain structures that allowed man to first create tools. In today's world, this signal is often seen during problem-solving situations. It's a favorite among politicians and corporate leaders because it communicates so many of the qualities they want to embody: authority, confidence, superiority, and reasoned thinking.

What to watch for: The interesting variations. Some would say that when you spread your fingers wider in the steeple, you take up more space and therefore reflect a higher degree of dominance. Steeplers can either raise their hands, to indicate superiority, or they can lower them, trying to reflect an openness and a willingness to be considered as equals. Either way, you are creating a barrier between you and your conversant, and depending upon the situation, you might take care not to put anything between the two of you, regardless of how powerful a gesture it is. The steeple is a better gesture in larger groups than in a one-on-one situation.

What to work on: Slipping it into your repertoire. When you use this gesture, you walk a fine line between arrogance and dominant power, so you must learn to use it appropriately and wisely. Experiment with different ways to do this until you find one that works for you. Maybe the steeple that's most comfortable for you won't involve the fingers touching at all; maybe the hands will lie flat against each other, as in a traditional prayer pose. Generally, any time you allow your palms to face one another directly, you'll transmit basically the same messages—competence, power, authority, and high status, with a sprinkling of condescension.

Body Signal: Thumbs-Up Gestures

As the digit that distinguishes primates from the rest of the animal world, the opposable thumb is our most powerful finger and, as such, a potent tool for expression.

You typically see the use of the thumb in gestures when people are trying to demonstrate confidence or authority. Typically, the thumb is seen as a bit phallic, so men are more apt to use this gesture than women.

What to watch for: People's idiosyncratic thumb gestures. Bill Clinton uses his signature thumbs-up so often that this gesture has become known as the Clinton thumb. He uses it to emphasize points, draw people into discussion, greet others or wave good-bye, or just generally to express optimism—and power.

President Bill Clinton gives a thumbs-up sign.

What to work on: Using it more, but not too much. The thumbs-up gesture has been used so much in our culture that it can sometimes be seen as sarcastic. ("Yeah, buddy, take a hike.") But there are still so many positive associations with this gesture that's it's worth tapping in to. Experiment with using it as Clinton does, as an unthreatening finger for pointing.

Body Signal: Preening

Preening is the conscious or unconscious act of grooming yourself in preparation for or in response to someone else's attention. A person who preens is both trying to attract attention to herself and working to present herself in the best light.

You'll see preening anytime people want to draw attention to themselves. Sometimes it can be as simple as a man pulling up his socks or brushing lint off his clothes, or maybe a woman fixing her hair or running her fingers over her lips. Preening goes across the spectrum from the simplest things that you don't even realize that you're doing to completely and utterly pampering yourself in front of another person.

What to watch for: How it changes in different settings. You might do it in a more subtle way during a meeting—straightening shirt-sleeves, buttoning coats, smoothing the front of a skirt. But with sexual preening, as in a bar or at a party, the gestures become more flamboyant. A woman might do a head toss to show a guy how glossy her hair is while also exposing a little bit of her neck.

Sometimes a woman can even preen when she's not interested in a guy—she might just want him to be interested in her: "Look what you can't have!"

What to work on: Doing it in an appealing way. Preening can be an incredibly seductive tool when done in the right way. Develop a confident signature move, such as a hair flip or a lip stroke, that you can break out in the right settings. Done well, preening will highlight your best assets; done poorly, it can function as a bull's-eye for your least appealing traits.

Ten Nervous Gestures That Turn Them Off

1. Jiggling car keys
2. Clicking pen caps
3. Tapping foot up and down
4. Chewing on anything other than food (nails, lips, pens, straw, toothpick, necklace, inner cheek, etc.)
5. Pacing
6. Swaying from side to side
7. Playing with your water bottle cap
8. Picking your fingernails
9. Picking your lip
10. Finger drumming or tapping

His Signals/Her Signals

The Heart Touch

The "heart touch"

When you look at a couple together, you can see the level of their intimacy and the level of their connection to each other in the way that they pose for photographs. If you see a wife standing or sitting to the side of her husband with her hand resting on his heart, there's deep affection there. We tend to clutch our neck to demonstrate our vulnerability and clutch our beloved's chest when we feel passionate about them.

Body Signal: Hands on Hips

Also referred to as "standing akimbo," hands on hips is a way of expanding your physical presence, another broadside gesture. If you put your hands on your hips, keep your shoulders square, and plant your legs firmly, you're making it possible to take up much more than your typical allotment of space.

If done from a position of authority, standing with hands on hips is an attempt to maintain dominance or intimidate others. Many parents will do this when they're confronting a child for bad behavior. Children will often return the gesture in defiance. While it's rarely seen among adults in a subordinate position, it can come out in moments of extreme anger and indignation.

When you place your hands on your hips, you're like a peacock, spreading your feathers so you can make yourself larger.

What to watch for: The one-hand variation. When you keep one hand on your hip, especially with one foot jutting out, it's seen as a slightly sarcastic or flirtatious position that denotes skepticism. The woman who does this—and it's almost always a woman—feels a little cocky or confident. People tend to perceive women who do this stance as tough-minded.

What you should work on: Using it to express defiance. The hands-on-hips gesture can make you look stronger and more dominant than you might actually be. It could come in handy when you feel like you're being ripped off. Let's say you dropped your car off at the shop for a simple tune-up, and the mechanic is now trying to rope you in to a major overhaul that you don't want. When you question the need, if he becomes disrespectful and patronizing, you can put your hands on your hips and demand he get his supervisor or return the keys immediately.

Body Signal: Hands over Crotch/Fig Leaf

Often used in moments of vulnerability, the fig-leaf gesture is seen when someone folds one hand over another and lets the joined hands hang in front of the lower body. While men might think they have the monopoly on this gesture, it's seen in women as well.

The fig leaf is almost always used in an attempt to protect oneself from pain, whether physical (in the case of a man defending his genitals) or emotional (as in the case of a mourner at a funeral, as shown here). We sometimes use it when we're being admonished as well.

Spanish royals use the "fig leaf" during a funeral for six UN soldiers killed in Lebanon.

What to watch for: If someone uses it. This gesture is, above all, a direct sign that the person is feeling insecure or vulnerable about something. Make sure you note what the situation is so you can better conclude why someone would need this type of barrier or protection. The fig leaf is not just done with the hands; it can be done with a briefcase or a pocketbook as well—anything that protects the lower body from exposure and risk.

What you should work on: Trying to remain open. Obviously you will not want to avoid this gesture when you're trying to prevent physical pain to your family jewels. But when the pain is more emotional, know that this gesture is perceived as weak. Recently, while attending a funeral, I found myself automatically succumbing to the fig leaf, silently and unconsciously protecting myself from the fear of my own mortality. I caught myself, however, and opened up, realizing that remaining open to others' grief might be more helpful to them than protecting myself.

Body Signal: Hands behind Back

When we're scared, we tend to curl up in a fetal position, probably to protect our heart and other vital organs from injury. In contrast, when we hold our hands behind our backs, we're telling others that they don't intimidate us.

This stance is not only about trust—it's about confidence and superiority. When a person clasps his hands behind his back, this position tells the other person, "You're so unthreatening that I can be entirely unguarded in front of you without fear." He is willingly exposing all of his nerve endings as well as his neck, heart, and gut, without a trace of anxiety.

What to watch for: When it's done in anger. When an individual clutches his wrist behind the back, which looks very similar to the confident hand-clasping gesture behind the back, he is unconsciously communicating frustration and growing anger, almost as if he needs to restrain himself.

What you should work on: Use it to present a sense of self-confidence to the world. This stance, when done well, can communicate your total ease and superiority in a situation. Clasp hand to hand, use lots of eye contact and smiles, and you'll be telling the person, "I'm confident you won't hurt me, and I am no threat to you either."

The body is a rich source of signals about who we are and what we feel. We can see displays of heartfelt emotion as well as clues to thoughts other people might wish we couldn't see. But none of these signals exists in a vacuum. We can't truly get the entire body language picture until we talk about the way our bodies react to each other in space. All of those facial expressions, all of those body signals, are in a constant state of flux—coming and going, approaching and retreating, touching and breaking away. Let's take a look at how human beings understand and define their own space and how those definitions determine who we allow to touch us.

CHAPTER 4

The Languages of Space and Touch

Man is the only animal that blushes. Or needs to.

—Mark Twain

During a break at one of my seminars, an attendee came up to ask me a question. Stephen introduced himself and told me he was a real estate agent. Then he took a deep breath and said: "You know, I just feel like clients are put off by me. They don't seem to like me. I try and I try . . ."

As he was talking, he stepped closer and closer to me.

Since that day in my psychology class, when Professor Mitchell made me do a backbend in my chair, I've learned a thing or two about body language. Now when people enter my personal space, I don't move. As he came closer, I stood my ground, and soon we were almost nose to nose.

I could see that he wasn't trying to manipulate me—he just didn't realize what he was doing. Finally, I said, "OK. Stop for a minute and just look where you're standing."

He just looked at me and blinked. "What do you mean?"

"Let me ask you something," I said. "When you talk to your clients, do you notice that they back away?"

His eyes widened. "All the time!" he said, clearly surprised.

"Well, what do you do?"

He squinted his eyes, turned his head, and thought for a second. "Well, I guess I just go forward or maybe touch them on the shoulder to try to connect and engage them some more," he said. He looked at me. "Is that wrong?"

I pointed at the approximately four inches of space between his shoes and mine. "You're in their face, my friend," I said. "You have to give them their space."

After the seminar, I didn't hear from Stephen right away. But about three months later, I got an e-mail. "I can't believe how much better things are, Tonya," he wrote. "All I'm doing is giving people their space, I'm not going toward them, and my sales have practically tripled. I can't believe such a little change would have such an impact."

Stephen's experience is a great example of how we communicate with our use of space and touch. If you take a step forward and you enter my personal space, I'll likely take a step back. You step forward; I step back . . . and on and on it goes, like a little dance, until you end up dancing me right out the door.

Each of us carries around us a bubble of space that experts call our personal zone. Your personal zone could be four feet; mine could be two feet. That zone is defined by the country you were born in, the city or village where you grew up, even how your parents played with you—or didn't—when you were growing up.

Many different factors go into creating the preferred sizes of our zones of space, including how we like to be touched—or not. The problem is, when we first meet someone, we likely won't know that person's preferences right away. That is, unless we breach them, and they retreat—but by then, it may be too late to undo the damage.

So how can we learn to use space and touch in a way that increases rapport rather than disrupting it? How can we learn to do that delicate dance in a way that draws people closer to us, instead of driving them away?

After years of putting people off and having his business suffer for it, Stephen learned that sometimes it pays to hold your own ground rather than pursue. He learned how to tap in to the power of body language to make his customers feel safe and respected, so they would trust him to help them make the biggest financial decision of their lives. In this chapter, I will show you the many factors that determine these deeply felt personal preferences, and how you can learn to use space and touch as effectively as Stephen did to improve his rapport with other people.

Decoding Space and Touch

Perhaps more than any other body language cue, the use of space and touch creates and defines our relationships with other people: Who is in the inner circle, and who is not? Who can come close, and exactly how close?

The rules of space and touch have a direct impact on our lives, day to day, second to second. They change depending on the location, the status of the players involved, even the desired ends of the interaction. A waitress who touches a patron while he orders a $10 plate of pasta will be thought of as warm and hospitable, and she'll earn a much bigger tip. At the same time, a real estate agent who comes within four feet of a client while discussing a $500,000 purchase will be seen as incredibly aggressive, and might be kissed off forever. A CEO who jokingly punches the arm of the mailroom employee will be seen as jovial and "in touch," while the mailroom guy who attempts a jab at the CEO might be escorted from the premises.

These rules can seem complex and arbitrary, until you begin to see the patterns. Just as with other aspects of body language, certain criteria—such as status, sex, age, and culture—dictate the unspoken rules of space and touch. For example, in all settings, higher-status people are afforded a wider berth of space, and people who touch others are considered higher status than those who are being touched. When you break those rules during a first impression, you're quickly scanned as "unsafe," a fast and definitive "no." But when you follow the rules of space and touch, it is much more likely that you will be seen as trustworthy, respectful, and, ultimately, a "yes."

His Signals/Her Signals

Don't Fence Me In

Men's and women's sense of personal space is actually quite different. Personal space between women is the smallest, between men is the largest, and between women and men is in the middle. Overall, women tend to keep less space between themselves and other people, but they are also more likely to withdraw when their space is invaded.

The crux of the rules is that at our most basic level, we humans are both fiercely territorial and desperate for touch. These conflicting needs create a space-touch continuum. We constantly move up and down the continuum, migrating back and forth from a huge circle of public space that can extend from thousands of feet around us, to mere inches as we seek the intimacy of a lover's embrace. Let's learn the rules of each stage on this continuum, starting with the most public interactions and moving toward the most private moments of human connection.

Defining the Four Zones of Space

Once you start looking for them, you'll see territories everywhere: the "assigned" seats at your family's breakfast table. The new fence your neighbor just built. The plants your colleague uses to block entry into his office cubicle.

As our status increases, so do the size and firmness of our territorial boundaries: from cubicles to offices to executive suites; from public housing to private condo apartments to penthouses; from the bus to the train to first-class air travel, with its private lounges with spacious seating areas. Like lions in their wild kingdom, the people with the highest status have vast amounts of territory that they consider their own.

Yet we still balance this desire for privacy with an equally strong desire to connect. Our personal bubbles of space expand and contract to suit our moods, our relationships, and the situations in which we find ourselves, while they also bounce off other people's expanding and contracting bubbles. We might feel perfectly comfortable standing shoulder to shoulder with a colleague on the elevator—but once the doors open, what happens when one of us follows the other a bit too closely and the other person scurries away, desperate to escape to her office?

Thankfully, to avoid the damaging fallout of such awkward moments, we can learn to master the dynamics of space. One of the first experts to do this was Edward Hall. In 1966, Hall coined the term *proxemics* to describe the study of how human beings interact within space. He defined four zones—public, social, personal, and intimate—and the functions of each within society. For the first time, people could clearly see and understand the differences in what had previously been lumped together in one amorphous area called "elbow room."

These zones are dependent upon culture—what is considered personal space in the United States might be considered social space or even public space in parts of Latin America. And we all have individual thresholds as well—how else to explain the attraction of the mosh pit? But Hall's zones give us a good framework to understand the dozens of cues that can show us where we are, and are not, welcome.

Sphere of Public Space

Hall called the outermost zone of space the public sphere. This area extends twelve to twenty-five feet or more. A familiar example of this sphere would be the space between a speaker and the audience at a rally, or a concertgoer and the musical performer. Politicians and celebrities are usually separated from the unwashed masses at this distance: they are close enough to the crowd to see and be seen, but not close enough to touch or be touched.

What to watch for: How it can change. Public space is the sphere in which you're most likely to be surrounded by strangers. On a sidewalk in a quiet residential neighborhood, you'd be in public space; on a city street at rush hour, you'd likely change to social space. Once you pack into the subway or train, you're talking about personal, if not intimate, space. These shifts in space zones happen constantly, and experts have found that how people handle these transitions can tell a lot about people's status.

One interesting study was designed to find out if gender had any impact on whose space was violated within a larger public space. In a bustling public area, the researchers had multiple sets of two people of both genders (female/female, male/male, and female/male) sit facing each other in chairs about twenty-six inches apart. The idea was to see how often each group would be "interrupted" by people passing through. They also left about twenty-one inches of space behind each chair, to provide the people approaching them the option of walking around each pair.

The results were astounding. Of the 1,081 people who passed the couples, the vast majority chose to go around them. But when people chose to go in between them, 53.3 percent of the time they walked between the two females, 29 percent of the time between a male and a female, and only 17 percent of the time between two males.

This study shows how people will react to each other differently within space, and invade certain people's space more often than

His Signals/Her Signals

Where You Place Yourself Can Change Your Luck in Love

When you're out on the town, trying to find someone special, where you sit and stand can make all the difference in how you're perceived. Many of us tend to cluster together with our friends and cast fleeting glances in the direction of people we're interested in—and then wonder why they don't get the message. Here are a few signals you'll want to send out if you're open to meeting members of the opposite sex.

- Keep your back to the bar (if you must stand at the bar).
- Stand next to a friend, but keep eyes out toward the club (the better to catch someone else's eyes).
- Point your body toward the middle of the club or the dance floor (or, preferably, get on the dance floor!).
- Move around the room (the energy of movement attracts attention).
- Stand by a window (many people look out the windows or gravitate toward them).
- Talk in the direction of the crowd (and laugh—a lot).
- Make eye contact (only with those you find interesting).
- Look directly at his or her lips (shows you are interested in meeting).

others', based on perceived status. The researchers commented that the fact that women's personal space was invaded much more often than men's personal space shows that women are still considered to be of lower status than men.

How to use it: Be aware of your surroundings. While public space is probably the zone over which you have the least control, certain body language techniques can influence how people react to you within that space. If you're walking into a conference hall and you want to make a good impression, allow your energy and enthusiasm to shine through. Walk into the room with your head held high, your shoulders back, and your best social smile. Focus on meeting the eyes of other people, and take the time to look around to determine who are the most powerful people in the room. Look for the individuals who have a crowd of people surrounding them, yet are given bigger areas of personal space.

Sphere of Social Space

The sphere of social space is found in those areas that afford about four to twelve feet of space between yourself and other people. Think of it as the "beach blanket zone"—even when it's really crowded, you typically wouldn't go within four feet of the neighboring beachgoers' personal space.

You might use this distance with business associates in meetings over a conference room table. Or, if you're a teacher, the outer edge of this distance would be where you stand during a lesson. If several people are waiting for a bus, they might maintain this distance until it's time to board, at which point they'd line up closer and enter one another's personal zones. If you're a salesperson, you might start the beginning of your sales call in the close end of social space, say at about four feet away from your customer, to get a sense of your customer's comfort level before you move any closer. (If you're selling something that the customer might want, but doesn't necessarily need, it's a good bet to start out farther away.)

What to watch for: How people move in and out of this zone. People may move back and forth within this four-to-twelve-foot zone, depending on what they want from someone. Women who want to get someone's approval move in and stay at about fifty-seven inches, or four feet, nine inches away, while those who weren't at all inter-

His Signals/Her Signals

A Room of His Own

Women are less likely than men to have their own private space within the family home.

ested in gaining approval average about ninety-four inches, or almost eight feet away.

Depending on how much you like someone, you might move from the social zone into the personal zone, and back again. Male college students who disliked their teacher but were asked to have a one-on-one talk with him said they would likely maintain almost five and a half feet of distance; when they liked their teacher, they said they would move to just over two feet away, well into his personal space. Women like to get even closer, moving from almost five feet from teachers they dislike to a cozy twenty-two and a half inches from a teacher they like.

How to use it: Learn how to manipulate perceptions of you with different sitting positions. Early in my career at a Fortune 500 company, I was working in the middle cubicle in a row of three. When a change in reporting structure moved my cubicle to the end of the row, I saw firsthand how positions equal power. I was asked to take messages for executives who had moved to new offices months ago, simply because I was in the cube closest to their old offices. Even if I were on international calls tending to my own business projects, people would drop by the executives' former offices, stand by my desk, and interrupt me with their questions, "Where's so-and-so?" "Can you tell so-and-so to please call me?" Suddenly, by shifting my desk a mere eight feet, I'd gone from being a mid-level professional to an administrative assistant.

The same principles apply in meetings. Where you sit in a meeting can speak volumes about your power and the value of your opinion—both to yourself and to others.

Best for Cooperation and Equality: The Round Table

The round table is the traditional peacemakers' arrangement. Because it tends to put everyone on the same footing, it's routinely used in diplomacy and peace talks, but it is tremendously useful in brainstorming meetings and other high-energy collaborations. Ideally, more conference rooms in the business world would have round tables, but they're usually reserved for off-site retreats or conferences.

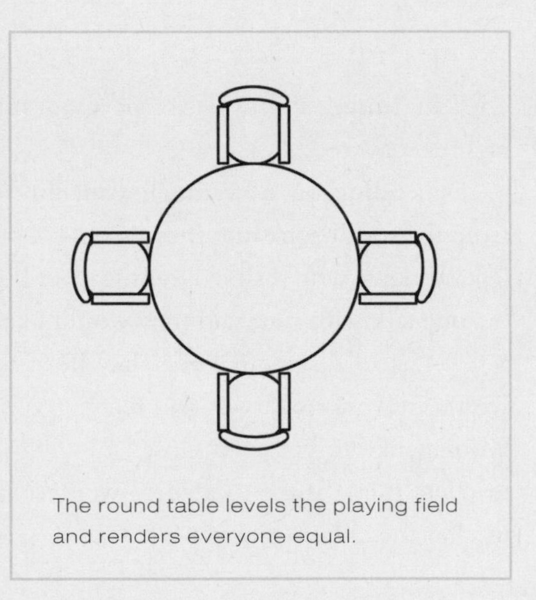

The round table levels the playing field and renders everyone equal.

Best Position for Collaboration: Side by Side

When you really have to work together and come to a common consensus on something, it's best to sit side by side, in the "roll-your-sleeves-up" position. Numerous stud-

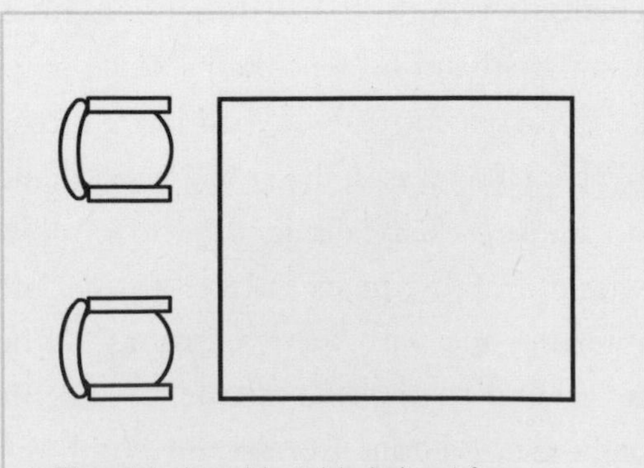

The side-by-side table is best for coming to agreement.

ies have suggested that people will work harder to come to mutually agreeable solutions in this position. Try to position yourself on your partner's right-hand side, which will unconsciously cue the other person that you are someone to be trusted.

Best Position for Confrontation or Competition: Straight On

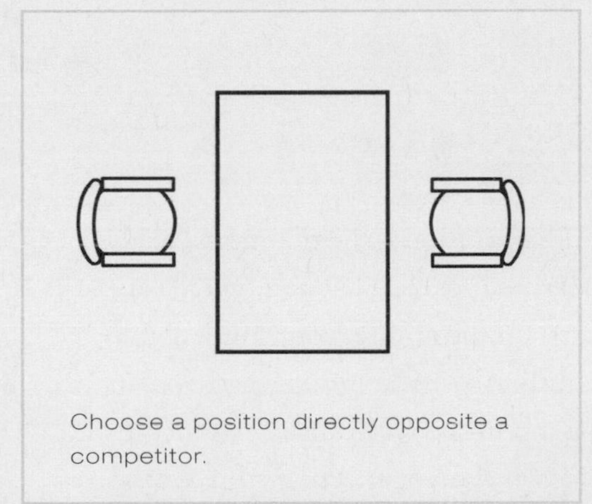

Choose a position directly opposite a competitor.

Sometimes the situation warrants a more competitive, confrontational approach. Interestingly, in research comparing the U.S. and U.K. attitudes toward seating arrangements, more people who were asked to compete with each other picked this position, but those in the States chose to keep a smaller distance between them than people in the U.K. Apparently, the U.S. sample sought to use the smaller distance to gain information about their competitors and possibly also upset them more readily.

Best Position for Conversation, Persuasion, or Seduction: At an Angle

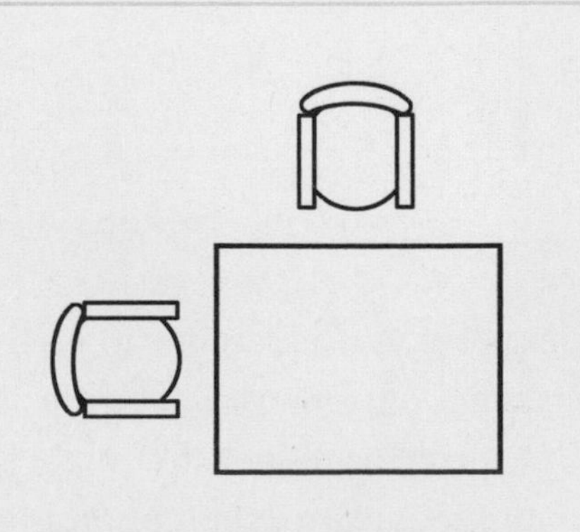

Conversations are best held at an angle from your partner.

This position is quite cozy, but still not restrictive. It affords both parties the opportunity to look into each other's eyes without a lot of furniture between them while also giving both the chance to look away easily. In many ways, this position affords the best of all worlds: the side-by-side feeling of collaboration combined with the frontal orientation that allows for any necessary negotiation.

Best Position for Traditional Authoritarian Leadership: Head of the Table

This position is the traditional leadership position. When you want to communicate your undeniable authority to a group, perhaps in a brass-tacks, we-need-to-buckle-down type of meeting, this would be the best spot for you. Beware, though: this position can also make you seem like the heavy and, depending on the content of the meeting, may make team members resent you a bit.

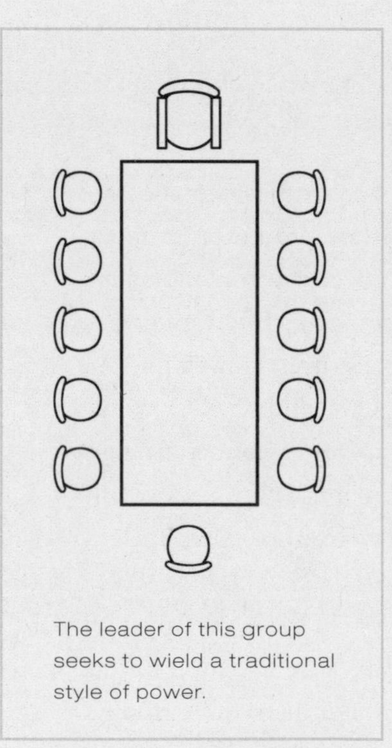

The leader of this group seeks to wield a traditional style of power.

Best Position for Coach-Style Leadership: Middle of the Table

This position is a great one to use when the atmosphere in a meeting is getting contentious, and you feel the team is not getting along well. (Of course, the round table might be best for that, but not many conference rooms have this option.) Particularly if you feel like productivity is suffering because people are not communicating, this would be a good position from which to solicit all opinions from the table.

Sitting here might endear you to the hearts and minds of your team, but again, beware. If you try to be too overly solicitous in this arrangement, you could come off as being weak or patronizing.

Interestingly, when people were placed in this seat by researchers (as opposed to choosing it themselves), they often spoke more—the more eyes on you, the more you might feel obliged to "live up to" this position at that table.

The leader at this table prefers a more collaborative approach.

Best Position for Being Seen (or Hiding) in a Meeting: Diverse

If you're an employee at a meeting, where you sit can also have a great impact on how you are perceived. The stars denote the places that are likely to make you more visible and give you a proverbial "seat at the table" instead of just filling the chair. Choose these seats when you have something to say and want to be seen and heard.

Now note the square positions at the table—these are the positions most likely to be chosen by neutral people who do not want to be

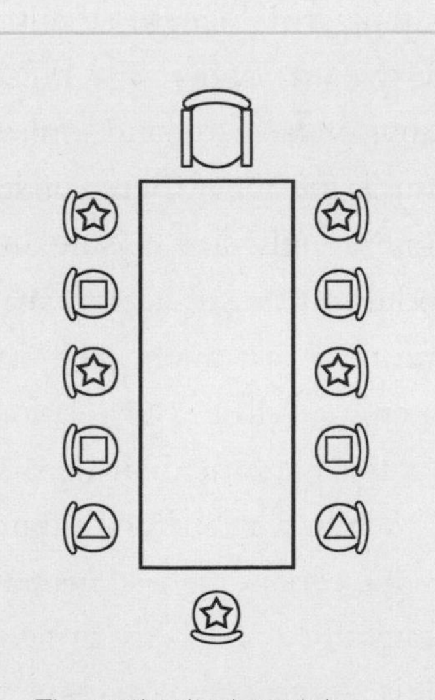

The authoritarian-style leader will view you as a bigger contributor if you sit in the star positions. You can hide best in the triangle seats.

involved in the discussion. As for the triangles, you might think of them as "meeting camouflage," as you're likely to fade entirely into the woodwork when you choose those seats.

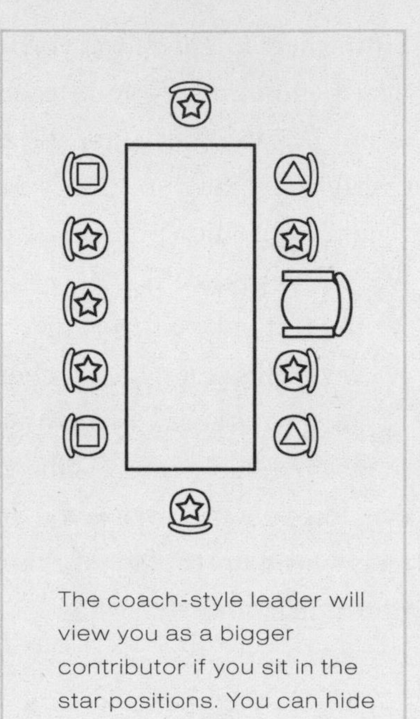

The coach-style leader will view you as a bigger contributor if you sit in the star positions. You can hide best in the triangle seats.

Sphere of Personal Space

Personal space extends from two to four feet. This "friendship zone" is the one we most frequently use with our family and the people we feel most connected to. You're within arm's length, the "cocktail party zone," where the music is so loud you have to stand somewhat close to hear what people are saying. This is the zone where you have your best conversations, usually with close friends, side by side on a couch or over a small table at a coffee shop. You step in here to shake hands with someone you've just met, and then you might step out again into the social zone, depending upon how close your relationship is with that person and whether or not this is a formal business setting.

While we generally do not like to have strangers in our personal zones, certain high-status people may be allowed in, sometimes even gratefully. A celebrity or an extremely attractive person might feel a certain entitlement to come very close without asking, in anticipation of our grateful reaction. Years ago my husband and I went to a U2 concert and sat in the front row. In the middle of the concert, Bono came toward our group of seats to find a woman to take up onstage to dance with him. Now, here is a male stranger looking to dance with a woman, and my husband is practically throwing me onstage to dance.

His Signals/Her Signals

No, Really, That's Close Enough

One fascinating study of married couples asked the husband to walk toward his wife and indicate the best possible conversational distance by stopping when he arrived there. The more satisfied the husband was with his marital relationship, the closer he walked to his wife, and the smaller the distance between them.

Typically, you would not find a male so willing to force his wife to dance with another man, but with a celebrity, normal proxemics rules do not apply. (By the way, Bono picked someone else.)

Often, even your boss might feel he is entitled to pat you on the back, and you're expected to feel honored by it—but he would likely be horrified if you returned the favor.

What to watch for: Signs that you've overstepped your bounds. The personal zone is the place where close connections take place, but it's also the zone that can get you into a lot of trouble. People regard their personal zone as an extension of their bodies; moving too close can be perceived as an immediate threat.

The personal zone is largest directly in front of the person. When people feel crowded into their personal space, they'll have a physical reaction: their heart rates increase, their blood pressure rises, their skin gets more tingly and sensitive, and EEGs show heightened brain activity.

Here are some signs you'll see when people feel their personal space has been invaded:

A threatening stare, then a turn to avoid your gaze

Increased blinking

Leaning away

Decreased smiling

Sudden halt to conversation

Stiffening or sitting up straighter

Turning feet and torso away from you

Increase in nervous gestures like preening, lip biting

Crossed arms

Finger or toe tapping

Blushing

Piling things up between you

Refusal to share any more personal details

Verbal hostility

People who feel crowded are unable to concentrate and perform less well on numerous thinking tests—people who are just asked to shop can't even do that! Research has found that even when people hadn't actually been crowded yet, just *the idea* that they would be crowded made them actively dislike the other people around them. Do you see where I'm going with this?

I recently analyzed a videotaped encounter between a reporter and Al Gore in which the reporter repeatedly entered Al Gore's personal space and, on occasion, grasped his arm. His response was to immediately shrink away from her touch. This minute movement would have escaped most people; however, I was able to view the interaction in slow motion, and was able to capture Gore's slight backward movement. Of course, it was obvious he did not intend to move away; however, it is usually an automatic response to pull away when someone enters your zone without permission.

What happens when someone unexpectedly enters our zone and we become uncomfortable? We also become aware of ourselves, and suddenly we forget to be *natural*. We tend to forget what we normally do with our hands, heads, and arms, and our movements become forced. When you see this kind of awkward movement, that's when you know you have made someone feel vulnerable and uncomfortable. Because you have the upper hand, if you use these few seconds

The Language of Smell

Tread Carefully or Risk Offending Someone Unknowingly

Our sense of smell is another interesting facet of body language. When we were still swimming around in the primordial swamp, our ancestors used smell to determine if another being was a friend or foe.

Certain smells bring us right back to early childhood memories because both are processed in the basal ganglia, the reptilian part of the brain. When my son was two years old, he found an old bottle filled with sour milk. He drank just a few sips, but that smell stuck with him, and even eight years later he cannot stand the smell of milk. This sense memory also occurs with pleasant things—apple pie reminds us of Mom, or a whiff of perfume reminds you of a friend you haven't seen in twenty years. But it is precisely because smells can illicit such powerful emotional associations that we need to approach them cautiously or risk offending someone unknowingly.

Let's say you are a female applying for a job with a male interviewer. You handle the interview flawlessly, and your references are impeccable. But you are wearing your favorite scent, Princess by Vera Wang, and as it happens, the interviewer's wife wears Princess and she just asked him for a divorce. What do you think is going to happen the minute he smells your perfume? He may not even realize why he suddenly dislikes you; all he knows is you are not a good fit for this position.

Could it go the other way? Absolutely. The interviewer might catch a whiff of Princess and suddenly recall a magical evening or a wonderful childhood memory. But don't take that chance; skip all scents. If you absolutely must wear scent, women should stick to universally pleasing scents such as musky jasmine, vanilla, or amber, and men should choose sandalwood, cedar, and balsam. We may think perfumes and colognes make us smell good, but research shows that our bodies are actually repulsed by these artificial scents.

appropriately, you may be able to get the other person to do what you want them to do.

How to use it: Don't enter someone else's personal space unless you know you are welcome. Here's the most important thing to remember about proxemics: very, very few people will ever tell you you've overstepped and you're in their personal space. They'll just gradually withdraw their attention, and eventually they'll flee. And apologizing is not going to bring them back. To them, you're now an aggressor, pure and simple.

That's why it is so important that whenever you're in doubt, or if you see any of the signs mentioned above, you should *just slowly and nonchalantly back up.* No amount of reaching out will help as much as simply stepping back and letting the other person approach you. The other person will tell you nonverbally exactly how much personal space she requires. Respect that from the beginning, and you'll be miles ahead.

The sole exception to this rule is when you want to use the invasion of someone else's personal space as a manipulation tactic. You can purposefully enter into the space of another individual who you recognize as insecure in order to overpower them and cause enough anxiety to have them submit to your request. Of course, beware that this can easily backfire if someone becomes angry instead of more insecure.

Some people have to be more careful about offending conversational partners than others, as they tend to have smaller personal zones. Interestingly, smaller people tend to be closer talkers, as are extroverts who are very confident and really like to bond with others. High-status individuals can and will take up more space with their bodies and their gestures. Especially with people who are normally introverted and anxious, you're better off letting them define their space and adjusting to their specific spatial needs. In fact, when people tend to prefer larger personal zones, they'll probably like you even more because you'll be mirroring their preferred distance, suggesting another similarity between you.

Now, what if you are a person whose space has just been invaded—how can you tell others to back off? To be honest, if that person has something you need, you don't. Just hang tough, hold your space—don't retreat at all—and stand there smiling. This is a way to increase your control of the situation. But if you really don't care what they think of you, and you want to maintain your personal space without fear of damaging your relationship, here are a few measures you can take:

1. As the other person approaches, take a quick step back. Usually you'll do this unconsciously anyway, but sometimes this one small signal is all it takes to let the other person know he's overstepped, and he will retreat, without anybody losing face.

2. If the person didn't get it yet, fold your arms to put a barrier between you.

3. If he still doesn't get it, move closer to him. Think of it as a martial arts move: you're turning his energy back on him.

It's critical, especially for women in business, not to allow people to come into your personal space without responding assertively, right away, until they relent. Once you're seen in a submissive light, you could have trouble reversing that impression.

Sphere of Intimate Space

Intimate space is touching space. From your body to about two feet away, this is the zone in which you're in direct physical contact with others or where you can easily touch each other. This zone is reserved for your absolute closest friends, your children, and your spouse or significant other. You use this space when you feel close enough to someone that you never worry about boundaries; it's reserved for people in your inner circle.

His Signals/Her Signals

Positioning Yourself for the Best Impression

Have you ever given thought to where you stand when you first meet someone? You should. Men and women almost universally prefer that when they first meet someone, that person stand or sit slightly to their right side, aligned with their right eye. Some believe this preference allows the person to evaluate the new acquaintance on a more cerebral level, as the right eye links with the left brain, the seat of rational thought. The right brain is associated with more anxious instinctual emotions, so sitting to someone's left might trigger more apprehension and uneasiness. On the other hand, once you get to know someone, it can sometimes work to your advantage to sit on their left side, to tap in to those emotions and strengthen any positive emotional associations.

It's also important to remember that men tend to find the head-on approach to be far too confrontational; as a result, it puts them off your message immediately. Women, on the other hand, prefer this kind of approach, probably because it feels the most open and communicative. Follow these rules of thumb to capitalize on these unspoken preferences:

A woman or man approaching a man: Men don't like to be approached from the front; they prefer to stand at a 90-degree angle to their conversational partner. Try to leave about thirty-five inches of distance. Also, consider talking while walking side by side, an excellent way to get the conversation "moving."

A woman or man approaching a woman: Women like to be approached from the front because they seek out more eye contact than men. About thirty-two inches is optimum.

What to watch for: When nonbeloved people use it. If you've ever been to one of those trendy small restaurants in New York City or Paris, you know the scenario: A person arrives at her appointed table in the restaurant, and the busboy actually has to move the table to the side so she can shimmy into her seat. Even though you may be eating in one of the most exclusive restaurants in the world, if you're seated at the next table, you're about to get a stranger's backside in your face. What do you do then?

Well, when you truly can't avoid the touch of a total stranger—as when you ride in a packed elevator, or stand in the five-deep crowd of parade viewers—that's when you develop what's called a "nonperson orientation": You and the other person silently agree to deny each other's existence and treat each other as objects, instead of as people. ("I know it's 90 degrees outside and we both smell like chimps in heat—but there's no way to prevent our bodies from touching until the train stops at the station.")

And then you have the people who consciously and willingly enter into your intimate zone with no apparent awareness of how it affects you. I know a woman who is a real sweetheart. But despite her very apparent desire to connect with others, her total lack of boundaries prevents her from connecting with anyone. She has no ability to read body language clues, and it devastates her socially.

I remember being at a party with her, years ago. Out of the corner of my eye, I watched her systematically approach eight or nine different women. She would first engage them in conversation, and once they responded, she would advance so abruptly into their intimate space that these women were visibly repelled. They leaned away, turning their faces in the opposite direction, nearly writhing under her gaze, until, one by one, they made excuses, turned, and ran.

Now, it bears mentioning that if you were so inclined to use this kind of behavior as an intimidation technique, it could be quite effective. But I don't believe that's what the friendly woman intended. By violating their boundaries, she lost opportunities for creating friendships with those eight or nine women. And she probably had no idea what was happening.

His Signals/Her Signals

Our Smells Bring Us Together

Our individual scents are as distinctive as fingerprints or genes, and they actually help our bodies communicate with each other. Six-day-old infants have been shown to prefer the smell of their mothers' breasts to those of other nursing mothers. Men and women's bodies emit odors called pheromones that are so subtle, we can't consciously detect them, but they have a powerful effect. A landmark 1998 study from the University of Chicago found that pheromones are responsible for the long-observed synchronization of menstrual cycles among women living in close proximity. Another study found that the closer women are to ovulating, the more they are attracted to the scent of men with higher levels of testosterone. Researchers believe this is perhaps due to an evolutionary preference that enhances humans' reproductive success.

How to use it: Enjoy intimate space wisely. To make sure you aren't unintentionally putting people off, continue to pay attention to their signals (see the list of signals people display when they believe their personal space has been invaded on pages 151–152). No matter what your relationship is with your conversational partner, you need to respect those signals. Sometimes even our closest pals need a little breathing room. Even if I'm at a party, the music is too loud, and the other person is screaming, "What?" I still let them lean into me because I refuse to enter anyone else's personal space, let alone their intimate space, without being invited. (Unless I have a specific motive, of course.)

At its best moments, however, intimate space offers some of the greatest pleasures of being human. Your most warm and personal moments, whether with your children or your loved ones, happen right there. I'm a huge believer in more hugs and more touch—I think we are, as Desmond Morris has said, a touch-starved society.

Once you've established the relationships that grant you access to this zone, I want you to make use of the intimate zone. Touch is an amazing tool for establishing bonds that last much longer than simple conversations. Increasing your daily level of touch can help you spark new relationships, build more enduring friendships, enjoy better sex, and create dynamic, confident, and loving children. Let's talk about the many ways that we can use touch to improve our world, always with an eye toward building rapport and stronger connections with other people.

The Fourteen Social Touches and How They Bring You Closer

Touch is one of our most vital senses. Every day, in every house in the world, people have a need to touch each other—they crave it. But most of us don't act on that instinct to get the physical contact with other people that we need—and that touch deficit can have drastic ramifications on our entire lives.

Touch is a form of body language that has physiological benefits beyond any other. Touch starts in the womb, when the contractions of the uterus, the gentle swaying of a mother as she performs her daily activities, lulls a fetus to sleep and helps acquaint him with the rhythms of human life. Once a child is born, that touch becomes even more critical to his survival. The giant leap forward in the development of a baby's nervous system happens, in great part, because of the tactile communication he receives from his caregiver's touch. In fact, research shows that while the normal dose of cuddling and nursing is wonderful for a baby, even more can have dramatic positive effects.

Just consider the experience of premature infants who are treated with what's called "kangaroo care," skin-to-skin cuddling with the baby tucked between his mother's breasts for several hours a day. Studies have proven that when the baby is cold, the mother's breasts will automatically heat up to keep the baby comfortable—as much as two degrees Celsius in five minutes—and then repeat the cycle all over again when his body starts to cool down. All of this happens without any external machines or assistance of any kind—and without a single word being spoken.

Now, that's what I call body language!

Numerous studies have also shown that in comparison to preemies treated in a hospital's normal neonatal intensive care unit, those treated with kangaroo care show a 75 percent greater reduction in apnea, better oxygen saturation, deeper and longer sleep, more rapid weight gain, decreased crying and longer periods of alertness, more successful breastfeeding, and earlier release from the hospital. Perhaps most amazingly, their newborn brains immediately fall into a patterned rhythm that full-term babies normally don't achieve until four weeks of age.

As the preemie babies' experience shows us, touch is not just something that makes you feel good—it's one of the most powerful ways to tap in to the body's own healing mechanisms. Massage has been found to help relieve the symptoms of dozens of ailments and diseases, such as anxiety, ADHD, high blood pressure, multiple sclerosis, Parkinson's disease, and many more. One study found that a thirty-minute massage lowered the fundamental frequency and sound pressure of people's voices. In other words, they sounded more relaxed, and had more appealing body language, because they had been touched!

This need for touch is just as hardwired into our bodies as our need for oxygen or water, and we never outgrow it. School-aged kids who are cuddled more are less aggressive on the playground. Adolescents who receive massage therapy are less depressed and more empathetic. Touch therapy reduces anxiety and stress hormone cortisol levels in depressed mothers, so they are better able to respond to their own children with loving touch.

His Signals/Her Signals

Share the Love

Boys under six months of age are touched, rocked, kissed, and held more often than girls of the same age; after six months, girls receive more positive tactile attention than boys.

So, if touch has so many beneficial effects, why is it such a taboo in our culture? Why aren't we all out there groping each other all day long? Well, maybe it's our roots as a puritanical country. Maybe it's our disconnected, media-drenched lives. Maybe it's just the evolution of preferences passed down from our forefathers' forefathers. Whatever it is, I think it's high time to reexamine that balance between our need for privacy and our need for connection, and make touch a bigger priority in our lives.

You know enough about body language by this point to know that I'm not advocating that you go out and touch total strangers, but I do encourage you to take advantage of the opportunity to regularly lay your hands on anyone who belongs in your intimate zone of space. I'm always encouraged to see the young people in my neighborhood hugging and touching each other more; it points to a larger social trend toward increasing levels of touch. In his book *Manwatching: A Field Guide to Human Behavior,* Desmond Morris created a list of fourteen ways that humans touch each other in social settings. Starting with the most versatile of all touches—the handshake—we'll talk about each one and how you can work them all into your body language repertoire.

Touch Signal: The Handshake

Most likely the handshake first came into common use in medieval times; soldiers would grip each other on the forearm to let each other know there were no weapons up their sleeves. We use it similarly today, to level the playing field before starting a new relationship. In the business world, deals used to be done "on a handshake," and it's still considered a very binding physical contact between two people.

What to watch for: The twelve wrong ways to shake hands. As the first physical contact you make with someone, the handshake is a critical opportunity to establish rapport. A handshake tells someone that you feel good about yourself and that you're "honored" to meet them. Don't be stingy with those handshakes! In the business setting, the more, the better—as long as you do it well. You'll find many ways to do it wrong, but there's only one way to do it right.

The limp handshake. One of the least appealing handshakes, the limp handshake feels like you're holding a lump of room-temperature chicken. All of the responsibility for the movement has been given to

Bill O'Reilly and I demonstrate a dominant handshake.

the other person, who is likely to feel put off and a bit resentful. Barring other evidence, this handshake says, "I'm weak, and I have poor self-esteem." Or a limp handshake could be a brush-off, as in, "You don't matter to me in any way, and I don't even want to touch you." The only time this is an acceptable handshake is when your hands are integral to your work—such as when you're a surgeon or a pianist—and you have to be very careful with them.

The dominant handshake. Any time you shake hands with your palm down, it's perceived as a dominant, overbearing handshake. If it happens to you, just give your wrist a quick twist so both of your thumbs are pointing straight up again. If the person resists, let it go—they obviously feel a tremendous lack of personal power if they need to dominate you that badly, or they simply don't know any better.

The submissive handshake. On the flip side, allowing your hand to be palm up when you shake hands can be a sign of submission. Also not advisable, the submissive handshake immediately pegs you as a doormat, someone less confident and easily malleable. Again, go for the wrist flip so you'll be in a more neutral position.

The fingers-only handshake. Some guys will sometimes offer just their fingertips for a handshake. Some women do it, too, in the mistaken impression that this is ladylike. Offering only your fingertips in a handshake is simply disorienting for the other person; she will feel like you just didn't reach forward far enough.

The overly affectionate handshake. This two-handed handshake should be reserved for celebrations with people you know. Sometimes called "the politician's handshake," this shake is seen as a synthetic attempt to be friendly and effusive. Reserve it for those times when you are truly excited and enthusiastic about meeting someone. You can also use it once you know someone already, as an extra sign of tenderness or respect.

The mini-hug handshake. When you shake with one hand and touch the person's opposite bicep or forearm with the other hand, the person will experience that as a modified embrace or hug. As such, it's completely inappropriate in business. The mini-hug is only OK for intimate settings if you really do know the person, and you know that extra touch wouldn't feel like a burden to them. The hand is the only part of a stranger's body that you're allowed to touch without further information being exchanged. Once you start touching them in other places, and you don't know them, they might get offended.

The sweaty handshake. Now, obviously, no one wants to do this one. Sweaty palms speak volumes about nervousness. Try to carry around a napkin to keep your palms dry, or spray antiperspirant on a napkin and rub your hands with it. If you shake someone's hand and they're dripping with sweat, you can either simply pretend that you didn't notice or give them a nice, warm smile.

The cold-hands handshake. Cold hands are sometimes caused by nervousness. Try to discreetly rub them together briskly before shaking hands with someone. A friend of mine who happens to suffer from cold hands due to poor blood circulation will always shake hands while saying, "Cold hands, warm heart!" to diffuse the instinctive negative impression.

The over-the-table handshake. I was once in a meeting in which a guy leaned so far over a big rectangular table to shake hands with someone that he tripped and fell flat on his face on the table. Try to avoid having huge pieces of furniture, or any barrier, between the two of you when you first shake. If you're sitting behind a desk, come out to the front.

The forward-lean handshake. Your body should not have to bend in order to make it possible to shake someone's hand—that shows you are too far away. Come within a distance that allows you to be standing straight up and down when you extend your hand.

The seated handshake. You never want to do handshakes in a seated position. They feel awkward and disrespectful. If someone is approaching you and you're still seated, get up to shake hands and then return to your seat. If you're both sitting down, don't force the issue by standing up, but know that it's much better to shake when standing up.

How to use it: Learn the only right handshake. This handshake will work with any person in any situation.

Go toward the person, lean slightly forward, look them in the eye, extend your right hand so that its right side is parallel to the ground, and simultaneously introduce yourself. (Step in, reach forward, hands meet; "Hi, Tonya Reiman, nice to meet you," as the hand pumps up and down two to three times.) Be sure to offer your full palm and have it meet theirs entirely. Your grip should feel easy and comfortable, the same pressure as if you were trying to comfortably hold hands with them. This grip suggests self-confidence and enthusiasm. All parts of your body should be pointed toward the person. If you keep your thumb pointing straight up, you'll ensure a neutral handshake.

Your elbow should be slightly bent. If your elbow is completely straight, you're obviously too far away from the person. Don't just shake the wrist or the fingers, but the entire arm. To finish, open your hand wide and release the entire hand at the same time. The whole handshake should not last more than two to three seconds.

I'll show you how to use this handshake to build rapport with other people when I explain the Reiman Rapport Method in chapter 9.

Touch Signal: The Body Guide

The body guide is a polite and effective way to control the direction in which another person moves. While you will always reserve your intimate touches for people who have consented to them, this is the kind of touch that you can use with a business colleague to help build rapport. Just take the person gently by the elbow (not the upper arm—that would feel too authoritative) and guide her through a doorway or to a table at a restaurant. Stay slightly behind the person so it's more of a gentle prod than a pull. This type of manuever is geared more toward woman-to-woman, woman-to-man, or man-to-woman

His Signals/Her Signals

Who Can Touch Whom When and Where?

Men and women differ dramatically in their levels of preferred touch from other people. Sex has a lot to do with it—and whether or not those advances are welcome help to define what's OK and what's not OK. Take a look at what's acceptable and what's not when it comes to touching a recent acquaintance.

1. **When a man touches a woman.** Keep it strictly chaste—only touch her hand or forearm. Anything more becomes way too personal. One study found that women find touch by an unknown man to be the least welcomed. (Men felt that way about a touch from an unknown man as well.)

2. **When a woman touches a woman.** Women have a bit more latitude. When a woman touches another woman, she can touch the hands, the forearm, the upper arm, and the knee without ruffling too many feathers.

3. **When a woman touches a man.** A woman can really touch a man anywhere on his body, but there are going to be consequences. Research has found that men prefer to be touched by a woman they know, but are almost as happy to be touched by a female who's a total stranger.

   Women have a tendency to touch early on in a relationship, and some men can misinterpret that as more sexual in nature. Overall, though, men don't get offended by a woman's touch that often.

4. **When a man touches a man.** Men can touch each other on the hand, shoulder, forearm, or upper arm. Any other touching would not be received well at all. In one survey, being touched by another man was the touch least welcomed by all men.

relationships. It should be used sparingly with man-to-man relationships, as it may cause discomfort on the part of the "prodded."

What to watch for: When someone does it against your will. This kind of touch can often happen without your consent. Perhaps it's from a person like a maître d' or an usher at the theater, someone whose job it is to guide. For example, most women do not like strangers of the opposite sex to touch them. If you get this touch from a stranger and you don't want it, you can just swivel your upper body away, ever so slightly—that usually breaks the connection.

How to use it: In a collaborative way. To make your direction feel like more of a joint decision, try this move. Instead of grabbing an elbow and pushing from behind, position yourself so you're at a 90 degree angle to the right of the other person's body. Take your left hand and place it on their right elbow. With your right hand, gesture ahead and slightly in front of them, as if to say, "Let's move this way together." You're welcoming them into the space at the same time you're supporting their elbow and moving sideways alongside them. They're likely to read this as a less authoritative version of the body guide.

Touch Signal: The Pat

The pat can be a very soothing gesture. We use it with kids, especially toddlers, when they're really wound up. Some experts believe it's especially soothing because you're mirroring the beat of a person's heart—very fast when they're wound up, very slow as they drift off to sleep. However, while the pat is very affectionate with kids, it can also be dismissive or downright condescending with adults.

What to watch for: When it reflects a suspected lack of intimacy. A pat can be a very efficient way to end a hug. I recently analyzed a tape of Hillary Clinton's announcement that she was running for president in 2008. She and Bill were up on the stage, she'd just announced, and then there it was—the pat. Bill gave her this "Gee, we're kind of like buddies" hug, and he patted her three times on the back. It was a very friendly gesture, but not one that you might expect of a couple with a long-term loving relationship.

How to use it: Use it with your male friends. As a guy, you can use the pat in a congratulatory way—"Hey, buddy, way to go." The pat is a more masculine touch, and whether they do them or receive them, men will likely recall this touch from their days on the high school football field. Both men and women sometimes use it to console others as well. But beware—the pat can at times seem patronizing and condescending. It's almost as if the patter is saying, "There, there, now, little one—don't fret."

I was away at a conference in the Southwest, right at the beginning of the campaign season, one year. While I sat with my fellow attendees at a luncheon, a local politician came in to do a meet-and-greet. He made his rounds throughout the room, stopping at every table to greet people. He was incredibly handsome.

"Wow, he's quite attractive," said one woman sitting at my table.

He approached our table, and I was stunned as I watched him lean over into people's faces, shake their hands, and then—completely without cause—pat them. Now, a lot of politicians do this because they're trying to be friendly and warm. The problem was, he was touching women right on their upper arm and shoulder, close to the zone that a strange man should never touch. When he reached me, I handed him my card and said, "We should talk."

After he walked away, another woman at the table said, "I would vote for him based just on his looks, but why did he touch me? Wasn't it creepy how he patted you on the shoulder?"

I was so sure the man was going to jeopardize his political career that I fully intended to send him a letter that said, "You may not win, and here's why." But before it came to that, he called me, and I visited his office several times before my conference was over.

The first thing we talked about was how he should never, ever hang over people while they're sitting down. By definition, the standing person has all the power, and the sitting person feels incredibly vulnerable. He was shaking hands, getting right into their faces, and then touching them. A lot of politicians do this because they're trying to be friendly and warm, but it's taking a huge risk. Then we worked on developing a correct, respectful approach—how you should bend over to shake someone's hand, how you want to smile at them, what the different smiles are, and, of course, where to touch people. When you're a politician, there are lots of good reasons to touch—you form an instant connection with people that will be hard for them to forget—but you just have to know how and when to do it.

Touch Signal: The Arm Link

More common in Europe, this signal is seen when either a male/female couple or two girlfriends who are comfortable intimate zone compatriots link arms together to walk down the street. In the heterosexual couple, the male is usually considered the anchor, and the female will link her arm through his.

What to watch for: Seeing it in American cities and urban areas. Because of its European ancestry, this touch signal is seen as very sophisticated and metropolitan in the States. Many also use this touch signal with elderly people, as the anchor's crooked arm makes a great balancing handhold for those who are no longer sure on their feet.

How to use it: With people you care about. This signal is really a lovely way of bringing more touch into your life because it's so

The Salesperson's Touch

How to Use Touch to Improve Your Numbers

As a salesperson, your primary objective is to gain your customer's trust. Touch can be a useful tool in building and solidifying that trust. Here are a few useful suggestions about when to touch—and when to absolutely *not* touch—a customer.

Touch them "accidentally." One study done on librarians showed that when they returned a library card, those patrons whose palms they touched were more likely to say they enjoyed the experience and would be inclined to return. Although librarians aren't money-focused, they are "selling" the library, and these kinds of accidental touches—handing someone a pen, showing them a folder of literature, handing them a menu—can create an instant bond where one didn't exist before.

Touch them when you're talking about the perks. "This car gets forty miles to the gallon" (tap, tap, on the hand or forearm). That touch will feel like you're coconspirators in marveling at the extraordinary perks of this car, as if to say, "We're both discerning people and we know how poor fuel efficiency usually is, but this one is truly amazing."

Touch them when you can see their interest is piqued. Let's say you're a real estate agent, and you've already brought your prospects around to two different houses—one beautiful, but out of their price range, and one horrific, but solidly in their price range. Now you're bringing them to a house you want them to buy—in their price range, very well kept. They walk in and, you can see their demeanor change—widened eyes, smiles, expressions of delight on their faces. *This* is your moment. Gently touch them on the arm, and say, "Look at this place. It seems to have everything you wanted." Don't touch too long—just about two seconds. Touch briefly and release, long enough to make a connection while they're falling in love with the place.

Touch them when you can see they're slipping away. You can also use this touch if you're sitting with them at the signing table and you sense they're slipping away a bit. Just reach out and touch with a comment like, "Just a few more places to sign and you are the owner of . . ." The touch lets them know you're on their side, and that you're someone to be trusted.

Touch them to reinforce a good experience. This touch goes especially for waitstaff. Research shows that if a waitress touches her customers as she returns the change or the charge slip to their table, she's more likely to receive a big tip. As you put the folder on the table, touch them on the shoulder and say, "Thank you so much for coming in. Enjoy the rest of your evening." Leave them with a big smile. No matter how busy you are with the rest of your tables, don't ever rush that good-bye moment, as that parting impression will influence what kind of tip they leave.

Don't touch them if they start to doubt you. If their eyes narrow at something you've just said, or they break eye contact suddenly, don't choose that moment to start pawing at them. Instead, begin the rapport-building process again and take the conversation in a different direction. If you touched them at that moment, you might be seen as trying to manipulate them back into the sale instead of appealing to their rising concerns.

versatile. You can use it with your parents, your spouse, your kids, your friends (unless you're a straight man who feels this will threaten your masculinity, of course). It's a warm, mutually loving signal that shows just how "linked" the two of you are. You wouldn't necessarily hold hands with your best friend on a walk around town, but you could link arms very easily—and present quite a united front while you do it.

Touch Signal: The Shoulder Embrace

In the shoulder embrace, generally the taller of the two people (often the man in a male/female couple) will drape his arm across the shoulder of the other person. Couples usually walk this way, especially if there's a discrepancy in heights—it's so comfortable for a tall guy to rest his arm across his girlfriend's shoulder and for her to wrap her arm around his waist (see "The Waist Embrace," on page 176).

What to watch for: When it's one-directional. In moments of celebration and congratulations, you might see a heterosexual man put his arm around another man's shoulder and say, "Good job." That one-directional shoulder embrace doesn't threaten either man's sexuality and is six times more likely to be seen than a full-frontal embrace because it is considered nonsexual. But sometimes a one-directional shoulder embrace is unwanted—and that's when you need a strategy to combat it.

How to use it: Only when you want to. When you see someone closing in for a shoulder embrace, and you don't want to do it, the best thing to do is turn your back to them fully and innocently walk out of the embrace. Done subtly, you needn't even betray that you knew of his intentions.

Touch Signal: The Full Embrace

Hugs are my favorite touch of all. What could be better than getting a big clincher from your spouse or a little child? Recent research suggests that people in the United States are actually becoming more connected by touch. One survey found that 60 percent of dads hug their school-age kids at least once a day, and 93 percent at least once a week, which is up 90 percent from a decade ago.

What to watch for: The increase in the social hug. As more and more young people are starting to hug socially as a means of greeting and leave-taking, the full embrace is becoming the rule, rather than the exception. But because this trend is still in its infancy, we don't have an etiquette book on hugging yet.

For example, what do you do when you get to a party and everyone's hugging, but you don't feel comfortable doing it? Or what if there's one person whom you really don't want to hug, but they're at the end of a long line of eager huggers?

Establishing your own hugging policy is a good start—and try to apply it equally across the board, if you can. You don't want that unhugged person to feel slighted. Or, instead of a hug for that one individual, you could just grasp their upper arms, just a quick greeting. Or, you could go in for a mini-hug, a handshake combined with an arm squeeze to their right arm. That makes the person feel connected and acknowledged without either of you having an awkward moment. If you're sure you're not going to want to hug anyone, you could always bring a prop such as a book and hold it up to your chest.

What if one of your friends is an "over-hugger," someone who holds every hug just a few beats too long? The pat can come in handy here. Just quickly pat—one, two, three—her on the back, the way Bill did to Hillary. That's the universal signal for, "OK, the hug is coming to a close now." If she still doesn't get it, you can do the pat and then pull your chest away and look in her face: "Boy, it's good to see you." Once your chests are apart, she's more likely to get the message.

How to use it: Know the preferences of the person you are hugging. Well, if you're a hugger, you can choose to hug those people who are warm and fuzzy and those who have already entered your intimate zone for a hug. You don't want to hug someone who has never approached you. If you touch someone in general conversation and she pulls her hand back as if you've just burned her, it's safe to say she is not a hugger. Before you attempt a hug, pay attention to a person's signals. You don't want your relationship to get off to a bad start or to sour because of misread cues.

Several years ago, I went to the house of a friend who had company I didn't know. Three of the people were men and two were women. I bonded instantly with four out of the five people, and when it came time to say good-bye, we were hugging and giving "I love you's" across the room. Unfortunately, this did not happen with the fifth person, and when it came time to say good-bye to her, it was an incredibly awkward moment—should I give her a hug, a handshake, a double handshake, or an arm embrace? I was at a total loss as to how I should leave, and instead I offered a quick, running-out-the-door "Nice to meet you." This was definitely not one of my finer moments in rapport building.

The next week when I was speaking to one of my brand-new buddies, he said, "Wow, you really blew Nina off last week. After you left she mentioned how you hardly said good-bye to her." I made a mental note to remind myself to keep things as universal as I can with each person I meet in order to avoid this feeling of discomfort.

Touch Signal: The Hand in Hand

The Beatles really captured the exuberance of this signal in their song, "I Wanna Hold Your Hand." We first used the hand in hand with our parents, when we're learning to walk, and it retains the same protective, all-encompassing feel of love throughout our lives. Young

The Man Hug

When Guys Embrace Guys

Recently, the "man hug" has become more prevalent. Not too long ago this was mostly acceptable only in the sports arena. Nowadays, however, the man hug demonstrates the hugger's self-confidence, as he is comfortable enough in his own skin not to worry about what others think. Man huggers tend to be quite extroverted.

Men typically hug with either one hand, one hand with a handshake, one hand with a back pat, one hand with a shoulder bump, two hands (aka bear hug), or two hands with a back pat. Straight men have also perfected the man hug to ensure that it does not appear feminine at all. Most of the hugs men partake in involve just the upper body; the lower portions of the body never need touch.

When two men hug with a handshake between them, it comes across as closeness with a small barrier between the two permitting each of the men to demonstrate their affection for one another while maintaining a sense of tradition. This differs somewhat from when men hug and slap or pat each other on the back, which offers a chance for each hugger to show regard while at the same time confirming their masculinity by hitting the other on the back.

The two-handed bear hug is the only one in which the lower body has a chance to actually touch; most straight men, however, will pull back their hips to guarantee there is no contact. This hug is usually reserved for men who are quite close or who have just experienced a life-altering event such as a celebration or a death.

Overall, the man hug is coming into its own. Men are much more comfortable touching other men today. To some, this might be alarming, but to others it is quite comforting.

children use it with each other to show their friendship, and young lovers use it to show connection.

What to watch for: How it can calm you down. We can tap back into that feeling of being cared for simply by holding hands with someone we love and trust. One study looked at the brains of wives under stress and found that just the act of their husband offering a hand to hold lessened their brain activity and decreased the release of stress hormones.

How to use it: Go for the full lace-up. When you hold hands with a child, usually the only way to do it is palm to palm because their hands are so small and cute. But if you're feeling intimate with someone, you and your partner's fingers will lace together more often. So if you're walking down the street with your boyfriend or girlfriend, husband or wife, and you want to encourage a bit more intimacy, lace those fingers together. Your partner will feel that you want to be closer to him or her.

Sometimes when married people have children they stop holding hands—not because they don't want to but because there is usually a child to be held or a stroller to be pushed. Once the children are old enough to walk without handholding, the marital handholding is gone. If this sounds like you, it's time to reacquaint yourselves with holding hands to regain intimacy. It might feel awkward at first, but handholding is a wonderful bonding mechanism, creating an exciting energy that connects people.

Touch Signal: The Waist Embrace

Similar to the shoulder embrace, the waist embrace is sometimes part of a walking signal. You're paired up alongside another person with one arm resting at your side and the other wrapped around the other person's waist. Or, you might be facing the other person, but instead of embracing him, your arms and hands just rest on his waistline. You'll see this signal mainly in close relationships, especially between younger children, teens, and new lovers.

What to watch for: Interesting variations. Every generation creates a new twist on the waist embrace. In the 1970s, when people kept those oversize combs in their back pockets, one lover would use the other's comb as a kind of a handle upon which to rest his or her hand. In the 1980s, people would shove their full palm into the back pocket of their lovers' jeans or trousers, almost as if they were giving them a nice cheek grab.

How to use it: Only with the people you are closest to. The face-to-face waist embrace brings the two people's genitals into proximity, which makes this embrace much more personal than the shoulder embrace. If anyone were to try this type of waist embrace on you at work, even just briefly, it would be considered sexual harassment.

The side-by-side waist embrace is a nice walking posture to try with your husband or wife to bring more intimacy back into your relationship. It's basically like a walking hug—you really have to coordinate well with each other to sustain this.

Touch Signal: The Kiss

One theory on the origins of the kiss is that it sprang from a primal urge to take in the other person's scent to determine breeding compatibility. Many anthropologists also believe that kisses originated when mothers fed their young by chewing up food and spitting it into their babies' mouths. Thankfully, we've moved beyond that particular mode of sustenance, but mouth kisses are still reserved for your very inner circle. If you've ever been kissed on the mouth when you didn't expect it, you know that it can be a very disorienting touch.

What to watch for: Different display rules for social situations. Some microcultures have their own very specific display rules about kissing. For example, in some industries, such as fashion, photography, or other highly creative fields, a kiss on the cheek is an accepted part of the business greeting. Other industries might use kisses after a business lunch. But for the vast majority of industries and professions, even cheek kissing is not acceptable in the office.

In social situations, some groups are huggers and some are kissers. Social kissing can also be subject to trends. About ten years ago in New York, it was common to see people greeting each other with a kiss to both cheeks; now that practice is considered passé in New York, but is still the norm in London and Paris. In some areas of the Netherlands, the standard greeting for acquaintances is three kisses on the cheeks: left, right, left.

Most women kiss once softly on the right cheek when greeting or saying good-bye to a friend. Women usually greet men, upon first meeting, with a nod or handshake. At subsequent meetings women will sometimes kiss men on the cheek. Some people do not actually kiss each other; instead they touch cheeks and kiss into the air. When in doubt about your target's intentions, go for the air kiss—it's much better than planting a big wet one on her cheek while she leaves you hanging on the other side.

Regardless of the rules of your group, try not to kiss hello if you are not comfortable with it. There is nothing worse than being smacked in the face with the hard lips of someone who is uncomfortable.

How to use it: Different kiss placements for different intents. Where you place a kiss changes its intent. Mouth kisses are usually strictly sexual. Kisses to the head are considered more loving, nurturing, and intimate. If they're kissing your hand, it could be respect, or it could be a very romantic come-on. Perhaps more important for conveying the intention of the kiss is the duration of the act itself—if it is just a second too long, it changes from just a greeting to something much more.

When you're thinking about initiating a kiss, try a touch to the forearm first. If the person pulls away, she's not open to touch. If that move goes ahead, move to the upper arm; if you try that and see the entire upper body pull away, she's not open to touch. But if you've touched her in these ways and she didn't pull back, go ahead and give her a kiss on the cheek.

A long, slow kiss can help you increase the intimacy of a committed relationship. Ellen Kreidman, PhD, in her book *Light His Fire* recommends that couples practice kissing for a full ten seconds at a time in order to deepen their connection to each other. Now that might not seem like a lot, but to some couples ten seconds of mouth-to-mouth connection can seem like an eternity if they have not been doing it regularly up to this point. You can make it feel natural again if you practice, practice, practice.

His Signals/Her Signals

To smell her is to love her

Napoleon Bonaparte once wrote to his love, Josephine, asking her not to bathe for two weeks while he was gone, so that upon his return he could enjoy her natural aromas.

Touch Signal: The Hand to Head

This touch is a very nurturing, affectionate touch. We touch our kids on their heads and stroke their foreheads to soothe them. Head touches feel very warm and comforting; perhaps that's why we pay people like hairdressers or facialists to work their magic all the time. Desmond Morris called these people "licensed touchers" and said that because we always want more touch than we're getting, we pay these people to give it to us.

What to watch for: When it feels patronizing. Because parents touch their kids on the head all the time—to comb their hair, to guide them through crowded areas, to grab their cheeks and kiss them—when adults do it to other adults, it can feel patronizing. In my mind, this touch should never be done lightly or taken lightly. Experts say that higher-status people feel more entitled to touch lower-status people, even on more private areas of the body such as the head. You would never see a fan permitted to go and ruffle Britney Spears' hair, but she'd likely feel perfectly entitled to do that to a fan because she believes not only that she has the authority and the right, but that the fan would be desperate for her touch. Be sensitive to your assumptions about how familiar you're really entitled to be, and take care not to overstep your bounds on this one.

How to use it: To bond with your mate. I know if my husband kisses me on the forehead, it can send chills through my body because to me it's such a loving, warm touch. Experiment with using it to bond more deeply; take your lover's head in your hands and gaze deeply into his or her eyes.

His Signals/Her Signals

Trading Touches

Before people get married, men touch more often than women. After a couple gets married, men touch less often than women. But overall, married couples are more likely to reciprocate touch than dating couples.

Touch Signal: The Head to Head

This touch might vary from two lovers pressing their cheeks together in a hug to good friends leaning their heads together for comfort when they're at a scary movie. Parents who read to their children in bed will sometimes lie side by side and position their heads to touch cheeks. The head-to-head touch allows for a prolonged moment of extremely personal contact.

What to watch for: When someone takes a big leap forward in closeness. This signal is usually only seen when people have achieved great intimacy. By "faking" it or creating opportunities for this touch—the scary movie, for example, or propping your head on another's shoulder after a fun day at a picnic—you tap in to a very primal connection. If you were looking to press fast-forward on a relationship and give the impression of intense connection, you could use this signal to your advantage.

How to use it: To connect more closely, without creating awkward discomfort. This move can sometimes be seen as a playful gesture as two people lean closer and closer to each other, looking into each other's eyes, and eventually bop heads. Or, you know that moment when you're sitting with your honey, whose arm is around you, and his arm starts to feel really heavy on your shoulders? Or you're holding hands, but one of them starts to fall asleep? The physical discomfort kind of cuts into the magic, doesn't it?

That's why I love this touch. When my husband and I watch TV, we sometimes sit with our knees up and our heads leaning into each other. It's another way to get that tactile connection. We're still touching, but we don't have to worry about holding hands. My three children have seen my husband and me sit like this so often that they now have started to do the same, either with Mommy and Daddy or snuggling together—all heads close to one another—watching a movie and having those few moments when they are just inseparable.

His Signals/Her Signals

Road Map to Sex

Body language icon Desmond Morris believed that heterosexual couples are no different than other animals that have a very specific progression from first encounter to copulation. If you've ever wondered how you ended up in someone's bed the next morning, here's Morris' road map of the visual and bodily contact that got you there. You might skip a step or two, but the destination is always the same.

1. Eye to body
2. Eye to eye
3. Voice to voice
4. Hand to hand
5. Arm to shoulder
6. Arm to waist
7. Mouth to mouth
8. Hand to head
9. Hand to body
10. Mouth to breast
11. Hand to genitals
12. Genitals to genitals and/or mouth to genitals

Touch Signal: The Caress

This touch can be very sexual in nature, but it stops short of progressing to sex. You could be stroking your fingertips down your lover's face. You'll often see this when a couple in the early throes of their sexual relationship "can't keep their hands off each other." It can also be a sign of affection, as when you lovingly stroke your child's face.

What to watch for: When it's done in a professional setting. Some couples feel very comfortable about expressing their mutual attraction so openly, but because of the intimate nature of this touch, it should never been seen at work. If it is, someone's either headed toward having an affair or having a meeting with HR!

How to use it: To communicate your connection privately, in public. This touch can be a very sexy prelude to a planned encounter later. While you'd never want to try this at work, if you're out with your lover in public—at a bar, say, or a party—you could rub his thigh or give her neck a nice, relaxing squeeze, signals that help you stay connected to each other while still hanging out with your friends. Mainland America tends to be very prudish about these behaviors, but in many other lands, such as Puerto Rico or France, young lovers engage in what in the States would be considered serious caressing and public displays of affection—with nary a passing glance from the crowds around them.

Touch Signal: The Mock Attack

The mock attack is usually a father's way of bonding with his son; or two guy friends will use it to show how close they are without showing actual affection. Sometimes business associates will fake a punch at the bicep of another to show how tight they are. Headlocks, ruffled hair, fake smacks, and other joking gestures fall in this category.

What to watch for: How kids sometimes use mock attacks to substitute for other touch. A series of interesting pilot studies compared the differences in touch between teens at a McDonald's in Miami versus one in Paris. Researchers found that Parisian kids were more likely to lean against, stroke, kiss, and hug their peers, whereas the kids in Miami were more likely to self-touch. When American kids did touch their peers, which was less frequently than their French counterparts, it was in a more aggressive, mock-attack kind of way. The researchers theorized that, due to cultural differences, the American kids had received less touch at an early age than the French kids, and this touch deficit caused them to become more aggressive and nervous later on.

How to use it: As a rapport-builder with friends. After you know someone pretty well, you can selectively use mock attacks as a way to gauge their sensitivity to touch. This playful act can sometimes heighten the intimacy of a friendship.

We've seen how we send one another signals with our faces and our bodies, and even by how far or close we place our bodies to other people's. Now let's talk about the signals that we send with our voices, aside from speech.

Types of Touch Situations and Likelihood of Touching or Being Touched

Others are more likely to touch you when . . .	Others are less likely to touch you when . . .
giving information.	asking for information.
giving advice.	asking for advice.
they're giving an order.	you're giving an order.
asking a favor.	agreeing to do a favor.
they're trying to persuade you.	you're trying to persuade them.
you're worried.	they're worried.
they're excited.	you're excited.
in deep conversation at a party.	in casual conversation at work.

Adapted from *Body Politics: Power, Sex, and Nonverbal Communication* by Nancy Henley. © 1977 by Prentice Hall. Adapted with permission of Simon & Schuster.

CHAPTER 5

The Language of Sound

Three things matter in a speech: who says it, how he says it, and what he says—and, of the three, the last matters the least.

—John Morley

"This one time? At band camp? I seriously jeopardized my career?"

A vocal tic that's quirky and endearing in a character in *American Pie* can be absolutely grating around the conference table. Yet we all know at least one person who has the habit of turning every statement into a question with the rising pitch of his voice. Conversations with such a person can be hard because you're never sure if you should be waiting for more information or answering the questions yourself.

Even without the use of words, our voice is a powerful channel of nonverbal communication. "Bandcampitis" is only one of numerous vocal idiosyncrasies that send certain messages about us. Our pitch, tone, rate of speech, and dozens of other cues betray many hidden, and not so hidden, cues about our personalities, backgrounds, and intentions. One person might be a loud talker, projecting power and possibly dominance. Another might have a high-pitched, squeaky voice that makes her seem chronically nervous. The speaker with "bandcampitis," for example, is thought of as less authoritative, hesitant, and probably pretty passive.

One client of mine, Samantha, knew this firsthand. Samantha came to me for help to remove this lilting pattern from her voice because she had begun to see how this habit was holding her back, both professionally and socially.

When we started our work together, I first asked her to take one paragraph of text—whatever she wanted—and read it out loud into a digital recorder. She selected a paragraph from the daily newspaper and read it into the microphone. As she listened to the replay, Samantha heard herself exactly the way the rest of the world heard her—and that only gave her *more* motivation to change.

We listened to the recording again and broke it down—how often did her voice rise like this? On what kind of statements? How extreme was the lift? Samantha left my office with instructions to record that same paragraph every day, over and over, and with each "take," to try to lower her pitch at the end of declarative statements and make her voice sound more authoritative.

This technique is progressive—by listening to the prior day's recording, she continually built on her success day by day instead of only comparing her voice to the initial baseline recording. As a result, Samantha was able to advance very quickly.

The results were amazing. In three weeks, she returned to my office and we compared her most recent recording to her first tape. Her bandcampitis had improved significantly. Once she had licked that tic, she was excited to do more to improve her voice. We used the same technique, even the same paragraph, to help her increase the speed of her words. Once again, she recorded herself every day and kept progressing. When she returned to my office two weeks later, we tested her on a fresh piece of text she'd never seen. She was delighted to hear that her voice had become more polished—confident, authoritative, fluent, and fast—in just a little over a month. With a few simple changes to her vocal signals, she had radically changed the way people would look at her for the rest of her life. Of course, she would need to continue practicing until it became second nature, but the hard part was now done.

The Seven Emotions and How They Sound

The Meaning Behind the Words

We've seen how the seven universal emotions have very distinctive facial patterns—but did you know they have vocal patterns, too? Take a look.

Sadness: The person's pitch will be average to low, and speech rate will be slow.

Surprise: The person's pitch, volume, and speech rate will rise.

Fear: The person's volume will be lower, but pitch and speech rate will rise.

Anger: The person's pitch will be higher, and the person will also speak louder and faster. The rate will slow down and the pitch will drop in moments of intense anger.

Disgust: The person's pitch will be lower, with lower volume and slower speech rate.

Happiness: The person's pitch, volume, and speech rate will rise.

Contempt: The person's pitch, volume, and speech rate will lower.

Tuning In to Paralanguage

Our voices hold a tremendous bounty of cues about who we are and what we believe. Paralanguage—the pitch, loudness, rate, fluency, and all other vocal signals aside from speech—accounts for almost 40 percent of our delivered messages. When we listen to people speak, we can immediately identify many things about them—if they are aggressive or passive, well educated or illiterate, high or low in status. We can even tell if a person is thin or overweight, simply by listening to him speak.

His Signals/Her Signals

He Is Listening

Women are much better than men at reading facial cues, better than men at reading body language, and only slightly better than men at reading vocal cues.

Vocal cues help us determine just how powerful a speaker is, and by extension, how persuasive his message is. We might listen to his words to determine what he's trying to say, but we listen to his voice to decide whether or not we'll believe it. In fact, researchers have determined that voice alone is an excellent indicator of deception. One study found that people who listened to an audio recording of a criminal's confession were better able to detect deception than people who watched an audio/video recording. While we can occasionally get distracted or misled by people's clothing, gestures, and other aspects of visual body language, because certain features of the voice are so difficult to control, it remains one of the most reliable sources of "leakage" in our interactions with others.

His Signals/Her Signals

She Should Trust Her Gut

Some evidence suggests that women are better at detecting nonverbal cues for lying, but are more likely to overlook them or believe the liar's words rather than his nonverbal cues.

One way that we use these cues is to pack our speech with what researchers call "metamessages"—the unstated message underneath our words. Just by emphasizing certain words, we can communicate entirely different meanings. Say these sentences aloud and consider the different metamessages buried in each.

> *I* usually enjoy a day at the beach. (As opposed to you.)
>
> I *usually* enjoy a day at the beach. (Today I wasn't particularly enthused.)
>
> I usually *enjoy* a day at the beach. (Today really sucked.)
>
> I usually enjoy a *day* at the beach. (As opposed to a week.)
>
> I usually enjoy a day *at* the beach. (As opposed to in the car, trying to get to the beach.)
>
> I usually enjoy a day at the *beach*. (As opposed to whatever *you* want to do.)
>
> I usually enjoy a day at the beach. (I usually enjoy a day at the beach—really!)

Beyond speech, we also use laughs, sighs, grumbles, and other nonspeech sounds to share our feelings about something—and the mirror system helps us reflect those sounds right back. In one study, researchers found that when one person hears another person laugh, specific areas of the brain associated with facial expressions are activated. The mirror system reflects the sound of the laughter by preparing the listener to laugh, way before a smile has time to reach his face.

His Signals/Her Signals

Look at Me When I Listen to You

Women with more power tend to be less skilled at reading faces and more skilled at reading vocal cues—probably because they are more tuned in to the speaker's status.

Deciphering Vocal Cues

Vocal cues are somewhat unusual in the study of body language signals because the subjective definition of vocal characteristics—whether it is high or low, loud or soft, fast or slow—exist on a continuum that is as individual as the listener. Researchers have found that some presumptions we make about other people's personalities based on their voices turn out to be false; others are incredibly accurate. But we do know that people with the voices that were judged most "attractive" were also perceived to be more credible, likable, open, powerful, conscientious, and secure.

Keep an ear out for some of the following characteristics that can help you make judgments about others based on their vocal cues. We'll discuss both ends of the spectrum of each cue and talk about some of the perceptions of each extreme.

Vocal Cue: Pitch

Pitch is the measure of how "high" or "low" a voice is, the quality that most easily helps us determine if the speaker is male or female. Girls' voices are higher in pitch than boys' voices at every age, except between the ages of five and six. While girls' voices steadily lower in pitch from age eight until adulthood, boys' voices drop suddenly around the age of fourteen. Studies show that attractive voices tend to be richer, lower in pitch, and somewhat varied.

Signals sent from the low end: Dominance; sometimes depression or anger. For the male speaker, low-pitched voices are perceived as more attractive, pleasant, and persuasive. Slight pitch fluctuation during conversation is normal, but a monotone pitch throughout an entire conversation can be a strong indicator of boredom or indifference and can slow comprehension by up to 10 percent. (Think of actor Ben

Stein playing the world's most boring teacher in *Ferris Bueller's Day Off,* lulling his class into a stupor: "Bueller . . . Bueller . . . Bueller . . .").

Signals sent from the high end: Insecurity; delight. Our pitch rises when we're stressed and feeling anxious, but also when we're experiencing great joy. Extroverts tend to have a higher pitch, but only up to a point—they're not shattering any glasses, they're just keeping the conversation lively. While a high pitch can indicate excitement, it can also be perceived as less truthful, less persuasive, weaker, and more nervous.

What you're aiming for: Varying your pitch. A dynamic, variable pitch should probably be the first thing you work on to improve your voice. Pitch variation is what keeps people interested in what you're saying. Strive to make your voice sound melodious, introducing many changes in pitch as you speak. Loosen up your voice by taking deep breaths and humming through your full tonal range. Then, every once in a while during conversations, just pique your conversational partner's interest by "bursting" a change of pitch into the mix. If your voice tends to be low in pitch, burst through with some higher pitch on words you want to emphasize; if your voice tends to be high, do the opposite. Think of giving your voice the kind of range that you must use when singing "Do Re Mi" or another singing scale. Or change your facial expressions as you speak; those changes will have a direct effect on your voice as well.

If I had to recommend one area of vocal cues to pay attention to, it would be pitch variation. We'll talk more about this important cue in the Reiman Rapport Method in chapter 9. Pitch variation is what keeps people interested in what you're saying. Studies have found that extroverts tend to introduce more contrast in their pitch throughout conversations. Introverts tend to have a more monotone delivery. One of my clients, Ron, found his pitch was putting people to sleep.

Ron needed some help with giving presentations. He called me in to watch his monthly presentation to his staff. As I watched him he stood behind a podium with a large PowerPoint screen behind him. The room was dim, and he became almost invisible. As he spoke about different statistics and how well the company had done that month, he stood motionless with the exception of his fingers, which fondled his PowerPoint clicker. Clearly, Ron hated public speaking.

We had videotaped the presentation so we could view it and go through it almost moment by moment. He made several fatal mistakes.

1. He put the lights down too low. Remember, as the speaker you are the focal point; the PowerPoint is just an aid to allow the information to penetrate.

2. He stood behind a podium. Anytime you stand behind *anything,* in essence what you are doing is putting up barricades. No one in the audience can connect to someone who is hiding behind a desk, podium, or table.

3. He stood motionless. Movement matters. When you move around you move the energy in the air. Instead, his staff was almost sleeping by the end of the presentation. If you want your staff energized, you must be energized.

4. He played with his clicker. There is nothing worse than watching a professional fidget—you'll likely wonder to yourself how they could have possibly gotten where they are when they are obviously insecure and anxious.

5. Perhaps most damaging was his lack of pitch variance. He rushed through his presentation with a monotone voice. A quick pace can be a good thing, provided it has varied pitch. In order to keep a group alive, you must change the tone and pitch of your voice; it keeps your listeners on the edge of their seats.

To tackle this daunting list of challenges, we broke his presentation up into five mini presentations of ten minutes apiece. We worked on anchoring good feelings into his speech by using his left hand while discussing negatives and his right hand while discussing positives. Each mini segment would end with a movement in his right hand to reinforce the positive.

Then we worked on increasing his energy level and the number of his movements naturally, without looking contrived. I told him about my own personal technique: walk into the presentation room at least an hour before the presentation and yell in your loudest voice to make the room your own, with the additional benefit of relaxing your vocal muscles.

As we worked together, Ron learned the benefit of moving around the room and staying away from the podium to connect with his audience. We also started placing four close associates strategically throughout the room so he could begin to make eye contact with his audience, scanning past some and resting on others. This was the first step to making him feel comfortable meeting the eyes of his own employees; next, he could move on to looking directly at the other employees. In addition, we adjusted the lighting and decided to have an assistant with him to change the screen on his command.

Finally, as the most critical piece, we slowed down his speaking rate ever so slightly, so he would have the opportunity to work on varying his pitch and tone. Ultimately the change was amazing. His employees were much more engaged in his presentations, and Ron felt confident enough to improvise and start adding a bit of levity. Breaking down his presentation into all of its individual components made it easier for Ron to imagine that he, too, could become a Master Communicator.

Five Strategies to . . .

Halt Inappropriate Giggling

Everyone likes a good laugh, but sometimes—during a wedding ceremony, at a funeral—having a giggle is not the most sensitive move. Problem is, those are the moments when, once you start, you feel like you absolutely can't stop. Try these tricks to get it together.

1. **Keep breathing.** Some nervous laughter takes a foothold because you're breathing so shallowly. Take ten deep breaths, even if you have to squash your lips together to squelch the laughter at the same time. By the end of the ten breaths, you should be back to your mature self again.

2. **Look down or close your eyes.** That will help you concentrate and collect your thoughts. It will also remove the visual stimulus—the snoring uncle falling out of the pew—that made you laugh to begin with.

3. **Make a stern face.** Moving your face into certain expressions will trigger those feelings. Try to tamp out laughter with a good dose of momentary anguish or sadness. Immediately think of one of the saddest movies you've ever seen, for example.

4. **Put a stick of gum in your mouth.** When you want to laugh, chew vigorously. Or, if you're at a wake or a shiva, bring your drink to your lips. It'll give you a second to compose yourself.

5. **Talk yourself down.** Mentally talk yourself through your to-do list—"I have to go grocery shopping, stop at the bank . . ." Changing the subject on your mental sound track and giving yourself something else to think about will be a helpful distraction in a way that thinking "Get a grip!" might not.

Vocal Cue: Loudness

Do you know the loud family? Every block has one. The house in which each person just seems to thunder over the next. Sometimes you feel a bit shell-shocked when you leave them, your nerves in shreds from the aural assault. But as jarring as a loud voice can be, an unmistakably strong voice is one of the biggest cues for dominance and power.

Signals from the low end: Insecurity; shyness; quiet power. Individuals who speak at very low volumes are sometimes thought of as insecure and shy. You'll know you're being perceived this way when people tilt their head and lean forward toward you as if they're straining to hear you. You're forcing others into your personal space, and you don't want that; it makes you seem weak. So if you're getting that look often enough, and it's not intentional on your part, it's time to raise the volume. (See the suggestion for how to project your voice below.)

But sometimes when a person speaks softly, the message can be, "I'm so important that you need to adjust yourself to listen to me." And sometimes silence can be the "loudest" indicator of mood; voluntary silence, especially when communicating disapproval, sends a very strong message of power and control.

Signals from the high end: Powerful; extroverted; Type A; dominant. Research has found that extroverts and dominant personalities speak louder than others. Type A personalities have particularly loud or explosive voices. To a certain degree, a loud voice helps you stand out and allows you to speak your piece. But there's a thin line between loud and rude, and it's sometimes difficult to know where you stand. You know you're too loud if you're in a restaurant and you find you're making eye contact with a lot of people at other tables; they're trying to tell you to keep it down. Speaking loud is considered disruptive and sometimes crude. If this sounds like you, ask a friend—or several friends—to give you a signal when your voice gets particularly booming.

Dominance is usually a good thing, so I don't want to discourage a loud voice. But volume can sometimes be an indicator of anger, and you don't want people to think you're an overbearing and aggressive person.

What you're aiming for: Projecting your voice with authority. Of the two extremes, it would probably be better to speak louder than softer. So how can you learn to project more? One way is to practice imaging your voice as a ball. Start by looking at objects two, five, ten, fifteen feet away. You're literally going to "toss" your voice to each place in turn. Do you see and feel how your voice changes? Keep practicing this, and you'll start to develop a feel for how soft or loud you should speak in every situation. Then next time you have to give a speech in a large hall and you need to reach the people in the "cheap seats," concentrate on lobbing your voice all the way to the back wall. Check in with the people in the back—"Can you hear me back there?"—early in your presentation to make sure you're not leaving anyone out.

His Signals/Her Signals

Girls Just Wanna Have Fun

Overall, women laugh more than men—and contrary to the stereotype of the sullen teenage girl, this difference is most pronounced between the ages of twelve and seventeen.

Vocal Cue: Rate/Speed

Consumers were delighted by the commercials of John Moschitta Jr., the fast-talking pitchman for FedEx and Micro Machine toy cars in the 1980s. Although his words were barely discernable, the speed of Moschitta's delivery points to a preference most listeners have for fast speech. Our normal rate of speech is 125 to 195 words per minute, but research shows that we prefer speakers on the faster end of the spectrum.

Signals from the low end: Introversion; insecurity; depression. Although speed-of-speech norms differ region by region, slower speech is typically seen as a sign that a person feels tentative about his words, or his thought processes have slowed, as in depression.

Signals from the high end: Extroversion; dominance; persuasiveness. Fast speech tends to increase your perceived credibility and persuasiveness. One theory is that when you speak quickly, other people don't have time to process the information, so the brain tends to just absorb the information as is and doesn't try to contradict it.

What you're aiming for: A faster speaking rate. We process about five syllables a second in normal speech, but we think people who speak faster than that are more interesting. Also, just as in pitch, you want to vary your rate of speech because it helps increase listener comprehension. Aim for a speech rate of 175 to 250 words per minute. Practice by reading one passage of text faster and faster, every day, just as Samantha did when she improved her bandcampitis with this technique. In a professional setting, the best way to increase your rate of speech is just to have your material down cold so you don't have to think about it at all. Being able to bat out information really quickly gives the impression that you're an expert in your field.

Vocal Cue: Fluency

The pause between successive phrases is typically 0.5 seconds in normal conversation. Some of us fill those pauses with stutters, hums, or junk words like *um, uh,* or *sooo.* But doing so can interfere with the fluency of your speech, and fluent speech is one of the strongest predictors of competence and persuasiveness.

Signals from the low end: Powerless; insecure; less persuasive. We all trip over our words occasionally. But if you find your conversation is littered with little stumbling starts and stops, you should know that it has a serious impact on your perceived competence. Parents: Once a person learns to fill his or her speech with *ah*s and *um*s, it can be a hard habit to break, so try to coach your children away from it while they're young.

I met Joel at a wedding. He was the best man and was getting ready to give the toast for the bride and groom. Joel was Mr. Calm, Cool, and Collected as we chatted in the lounge. A few minutes later, Joel was up at the microphone giving what seemed like the longest, most un-thought-out toast I had ever heard. He filled every pause with, "Well, you know, like," and demonstrated staggering abilities to lengthen sounds such as *ummmmm, uhhhh, ahhhh.* It was painful to listen to him.

When he saw me afterward, he walked right over and, beet red, said, "Man, I thought I was going to die up there."

"Why?" I asked, although I had a pretty good idea.

"I just hate public speaking," he mumbled.

I told him that he was in good company—I don't think anyone likes public speaking, except perhaps those of us who get paid to do it.

He asked what he could do so he wouldn't have to go through that agony again. I told him the most important thing he could do was to cut out the extra sound effects—even when nervous—and keep quiet during the seconds when he had to collect his thoughts.

I was grateful that I'd talked to Joel before his speech, so I knew that he was an intelligent man. But I'm sure my first impression would not have been that favorable had I not met him before he gave the toast.

Signals from the high end: Extroverted; competent; persuasive. Extroverts tend to use shorter pauses and few hesitations within their speech patterns. They also react faster when the conversation turns to them. If you find you lose your train of thought often when you're speaking, you might increase the fluency in your speech by focusing exclusively on the conversation and reducing the attention you pay to distractions such as other people's conversations or your own random mental wanderings.

What you're aiming for: Variety, fluency, and confidence. Instead of filling pauses with junk words, just be quiet while you collect your thoughts. Filling pauses with junk words delays your own thought process, which in turn makes you seem even less competent. In contrast, pauses make you appear confident, intellectual, and more powerful; they suggest that you're in deep thought, and you're self-assured enough to be quiet while you pause to think.

Vocal Cue: Total Talking Time

Some people, by nature, do not like to speak that much. Other people just love to talk and talk. Unlike some of the other characteristics of speech, both of these ends of the spectrum have distinct advantages and disadvantages.

Signals from the low end: Thoughtful; timid; insecure. When you do not speak as much as other people, sometimes you are seen as being aloof, shy, or insecure. People may discount you and think you don't have much to contribute. On the other hand, in today's world, so many people are in a rush to talk that your more reserved communication style could actually benefit you. People might be more inclined to pay attention to your words when you speak, so each of your individual messages carries more weight. Also, when you let the other person drone on, you can often gather a great deal of information that the other party perhaps didn't intend to share, just by being a patient listener.

His Signals/Her Signals

Contrary to What He Might Tell You

In groups of men and women, men spend more time talking than women do, and women spend more time watching people talk.

Signals from the high end: Entertaining; self-absorbed; narcissistic. Extroverts talk more in two ways—they contribute a larger number of words, and they speak for a longer time than their conversational partners. People tend to see extroverts as more engaging than more reticent folks. But there is a fine line between amusement and domination. Someone who does not know when to stop talking can drive other people away. In our excitement, we sometimes miss the fact that our conversant's eyes have glazed over due to boredom, indifference, or overload. We might misinterpret their blank look as confusion and make matters worse by trying to overexplain.

Incidentally, most people who talk too much do not think they are perceived by other people as talking too much. This is a terrible stigma that can be tough to get rid of. Remember, one of the key components to effective communication in a conversation is sharing with your partner.

What you're aiming for: If you don't have a specific goal for the conversation, just share. To figure out how much floor time you need in a conversation, determine what you want to get out of every conversation. When you're talking to a friend, a colleague whose status is similar to yours, or an established contact, aim for as close to a 50-50 split as possible. That will result in both conversants feeling heard and entertained. When you're meeting someone for the first time, try to be a bit more quiet than usual so you can truly hear everything the other person has to say. People feel important when they're listened to closely. (You'll also find that most people don't like quiet, so they start to panic and fill the void. Sometimes you can learn so much more about people when you let them run on than you would normally have learned.)

Five Strategies to . . .

Cut Off a Blowhard

Nothing's going to stop him. He's on a roll, with no signs of taking a breath. Here are a few ways to trip up the person who feels compelled to add way more than his two cents to every team meeting.

1. **Sigh in exasperation.** But not the standard way. Just expel a large enough breath to attract others' attention, and then disavow any ulterior motive. "Sorry," say, "just had to yawn." The others will be grateful for the distraction—and the inside joke.

2. **Avoid eye contact.** When you look in someone's eyes, it means you're interested. You're not. So don't.

3. **Angle your body away, especially your feet.** The direction of our feet and the rest of our body indicate our interest. Point every available body part toward the door.

4. **Keep your head very still.** Sometimes when a person doesn't see any movement in the person he's talking to, he starts to wonder why and he instinctively stops speaking.

5. **Very, very slowly, shake your head.** Even if he doesn't see the whole sequence of a full head shake, he'll subconsciously pick up on the movement. And, hopefully, stop talking. Just. Stop. Talking.

Vocal Cue: Turn-Taking

Turn-taking is the corollary to total talking time—how skilled are you at alternating turns in a conversation? How long do you pause before responding? You might think taking turns is something we do quite naturally. But some people really don't get it—they'll either talk over you, or finish your sentences, or won't respond in a predictable interval when you're done talking.

Turn-taking also makes use of backchannel responses, those clues such as increased eye contact, nodding, and "uh-huh"-ing that we give the speaker to acknowledge we understand what they are saying. Backchannel responses such as "hmm," squinting, or decreased eye contact are also used to let the speaker know we would like to take a turn and speak. If the speaker doesn't see any backchannel responses, he might not feel confident that you understand him, and might start asking, "Do you know what I mean?"

Signals on the slow end: Depression; insecurity; social awkwardness. The "response latency" in a conversation is the period of silence between turns. Usually, we respond to a pause in conversation in less than two seconds; if you wait longer than three seconds, your conversational partner will become uncomfortable. Many people, including those who are depressed, tend to leave long, silent pauses before responding to another's comments.

If you have trouble detecting when it's your time to talk, look for these signs: a period of silence longer than three seconds; the other person stops gesturing and looks directly at you, resuming eye contact; someone states a fact while also tilting her head, as if to say, "What do you think about that?"

Signals on the fast end: Extroverted; aggressive; impatient. Being fast on your feet is usually a good thing—you don't have to deliberate too long on your responses, so you come across as much more knowledgeable and intelligent. But when you tend to have shorter latencies, you run the risk of interrupting. Extroverts tend to have shorter pauses, which is good, but Type As tend to interrupt more.

Keep an eye out for signs that people are not finished talking. When someone is speaking, they will usually look at us while they're talking and then look away during a pause in order to not hand over the floor. If they think you are trying to take over the conversation, they will fill their pauses with *ahs*, *ums*, and *uhs*, hold a gesture longer, increase their volume and rate of speech, or sometimes even touch your forearm or hold up a hand as if to say *stop*, don't interrupt.

One caution to fast responders: Slow down. Sometimes in our eagerness to respond quickly, we say things we regret. I recently analyzed a tape of Carl Bernstein, the author of *A Woman in Charge,* a book about Hillary Clinton, when he was speaking with Bill O'Reilly about Senator Clinton. Take a look at this exchange:

O'REILLY: Did she break the law?

BERNSTEIN: Yes. [*Immediately furrows brow.*]

O'REILLY: OK. Good I like this. How did she break the law?

BERNSTEIN: [*Smirks, nervous laughter.*] She broke the law—if indeed she perjured herself. [*Close eyes.*] You know what? Let me be really straightforward. I don't think she broke the law. I think there was a time that she did not tell the truth.

O'REILLY: Under oath?

BERNSTEIN: [*Visibly uncomfortable.*] You know, I wasn't in the room. [*Smirk.*]

Had Bernstein taken his time and not reflexively answered O'Reilly's first question, he wouldn't have had to backtrack.

What you're aiming for: Active listening, equal air time, and short pauses. Ideally, you won't take a long time to respond when your conversational partner is done talking, and you also won't step on their words. But what happens when they're yammering on, and you're indeed *trying* to interrupt them? Make direct eye contact with the speaker to let her know you want a chance, or hold up a finger, putting an imaginary hole in the conversation. Also, you can lean forward while taking in a deep breath and increase your backchannel responses—nod your head quicker than usual, say *ahh, um-hmm*, and *yes* more often—as if to say, Hurry, finish up, I want to go. (For more tips, see "Five Strategies to Cut Off a Blowhard," on page 201.)

Vocal Cue: Articulation and Pronunciation

Perhaps no other vocal cue tells a listener more about your background, intelligence, and social class than how you articulate and pronounce your words. Excellent grammar and diction can elevate your status in your listener's mind, even if you come from humble beginnings. If you have an accent or speak in a dialect, that allows people to place your geographic home. For some people, their accent might be a point of pride. For others, their dialect might be associated with lower intelligence and could be something that they seek to remedy to broaden their career possibilities.

At the end of one conference I did overseas, Niko approached me and introduced himself as a businessman who traveled to the United States quite often. He felt he was not taken seriously because he had an accent. His accent was so thick that people would constantly ask him to repeat himself, and his insecurity about his voice had an effect on his ability to negotiate effectively. He became so self-conscious about his accent that he dreaded traveling to the States.

After speaking to him for just a few minutes, I could understand why his business associates were having a hard time getting past his accent. When speaking with him, you had to focus all of your attention on what he was saying, which can certainly cut into the development of rapport!

The accent was one thing—but as I talked to him, I discovered that when he spoke in English, he had other verbal tics that made him seem less secure than he obviously was: he spoke at a higher pitch and a slower speed, and his grammar was choppy and not polished. He, too, had a case of "bandcampitis," and his statements ended in question marks. In addition, because of his insecurity, his body language would also come across as forced and unnatural.

The first thing I instructed Niko to do was to lower the pitch of his voice. Together we put together standard presentations on his business, and we practiced them over and over, focusing on increasing his speaking rate and ending his sentences with periods instead of question marks.

After a few weeks, Niko sent me some mp3s of his speaking presentation, and the results were dramatic. Niko was coming across as more dominant and secure. As he began to feel better about himself as an English speaker, his body language became spontaneous and congruent. He regained his native confidence, and his U.S. business started to take off.

Signals on the low end: Ignorance; lack of credibility. One of the best examples of how diction defines you as a person is seen in James Gandolfini's performance as Tony Soprano on *The Sopranos*. The way Tony skips letters and combines his words—saying things like, "Djeet?" instead of "Did you eat?"—makes him seem less cultured. Now imagine what he would sound like if he pronounced every single letter. Very different, right?

Signals on the high end: Intelligence; social status; eloquence. Certain accents and speech patterns are more often associated with intelligence and high status. Americans tend to associate a British accent with higher intelligence, for example, whereas a New York accent might sometimes be perceived as less intelligent. (I can say that—I'm from New York.) In business settings, a regional accent could be a liability. As a result, a growing number of people have begun to enlist help from speech pathologists to minimize their regional accents in the workplace. They can and do "code-switch," or use their native accents—which are a big part of their identity, after all—with their family and friends.

What you're aiming for: Excellent grammar and an accent that doesn't distract. Reading can help you on both of these counts. If your grammar isn't as sharp as it could be, make sure you're reaching high enough with your reading materials—whatever words you put into your brain will come out of your mouth. Also, continue to practice with that favorite passage of text. Pronounce each word, enunciate every syllable clearly, and practice punching up the consonants, making sure they really stand out. Think crisp, clean, precise.

Five Strategies to . . .

Communicate with Non-English Speakers

Whether you travel on business or pleasure, at some point you may find yourself in a place where you share no common language with the locals. Of course you'll already have scoured your guidebook to understand any culturally specific body language cues, so you don't insult or offend. From there, try some of these suggestions to get your message across without words.

1. **Exaggerate your tone and pitch.** Vocal cues tell a great deal about the content of your message. Even if you don't have a language in common, ask your questions in your own language with exaggerated tone and pitch (but not volume—being loud does *not* aid comprehension). Most important: elevate pitch at the end of questions.

2. **Talk with your hands.** Channel your inner Charades champion and act out every idea with larger-than-life gestures, repeating as necessary.

3. **Tilt your head to the side.** This universal sign of vulnerability and trust shows the person that you are very interested in hearing what they have to tell you.

4. **Use smiles as positive reinforcement.** Smiling is a universal sign that you are not threatening. Smile and indicate grateful agreement whenever someone gets even part of the message right.

5. **Show thanks.** You'll truly know the power of body language when another person actually *gets* your message and is able to help you, without a single word being understood. Put your hands together, palms touching, in prayer position and lower your head slightly. This signal is a common greeting and thank-you gesture throughout Asia, but is understood as a sign for gratitude in many parts of the world.

The one situation in which body language is perhaps more critical than any other is when you first meet someone. No other information you present to them will be as significant to the future of your relationship as what you show them in those first few seconds. I'm not kidding when I say that that first meeting can make or break your entire relationship. Don't take any chances. Let's look at all the ways you can maximize your body language so you can nail every first impression.

CHAPTER 6

Mastering First Impressions

Do you believe in love at first sight, or should I walk by again?

—American pickup line

Recently a television news show called and asked me to evaluate footage of Joran van der Sloot, a suspect in the mysterious disappearance of Natalee Holloway, an American woman who vanished while on vacation in Aruba. The producer asked me to look at van der Sloot's body language, listen to his voice and try to ascertain the meaning of his movements.

As I watched the clip of van der Sloot speaking with a male reporter, I talked about his darting eyes, a momentary lift of his eyebrows, a hint of a smug smile that crossed his lips as he talked about Natalee during an interview. I talked about how he did an inward lip roll, a facial signal that typically indicates nervousness or anxiety.

Basically, I was asked to watch a brief flash of his body language and draw a conclusion about him. Form an impression.

Seems a bit reckless, doesn't it? Judging a man based on just a few short moments of his life?

And yet we all do it, every single day.

Each time we meet someone new, we take a tiny sample of his entire life and assume this one small sliver portrays 100 percent of his personality. We take in details about the lines on his face, the set of his eyes, his slight vocal tics, the cut of his suit, the length of his hair, his tattoos, rings and other body adornments, even the way his mouth is curved. We scan our mental database, link these details to presumed characteristics, and reflexively judge: Safe or unsafe. Yes or no.

Every single first impression involves the same kind of scan and could mean the difference between scoring the job/account/phone number—or being turned down flat. Once you've truly nailed all the elements of your first impression, most people you meet will automatically like you—even if they have no idea why.

Perfecting Your First Impression

I've helped many people dissect and analyze their own first impressions to help them understand what messages they send. Along the way, I've discovered several surprising things.

- Most people have no idea of how they're being perceived. They may believe they do, but they don't, and that lack of awareness hurts them.
- A great percentage of people unintentionally put out the exact *opposite* messages of what they intend to convey—again, without realizing they're doing it.
- A smaller, but still surprising, number of people believe it is dishonest to consciously alter your body language in order to make a positive first impression. They think that you should present the "real you," no matter what the setting or audience.

The first two points will be addressed and hopefully solved in the balance of this chapter. But let's talk about this last one.

I'm all for honesty. When you present yourself in a genuine way, you're much more appealing than when you're a phony. But the "real" you can sometimes be improved. You might not want to change simply "to make other people happy." However, when you choose not to change, you're the one who suffers the loss of potential income, increased status, admiration, or dance partners.

Other people have no conscious control over how they react to you. They might think of themselves as open-minded and unlikely to cast judgment based on something as superficial as your weight or grooming—but they do. People always have and most likely always will.

Making a good first impression is a sign of respect. You're telling the other person, "I care about what you think of me; I want to give you my best." That's a tremendous compliment, one that is more likely to curry favor than, "This is me—take it or leave it." Remember, your actions give the other person's brain an image that her mirror neurons are going to reflect immediately—and who wants to imitate an unappealing person?

First impressions are a fact of life. Instead of making people work to get to know the best that you can be, let them see it the very first time they meet you. You're not lying about yourself—you're clearing away any debris that might get in the way of your objectives. Without the distractions of a bad first impression, people will see and accept the messages you actually *intend* to send, and you won't have to play catch-up for this easily avoided misstep. The sooner you own your first impression and make it work *for* you, the further you can go in all areas of your life.

Maximizing Each Stage of a First Impression

First impressions occur so regularly, we hardly acknowledge them. Most of us interact each day with someone new, be it a deli clerk, a new colleague, a parent at a school meeting, or a waiter at a bar. You can use your body language to assure yourself of the best possible outcome from every first meeting. Once you get a firm handle on how your particular traits might generate certain assumptions from other people, you can start to manipulate those assumptions in any direction you wish.

Every first impression is made up of three stages. Let's look at each stage, what kinds of decisions are being made based on what kinds of signals, and how you can use your body language to your advantage. We'll look at signals that range from your body shape and the way you dress to how you can use specific movements to tap in to the other person's mirror system and connect with that person on a subconscious level.

(Note: Our focus here will be on how you can make the best first impression. We are programmed to *receive* first impressions, so you don't have to learn how to interpret them—your gut will do that for you.)

Stage 1. The Snap Judgment: The First Few Seconds

In the introduction, I shared the shocking fact that within 1⁄10 of a second of seeing your facial features, that guy you've just met has already made a judgment about whether or not he is attracted to you, if he can trust you, how competent you are, or even if he will like you as a person. If you give him half a second, or even a full second, those judgments would remain the same and just become *more* solidified.

Your entire shot at the job, the account, the date, over in 1⁄10 of a second. Most people can't even blink their eyes in that amount of time. All this occurs before you open your mouth to say a word.

Princeton University psychologist Alex Todorov, coauthor of the study that revealed that remarkable one-tenth-of-a-second window, believes that certain judgments, such as whether or not a person is trustworthy, are made by our amygdala, a part of the mammalian brain that evolved before humans had the capacity for rational thought. The

The Beauty Benefit

Pretty Faces Are Easy on the Eyes

Given that attractive people tend to have better careers, earn more money, and have higher social status than less attractive people, it's no wonder we all would like to be attractive. But what does that actually mean? Research tells us that for women, attractive equals clear skin, high cheekbones, shiny hair, a high forehead, full lips, small jaw, small chin, big eyes, and a small nose. For men, attractive is large expressive eyes, smooth skin, a straight nose, and a strong jawline. But the most important characteristic of attractiveness for both? Symmetry.

In all of nature, symmetry is code for resilient health and strong genes, making people with symmetrical faces seem like a pretty good reproductive bet. Plastic surgeons have condensed this symmetry down to a science. Dividing the face horizontally into three areas and vertically into five, they've precisely calculated the "perfect" proportions for each feature in relation to the other. For example, in Caucasians, the distance from the outer edge of one nostril to the outer edge of the other should be equal to one eye width; for Asians and African-Americans, it can be slightly wider. The lower lip should be slightly fuller than the upper lip, and when the face is resting, the lips should naturally spread no more than 3 millimeters apart. A "beautiful" smile is one that does not show any gums, and no more than two-thirds of the eyeteeth should show.

Wow—turns out there's a lot of math involved in being beautiful.

Perhaps the cosmetic surgeons work this hard at beauty because our brains don't want to. A study from the University of California, San Diego, found that we prefer to look at things that are symmetrical because our brains are lazy. We're drawn to symmetry because it allows our eyes to take in information faster and our brain to process it more quickly with less effort. Visually, we prefer things that are "easy to love," that don't make us work to understand them.

Humans show this preference from birth: babies under six months old will stare longer at faces judged more attractive than less attractive. One-year-olds prefer to play with attractive strangers rather than unattractive strangers. Later, students rate good-looking professors as better teachers. Professors give higher grades to more attractive students. Attractive women tend to get fewer traffic tickets. Attractive defendants are less likely than unattractive defendants to be sent to jail.

But wait. Before you start railing against all the beautiful people, know that you can make this "lazy brain" tendency work for you. You just need more face time. After repeated exposures to a certain stimulus, your brain becomes trained on what it has seen. Once a person has seen your face a few times, you'll become more attractive to them, regardless of your degree of facial symmetry. Guess it's time to stop by for a few more impromptu meetings with the new boss!

"top level" of our brain, the prefrontal cortex, might not even get a say in the matter at all.

The snap judgment is the biggest part of the first impression, but it's made so quickly, you'd never be able to adjust in the moment when it's actually happening. That's why you'll need to prepare beforehand and have everything in place for that first brief, shining moment.

Seventeen Things That Turn Them Off Immediately

1. Scratching your head
2. Nervously biting your lips
3. Raising your eyebrows incredulously
4. Shifting in your seat
5. Crossing arms or otherwise displaying superior, conceited, or overbearing body signals
6. Looking distracted and losing concentration or attention
7. Looking down or avoiding eye contact
8. Standing rigidly in place
9. Keeping your hands in your pockets
10. Not using any hand gestures
11. Rocking
12. Slouching
13. Self-touching, such as picking off invisible lint or brushing your sleeves
14. Jiggling your leg
15. Twisting your hair
16. Clicking your pen
17. Biting your nails, even briefly

How to Prepare for the Snap Judgment

Way down in our evolutionary DNA, we have the perpetuation of the species to think about. We're hardwired to look for people who are healthy, energetic, and fertile, the characteristics that helped perpetuate the species and bring home the brontosaurus bacon in times past. The only way to get past the hair-trigger sensor is to prepare to display those positive traits as quickly and confidently as possible within that brief window. Here are some ways to start.

Gather information. Forewarned is forearmed. Before you make contact with another person, even by phone, try to gather as much information about that person and the context of the meeting as possible. Is this a man or a woman? What's his or her title or position in the company? What exactly do you want out of the encounter? Any information you can gather will help you prepare in other ways—how you'll dress, how you'll greet each other, what unspoken messages you'll exchange in that first second. Let's say the person you're going to meet is named Pat; you wouldn't know she was a woman unless you had Googled her androgynous name and found a profile about her from her local newspaper. Imagine how refreshing it will be for her to meet you and *not* see that brief look of surprise that so often greets her during first encounters.

Lose the weight. You certainly don't need a lecture from me about being physically fit. But did you know that the rounder you are, the less money you will make?

Fat bias is one of our culture's most prevalent and enduring prejudices—and the most damaging to your financial bottom line. In 1993, a landmark Harvard study found that overweight women earn an average of $6,710 less a year than women who are not overweight—and that was almost fifteen years ago! Newer research has found that larger women earn at least 12 percent less than thinner women who have the same qualifications.

But that's once you get the job—you still have to get through the interview. Some overweight people sail through the phone meetings, only to be cut at the first in-person meeting. One study found that 16 percent of employers said they wouldn't hire an overweight woman under any circumstances.

This bias not only prevents you from earning what you deserve, it could stop you from finding the love of your life. The Harvard study also found that obese women are 20 percent less likely and obese men are 11 percent less likely to get married than thinner people.

You work hard; you deserve to earn as much as everyone else. Don't let your weight hold you back. The obesity bias effect is so widespread that it's unlikely we'll see much of a shift on this stigma within our lifetimes.

For women, the ideal is a 0.7 waist-to-hip ratio—researchers have found that having a waist that is 70 percent as wide as your hips telegraphs attractiveness and fertility. This ratio guarantees that women will have a curvy, hourglass figure, one synonymous with childbearing. For men, the waist-to-hip ratio should be 0.9. This ratio gives off messages of virility, stamina, and good health. Don't forget: Future employers and prospective spouses want to believe you're a good long-term investment. These aesthetically preferred waist-to-hip ratios also happen to be directly associated with a much lower risk of many chronic diseases, such as heart disease and diabetes.

Women, call attention to your bottom. People always react to attractive members of the opposite sex. Even if a guy is happily married, has five kids, and would not ever think about ever having an affair, if he sees a beautiful woman, he will suck in his gut and fix his hair. It's not because he's thinking, "I want to go home with this woman." It's because we instantly try to look our best when we see somebody else who's attractive. We don't do it intentionally; we're merely pawns in the evolutionary drive that makes the entire human experience revolve around sex.

That's why, even in professional settings, men like to see women with a bit of "junk in the trunk." Are you shocked? Don't be. A rounded derriere is a powerful subconscious reminder of the rear-entry sex preferred by most primates. Your interaction with your prospective boss might be all business, but even without trying, you will still appeal, in a subtle way, to his procreative urge.

Even if you're overweight, make sure the cut of your suit makes a distinction between your waistline and your hips. Most women's suits these days are cut with a little hourglass figure. If you have a twenty-four-inch waist, let people see that. If you don't have one, pick a suit that provides the illusion of that 0.7 ratio. When you accentuate your body and therefore your health, you look like a more confident, positive person who's not afraid to show off her best assets. You work hard on yourself; you're going to work hard for the company.

Whatever you do, don't go for the potato-sack look—you're not hiding anything, you're making matters worse. On the flip side, don't wear a suit that's cut so tight that you can see your bra strap digging into your side—that shows a total lack of awareness of how you're perceived. As soon as we see a button bulge, we start thinking along more sexual lines—and while some appeal to men's evolutionary procreative drive can help your cause, overt sexual overtones are likely to damage your credibility in all situations other than a bar.

Very few interview settings will reward you for being individual in your dress. Sure, if you're hoping for an apprenticeship on Seventh Avenue, wear something that shows your unique fashion sense. Otherwise, if you're going for any other corporate job, let your personality and your résumé set you apart—not your clothing. Invest in an understated suit of the highest quality in blue, black, or gray. Wear a button-down shirt that reveals your neck dimple, the slight indentation in the middle of your collar bone; that hint of vulnerability tells the world that you're warm and open without the blatant sexual overtones of cleavage.

Men, play up your wedge. In men, both men and women prefer to see a wedge shape—a narrow (thirty-three- to thirty-six-inch) waist that fans out into a V shape at the shoulders. That means any work at the gym should include shoulders and upper arms, to create the bulk that will distinguish the upper half of your torso from your waist. If you're packing a belly, make sure you buy your suits big enough that the buttons never strain. You want to be able to open and close at least one button very quickly and easily, without the slightest pull on either side. When buying a suit, it's better to buy too big than too small, but just as with women, it's best to seek out a tailored suit that will create that desired wedge shape for you.

One caveat about those muscular shoulders: crafting a wedge shape doesn't require you to become Cro-Magnon Man. Prospective employers associate bodybuilder bodies with men who prefer gym time to more intellectual pursuits, although women might find them more attractive.

Try to look taller. Something you can't do too much about is your height, but it's good to know that just a couple of extra inches can play in your favor. One study done at the University of Pittsburgh found that men six-foot-two and taller are likely to make 12 percent higher starting salaries than men shorter than six feet. Emerging research suggests that this effect pertains to both men and women, and that each inch of height could translate to an extra 1 to 2 percent higher salary.

The root of this effect is somewhat controversial, but regardless of the reason for the difference, the bias is very likely entrenched in your future boss's mind. Stretch for every extra half-inch during your first few encounters, and eventually those inches could translate into cold hard cash. For women, that might mean wearing a slightly higher heel, provided it is still professional and you can walk in it; for men, perhaps a slightly thicker sole or an unobtrusive heel. For both sexes, good posture is critical and can literally add an inch or two to your height.

Choose your accessories sparingly. You don't need a lot of extra accessory baggage when you're meeting someone for the first time. If you're headed to an interview, pick a maximum of three accessories and make sure they reflect the values of the person you're going to meet. Eyeglasses could be an excellent choice for an interview at a law firm or a software company—overwhelmingly, most people label eyeglass wearers as intelligent. But to communicate rugged, ready-for-anything spontaneity when applying to be a personal trainer or a camp counselor, you might go with the contacts.

Context will also determine which accessories are group signifiers and which are deal-breakers. To be safe, take out your nose ring and cover up your tattoos—unless you're applying at a biker bar, where those adornments might work for you. Leave your engagement ring at home—unconsciously, your female interviewer might feel threatened by it. Think pearls and small earrings—nothing big and dangly, no big bracelets—and just a wedding band. A watch is the best accessory for job seekers—it immediately communicates that you are deadline-oriented. Invest in a model that shows you know quality, but don't go for flash. You don't ever want to have a more expensive watch than the person who is interviewing you.

The cardinal rule for accessories: they should add to, not detract from, your overall message. If your briefcase is scuffed up, pitch it—it's better to go without.

Groom as if you care, but not as if you're obsessed. Your grooming should be so flawless that it's invisible. The essentials: Clean hands. Clean fingernails. Clean teeth. And this one's critical: No hair hanging out of any orifices or otherwise inappropriate places. You might laugh, but it's amazing how many people will overlook the most obvious grooming mistakes. I kid you not, I once interviewed a woman who had an eight-inch hair hanging off her chin. I hardly heard a word she was saying; all I could focus on was that hair. (I felt like Austin Powers meeting Number Three in *Goldmember,* when all Austin could do was fixate on that gigantic mole on his face.)

For both sexes, hands are an extremely important part of nonverbal communication. To use your hands to maximum effect, your nails should be nicely manicured but not too long, especially on a job interview. You want to show the interviewer that you're a worker, and you have better things to do with your time than focus on your nails. Even if you bite them, make sure you get a manicure before a big meeting. Short manicured nails are considered the most professional. The French manicure is a hit because it's the perfect combination of natural and polished grooming.

Many guys are pretty oblivious when it comes to their nails—but you don't want to sabotage those strong nonverbal messages with black crescents of garden dirt under your nails. It is not unusual today to walk into a nail salon and see men having their nails cleaned up. Guys, consider getting your nails professionally cleaned and buffed before a big meeting. (You might even enjoy the experience as much as women do!)

His Signals/Her Signals

She Gets, and Gives, All the Smiles

Many studies have found that boys and girls smile an equal amount, but women smile much more than men. Women are also much more likely to be smiled *at* than men.

Use neutral makeup, even on your lips. Humans have been wearing makeup for a very long time. Experts believe Neanderthals may have used natural pigments to paint their bodies. Egyptians loved to mix diverse colors of lip tint and prided themselves on precise application. In today's world, we still use makeup to draw attention to our best assets and away from our flaws—but we definitely want to stay far away from anything that might be labeled as "body paint."

For the best first impression, you want the other person to focus on you, not your eye shadow. Stick with neutral colors for your base, blush, and eye makeup. Even out your skin tone and cover any blemishes, but stop way short of a complete "mask." One study of 136 people found that a woman with no visible makeup was perceived to be more qualified for a professional job and was recommended to receive a higher salary than other candidates who wore more makeup. Another study found that women who used "appropriate" amounts of makeup at work said they believed their peers judged them as more healthy, credible, and more likely to be heterosexual than people who wore inappropriate amounts or none at all. I suggest to all my female clients that they get a makeup consultation at some point in their professional lives (preferably early on). The investment could continue to pay dividends forever.

One exception to the neutral rule *might* be lipstick. I still recommend neutral tones in all makeup, especially for a first-impression situation, but I know many women like to wear bold lipstick. In one study, 82 percent of women said that lipstick made them feel "really good about themselves." That confidence is going to carry over into the way you present yourself, and confidence is very important in body language. But be aware: anthropologists believe that men respond to red lipstick because it reminds them of the flushed colors and wetness of sexually aroused labia. If you're headed to an interview, this is probably *not* the effect you're going for—and a neutral-colored lip gloss (hint: also glistening) can play on the same impulses without being so overt.

Recently when I appeared on *The O'Reilly Factor,* a different makeup artist did my face before the show. That week I got fifteen e-mails from viewers that said, "Oh, your lipstick was darker this week." And I thought to myself, It was? If I were going to an interview on Wall Street, would I want the interviewer to say, "Oh, what a pretty color lipstick that is!"? No. I wouldn't want them to recognize any of those things—in fact, I'd prefer if they didn't even notice I had makeup on at all. I firmly believe that flair should be in your personality, not in your appearance. In professional settings, work your way toward more neutral colors in all your makeup.

Perfume and cologne should be applied very lightly if at all. Natural aromas are the most attractive to everyone, but perfumes and deodorants hide those scents. Studies show that natural scents stimulate the hypothalamus of both men and women and result in positive changes to blood pressure, respiration, and heart rate. Now, you don't want to be offensive, but trace amounts of your own natural scent can send a warm and emotionally arousing message. If you are looking for a very light coverup, use musky, jasmine, and fruity scents layered with vanilla or amber. (You want to make an impression, not clear a room.)

Be conservative with your hair. Ladies, long hair, worn down, no matter how nicely it is kept, no matter how good it looks, is not usually considered professional. If you're heading for a job interview, make sure your hair is up and coiffed appropriately. (Early in my career on Wall Street, nobody knew I had more than a few inches of hair on the back of my neck because I would never take my hair down.)

Short hair and shoulder-length hair is entirely appropriate, but experiment with new hairstyles or blow-drying before the day of your meeting. Get a haircut at least a week in advance so it can "settle in," but definitely don't skip the haircut before going—you would have to get quite a butcher job before it would look worse than raggedy split ends. As far as the dividing line between appropriate shoulder-length hair and inappropriate long hair, my rule of thumb is: if it's long enough to put up, put it up.

Men should make sure the fuzz on the back of their neck is gone. It's worth a quick stop at the barber to clean it up the day before your meeting. And men who go on job interviews in corporate America should avoid having ponytails.

One of the most common grooming mistakes that people make is not to pay attention to major dandruff. They don't realize that one finger to the scalp for a quick scratch leaves twenty little white flakes hanging around them. Check your shoulders on a regular basis. If you find *any* dandruff, remember to check before you're about to meet someone so you can do a quick wipe. In the meantime, stock up on dandruff shampoo—it really works.

Right before your meeting, do a quick de-stress drill. If your hands are chronically sweaty, consider spraying antiperspirant on your hands for a few days before the day of the meeting. Also, try this trick: Immediately before you will have to shake hands, go to the bathroom and let ice cold water run over your wrists for as long as you can stand it, ideally up to sixty seconds or longer. This will make your entire body cooler and will keep your palms cool for at least a few minutes. (They're not going to stay cool for a half hour, but they will stay cool for a little while, and sometimes that's all you need.) Don't use the hand dryer; dry your hands with paper towels. Once you leave the restroom, don't clench your hands again. Once you begin to clench them, they'll start sweating again. Keep them open and at your sides until the handshake.

While you're in the bathroom, check for anything in your teeth, dandruff on your shoulders, runs in your stockings, scuffs on your shoes, crumbs on your shirt—anything you can deal with in the few minutes before the meeting. Then take a series of five to ten very deep belly breaths and let them slowly out; this will help decrease your heart rate and initiate a relaxation response that will make you seem more confident and less nervous—and help you to ace the snap judgment of the person you are meeting.

His Signals/Her Signals

She's Wired for Stress

Stressful situations affect men and women differently. Men's brains have fewer connections between the amygdala—the "emotional" part of the brain that reacts to stress—and the parts of the nervous system that control blood pressure and heart rate. Women are more likely to experience their hearts pounding in stressful situations, whereas men can remain more detached.

Stage 2. The Database Scan: The First Three to Four Minutes

Whew, you made it past the first one-tenth of a second. You prepared yourself so the snap judgment would be positive. She's smiling; so far, so good. But you've still got some work to do. The amygdala, the middle brain, registered her immediate sense of you, and started her reaction. Provided her snap judgment of you didn't scare her or make her distrust you, her rational neocortex will step in to modulate her reaction and allow her to evaluate you more evenly and comprehensively. If your first one-tenth-second impression made her dislike or distrust you, you have your work cut out for you, but there's still time to convince her that you're "safe" or a "yes."

These next three or four minutes are when true body language enters the picture. Do you know how when you've typed a query into your computer and hit "search," the little icon waves or spins or turns colors to let you know the computer is thinking? That's what's happening in this person's brain. She's inputting dozens of search terms—your rate of approach, smile, handshake, proximity, smell, and hundreds of other details—then combing her database, seeking out comparisons, trying to match you up with any person she's ever met, any book she's read, any movie she's seen, song heard, Web site visited, and so on, to solidify her first impression with plenty of "hits."

I found myself on the wrong end of this database scan just recently. I had been hired to give a seminar on body language to a group of executives as part of a French Canadian manufacturer's business conference. It happened to take place aboard a cruise ship in the Bahamas. Having never been on a cruise ship before, how was I to know I was not the seafaring kind?

I was fine while the ship was at port, but the second we pulled away from the dock, my equilibrium deserted me as well. My ears became clogged, I couldn't tell which end was up, and my gut went into complete revolt. I could not stand up straight, for fear I would fall on my face or vomit.

We must have been quite a sight, my husband and I, as he literally held me up while we staggered down the ship's corridors. Unfortunately, I had no time to get my "sea legs" before I was due to meet with senior management in the lounge to discuss the next day's seminar. While my husband ordered me a club soda, I held on to the bar as if it were a life raft. The drink arrived at exactly the same time as the executives, who took one look at me and started talking excitedly in French, asking my husband what was wrong. Naturally, the translator had not yet arrived and my husband could not speak French, so I began pointing at the club soda while clutching my stomach, thinking those gestures might send the message. The executives continued to look at me and back at one another with widened eyes, worriedly chattering.

I was very touched by the level of their concern. It was only when the translator arrived fifteen minutes later that it became clear my body language and gestures were not as clear as I'd hoped. The executives had taken my pointing at the glass to mean I had drunk too much and I was either still hammered or extremely hungover from the night before. Not exactly the first impression I'd hoped to make.

Perhaps the businessmen, like me, had never been on a cruise ship before and had never encountered someone with such a pronounced case of seasickness. Or perhaps they'd seen colleagues get drunk at conferences before and, seeing the bar, my drink, and my demeanor, were primed to suspect the worst.

Everyone's prior experience of the world is different, so everyone's database is filled with different data. We can only search for what's in our own personal database. That's why people with more world experience are likely to find more matches—their mirror neurons have been hard at work!—and are less likely to judge people based on a single trait.

Let's say you resemble a friend from the woman's high school days, someone she has a really good feeling about. She might be predisposed to like you before you open your mouth. That's one more "safe" or "yes" hit in your favor. You can't control her memories, but you can control other aspects of that three- to four-minute database search.

His Signals/Her Signals

Here Comes the Judge

Women may be better at sizing up people quickly and making judgments about their intentions because the neural connections in their decision-making centers, the frontal cortex, are more highly developed.

How to Present the Right Data to Scan

Studies show that job interviews are basically decided within the first few minutes, and are based more on how much the interviewer likes the applicant than on the applicant's professional background and his likelihood of fulfilling the requirements of the position. Let's look at how you can continue to present all the right data for her to scan.

Project confidence—even if you have to fake it. One of the main aims of this book is to help you project more confident, assured, open body language—but it has to start with your own mind-set. If you don't believe you have anything significant to say, why would others think you do? Insecurity scans as a big "no" because it shows up as fear. People want to feel safe, and your fear makes them feel unsafe. Insecurity makes other people question your ability, credibility, even your likability. It's one of the first things people see, and often it's the only thing that matters.

Remember mirror neurons—when you project warmth and confidence, the other person will absorb those positive feelings in his body and reflect them back to you. Everyone benefits. If you are nervous, remind yourself how well you've prepared for this moment. Create a little personally meaningful mantra for yourself, with words to psych you up for any meeting, something like, "Warm, smart, confident." Repeat these words to yourself as you prepare for the meeting and then again as you stand in the reception area or approach the door of the meeting place.

His Signals/Her Signals

Speed Dating

The phenomenon of speed dating puts the first impression to very practical use. In highly organized meetings, singles rotate through five-minute "mini-dates," during which they exchange information about themselves and try to feel out any mutual interest. This highly efficient mating ritual may be a very twenty-first-century way of culling the field quickly, but a recent study on speed dating suggests that the qualities we look for have remained the same since the dawn of time. Men value physical attractiveness 18 percent more highly than women do, and women are twice as likely to view intelligence as necessary for a "yes" as men are.

Assume a high social status—but not too high. For better or worse, humans, like all animals, are hardwired for hierarchy. Affiliating yourself with the strongest members of the tribe, the ones who are most likely to score food and fight off the wolves successfully, has proven to be a sound evolutionary strategy. That's why one of the first yes/no hits we're looking for is "Does this person look like a leader?" Subconsciously we believe that people with status have access to more resources. When we look at them, we reflect their emotions and stature, and we, in turn, feel higher in status as well.

Now, that's not to say you want to present yourself as "above" the person you're meeting with. Perhaps the most versatile approach is to be impeccably polite and self-confident. Starting off any encounter with this approach will not only work with people who truly do have more power over you—such as new clients or hiring managers—it will also charm any employee at a store, restaurant, or other service setting. (When you disarm them this way, any extra favor you ask of them will make them feel as if they're bestowing an honor on you.)

Many magnetic, high-powered salespeople tend to project a high social status, which works for them. Their new clients and associates are drawn to these movers and shakers—they admire the guys making the big deals for big money. Long-term, however, they must live up to this expectation—otherwise, we tend to be turned off by those people.

Walk like you have someplace to go. Sometimes your walk is the first thing the other person sees. If you approach someone from thirty feet away, the way you walk is going to be a big part of their one-tenth-second snap judgment about you. If you're being brought into a room for an interview, often the interviewer is seated behind a desk and sees your approach. Bouncing around and looking in all different directions makes you appear lost. Walking while slightly slouching over gives the impression that you are exhausted. At best, the way you walk tells people, "I'm comfortable in my own skin." At worst, it can tell people, "I'm lazy" or "I'm late."

The best walk is one that starts with your shoulders pulled back and your neck elongated. Start your step on your heel, roll forward through your foot, and press off with your toe; each stride should be about one to two feet wide. Allow your arms to swing naturally back and forth. People who are nervous because they're late tend to swing their arms up higher. Also, avoid the shuffle walk at all costs. (See "Total Turn-Offs: The Shuffle Walk," on page 229.)

Total Turn-Offs
The Shuffle Walk

What is the shuffle walk? Taking slow, lackadaisical steps with your pelvis thrust forward and shoulders slumped back, and your head lolling around very low. The shuffle walk screams, "I'm lazy! I don't have a care in the world. I'm just getting where I have to go, at my own speed, my own pace." Not the message you want to send to anyone, unless you're on vacation. Your business walk should say, "I am going someplace. I have to attend to something important. I'm not going to rush, but as a professional, I know where I have to be."

Once you've been acknowledged by the person you are meeting, walk directly to him, with every body part pointing in his direction. Maintaining eye contact with occasional breaks to the side will ensure that you seem more confident about meeting him.

After you've greeted each other and you start to walk together, match your speed and gait to his. (If you walk faster or slower and he has to struggle to stay in step with you, he is going to scan that frustrating mismatch as a "no.")

Smile—and make sure your smile is something to look at. We can identify a smile more easily than any other expression, even from a distance of up to 300 feet. The smile is the surest way to guarantee a "yes" from the first-impression database scan. When you smile at another person, his mirror neurons light up and cause him to mimic that smile immediately—in some cases, even against his will! And once he has smiled, his body rewards him with the neurochemicals of happiness. Physiologically, a smile tells our brains that we are safe and that we can relax. So when we smile at others, they see us as open and approachable and automatically receive a message of trust and sincerity. What a bargain!

As we discussed in chapter 2, "The Language of the Face," the smiles perceived as most genuine will involve the eyes and the whole face. You'll see little crinkle lines next to the eyes. I work with many of my clients to develop their own social smiles for occasions when they want to make a good first impression. (See "Flash Your Social Smile," on page 282, for tips on how to create your own versatile social smile.)

The most important aspect of the first-impression smile is the color of your teeth. In today's world, having yellow teeth is like dying a slow social death. We have so many economical, quick ways to fix yellow teeth, either by using over-the-counter whitening strips or by dropping a few hundred dollars for a dentist-grade whitening treatment. In the U.K., the demand for tooth-whitening procedures is predicted to grow by 40 percent a year for the foreseeable future. You have so many options for tooth whitening, it's so inexpensive, and so many people are doing it that when you choose not to, you really stand out—and not in a good way.

Listen, I know what I'm talking about. I grew up without dental insurance and had problems with my teeth for my entire young adult life. Every time I laughed, I would cover my mouth with my hand. Finally, at a certain point, my dentist mentioned what an impact my teeth made on my appearance. I gave in, had my teeth bleached, and it literally changed how I felt about myself and how others viewed me.

You could spend tons of time trying to figure out the right way to stand and point your feet and millions of other body language signals, but if you open your mouth and you have yellow teeth, you're undercutting everything. If you haven't done so already, go immediately to your local drugstore and buy some Crest Whitestrips or look into one-hour whitening with your dentist.

Perfect your handshake, your most important body language signal. When someone is doing their first-impression database check on you, a lousy handshake will quickly be scanned as a "no." If you cannot even shake hands properly, how can you possibly be a good business partner or employee? A poor handshake automatically leads to feelings of awkwardness and can derail an otherwise pleasant first encounter.

In contrast, a good handshake is an excellent way to exhibit professionalism. Typically, the person who initiates the handshake is seen as the more confident of the two, the person in power. But don't let that stop you from sticking your hand out to greet your interviewer, boss, or the CEO. Done well, initiating the handshake shows that you are very assertive, a go-getter.

Give more space rather than less. While leaning forward can be a rapport-building part of the handshake, be sure to back off just a bit during the next part of the conversation. Invading someone's personal space can cause him to have a visceral reaction, as humans are by nature extremely territorial. No matter what, do not remain in someone's intimate zone, which is roughly eighteen inches around them. The general rule is to maintain one full arm's length from each other, which generally turns into about three to four feet. Find a good solid middle ground to ensure comfort for all.

Stand or sit up straight, and don't slouch for a second. Whether sitting or standing, maintain excellent posture. Imagine an invisible vertical line dividing your body in half. Try to create a sense that each half is a mirrored image of the other. If you have to lean, make it slightly forward, as this will help you appear more interested. Think of your spine as a column of dice, stacked one on top of another. Try to keep them balanced at all times, whether you're sitting or standing. Pull your shoulders back and down, keep your chest high, and elongate your neck. Keep your head high and even, both horizontally and vertically.

To really get a feel of how your spine is supposed to be aligned, lie down on your back and bend your knees, so your feet are planted on the floor. Take a few deep breaths and allow your body to relax

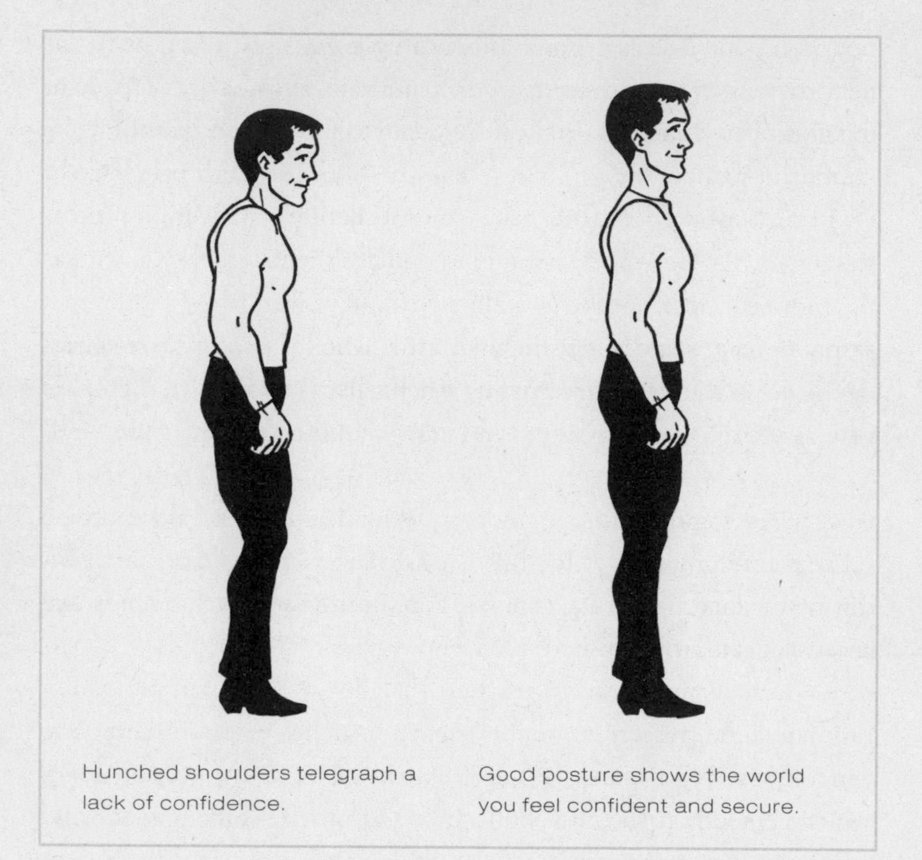

Hunched shoulders telegraph a lack of confidence.

Good posture shows the world you feel confident and secure.

into a natural state. This is the feeling you should have when you are standing.

Women sometimes misinterpret the advice to keep one's chest high. Occasionally, you'll see a woman with her chest pushed out and her butt sticking out the back. You want to make sure that you keep your spine straight down so your booty doesn't stick out too much. Also, women often lean to one side, putting their weight on one foot, and jut out their hip a bit. Unless you are mirroring someone else's posture, that stance detracts from your overall appeal, as it scans as a lack of symmetry.

Keep your feet pointed in the direction of your interest. Many of our emotions "leak" out of our feet. That means if you're talking to someone, and your face and trunk are both pointed toward her, but your feet are pointed toward the door, the truth is that you really don't want to talk to her. Subconsciously, she's going to pick up on that fact. She might not realize it; she might just think there's something not right in the conversation. Just remember: Our feet always indicate our interest.

Arms at your sides. Crossing your arms when you first meet someone is almost always perceived as a defensive gesture. On the other hand, you don't want to put your hands behind your body either, because that could be perceived as a power stance. So typically, unless you have something in your arms, your arms should be down at the sides. Although it might feel a little "boring" to have such a straightforward stance, it's actually very pleasing to the other person's eye because, again, it's symmetrical.

When you sit, think right angles. If you're walking into an interview, you'll be offered a seat. When given a choice, pick a seating arrangement with no barrier between you and the interviewer. When speaking to men, try to sit at a 90-degree angle to his chair, as a straight-on approach can come across as adversarial or confrontational. Women, however, prefer a more direct and frontal approach.

Resist the temptation to go for the comfy soft chair—you'll sink in and look weak and swallowed up. Sit on the firmer chair, but don't let your back rest against the chair; sit slightly forward. Your knees and waist should be bent at 90-degree angles. You want to look comfortable but not too relaxed. If your seat has arms, use them so you can avoid crossing your arms in your lap.

Men's feet should be planted firmly on the floor, legs parallel, not crossed. Some women feel they have to cross something. If so, you can cross your legs at the ankle. Women should not cross their legs at the knee, as it tends to be distracting. Your best bet is to keep both feet on the ground.

Women are often tempted to do a leg twine, crossing their legs so their calf muscles look tight. This sitting position is very attractive to men and can also be distracting. As I mentioned earlier, men and women work off of procreative urges; while this position can appeal to a man's procreative urge, that won't get you the job.

Men shouldn't cross their legs by resting an ankle on the knee of their opposite leg, a position called the "figure four." The figure-four position closes your body up and makes it look like you're trying to be the dominant force. It's best to keep your feet planted on the floor, so you can give the other person the feeling of balance and equality.

At the end of the three- to four-minute window, your baseline first impression is fully formed. Unless something really big happens after the first meeting to change the person's mind about you—perhaps you unexpectedly win a major industry award, or perhaps you are exposed for accounting fraud.

Here's an all-too-common scenario. Let's say we meet each other for the first time, and I'm having a really bad day. Maybe I'm not talking to you as much as I should be, and you think, Well, she's just cold. I could be experiencing some catastrophe in my life, but you walk away from our first meeting thinking I'm cold, standoffish, and arrogant.

Now the second time we meet, it's already in your mind that I'm arrogant. You're going to be more tentative, because your first database scan yielded the results: cold, standoffish, and arrogant. Now you're really just looking for more information to confirm this initial impression of me—but you're highly unlikely to change your mind. In order for me to show you that I'm absolutely wonderful, I'm going to have to do the work of ten people.

It's impossible to retract a bad first impression. That first impression is the benchmark for everything. But each new impression is layered over the first one. You won't be able to start from scratch, but you can make the next several impressions demonstrate who you are more accurately. That's why I advise people not to have to make a second impression. Just make that first one the best.

Now that you've learned how to create the best baseline first impression, you can solidify this positive glow immediately with some rapport-building techniques. These will add even more "yes" hits to your baseline first impression and build up a long-lasting reservoir of goodwill.

Stage 3. Building Rapport: Five Minutes and Beyond

The first impression is based on our biological hardwiring to assess and categorize—we're collecting information to see how this person "fits" with us in the larger social network. Am I safe with him? Is she like me? Once we've cleared the database scan and have gathered lots of "yes" hits, the next job is to solidify that rapport. Rapport is the sense that the two of you are "in tune" with each other—that the two of you "click," that your mirror neurons are singing out to each other in tune. Rapport becomes the glue in this new budding relationship; it will spring naturally from your mutual mirror systems—but you can also help it along with a few simple techniques.

Make it all about the other person, as much as possible. You know that joke, "Enough about me—what do you think of me?" In a first impression, go with the exact opposite approach. When you're trying to win favor, instead of trying to sell yourself, focus entirely on the other person. Constantly focus on sending a nonverbal message of "Tell me about you," and reinforce thoughts of interest with your body language. Does this person think he's very polite? Underscore that by smiling broadly and widening your eyes to thank him for holding the door open for you. Does this person value his car? Let out a whistle and run your hand along it admiringly. Is this person going through a rough time? Tilt your head to the side and shake your head, as if to say, "I admire your strength so much."

Maintain eye contact 70 percent of the time. When you meet someone's gaze, you're telling them that what they have to say is important and meaningful to you. Eye contact is crucial to demonstrating sincerity and establishing trust. In the United States, the inability to maintain eye contact is taken as a sign of disrespect, a lack of personal confidence, or a short attention span—and in some cases, people might assume you're a liar. Keep in mind, some cultures (such as those in South Asia) regard direct eye contact as threatening, rude, disrespectful, or impolite. But when you maintain eye contact in our culture, you're likely to be perceived as attentive, competent, and powerful.

While a reasonable amount of eye contact is good, outright staring can be insulting, even scary. (Review the facial signals in chapter 4 to be sure you know the difference between quality eye contact and a "stalker stare.") If you tend to stare, try visualizing a triangle on the other person's face, made up of the two eyes and the nose. Move your eyes around within that triangle, so you can be sure you have appropriate eye contact without staring the other person down.

Ask friends to be honest with you and let you know if your level of eye contact is appropriate. Although sometimes maintaining eye contact is uncomfortable, it is essential that you learn this skill to help build rapport and gain confidence.

His Signals/Her Signals

She Might Be Checking You Out—But You'd Never Know

Women have better peripheral vision than men do—they can take in a much broader visual picture than men while looking straight into another person's eyes. Men don't have this advantage, which is why they often use full-body, head-to-toe-to-head eye movements to check someone out. (Women can get the same amount of visual information without anyone being the wiser!)

Listen with your whole body. Sometimes when we first meet someone, we're so worried about constructing our responses to their words that we don't truly listen—and that's a big mistake. We can spend up to 75 percent of the time other people talk to us being distracted or preoccupied, and as a result we don't retain what they are saying. When listening to someone else speak, always look the person in the face, maintain eye contact, occasionally tilt your head to the side to indicate interest, and nod at appropriate times. Focus on the content of her words, and your responses will automatically become more natural, less forced. Several studies have found that leaders are perceived to be excellent listeners; one study in particular found that listening accounts for approximately one-third of the characteristics that coworkers say are important when it comes to being an effective communicator. There is no bigger compliment you can give someone than your full and focused attention.

Talk in a low tone of voice. Stress impacts every muscle in the body, tightening everything up, and our vocal cords are no exception. When we're nervous, our voices become more high-pitched, which is unfortunate—a high-pitched voice in women comes across as ditzy, and in guys it is perceived as effeminate. On the other hand, a low voice is considered dominant (and very sexy). Before you go to the meeting, practice doing deep breathing exercises, as they'll slow down your heart rate and allow your vocal cords to loosen, which will keep your pitch normal. A strong approach is to use a low-pitched voice when you are stressing a point as that comes across as powerful.

To build rapport, listen beyond the words—do you hear any other emotions? Anger or hostility? Boredom? Happiness? Excitement? Disbelief? What about the pitch—high or low? Take a moment, listen to the other person's voice, and then try to make your voice sound similar. This also applies to how fast or slow you speak. If you're a fast speaker and you're speaking with someone who usually speaks slowly, she may have problems understanding you, trusting you, or building any kind of rapport with you. Even if it's frustrating for you, you need to try to match her pace. The reverse is also true—if you're from Indiana and you are speaking with a Manhattanite, it might be difficult, but you'll have to speed up so you can be on the same page. You want the other person to have that subconscious, "Yes! You're just like me" feeling in any conversation with you.

Control your movements. Few things are as annoying as a person jiggling their leg, tapping their pen cap, drumming their fingers on the table, or any other repetitive movement that serves no other purpose than as an outlet for nervousness. For years, experts have recommended that people just not do it, but very recently, German scientists actually discovered the "fidget gene." People with this gene are those who "just can't sit still." It's no wonder that people who fidget are usually on the lean side—their excess movements can burn up to 700 calories a day. That weight-loss benefit, however, doesn't help you make a good first impression. When you move around restlessly, the person you're with will think, "She's nervous, impatient, or perhaps getting bored." The extra calorie burn is hardly worth putting people off with a perceived lack of confidence, control, and competence. Recognize that each movement says something about you and your state of mind at any moment.

Keep your gestures within the range bound by your hipline and your shoulders to demonstrate that you are in control. Natural gesticulators can make use of their hands and arms to deliver a clear and concise message and do so with ease. Wildly erratic or overly exuberant gesticulators are sometimes seen as overbearing and obnoxious. Gestures should emphasize verbal statements and consistently take place in the square area surrounding your torso.

Mirror, mirror, one and all. Once the initial impression is formed and you are off to building rapport, one of the easiest ways to do so is to mirror the other person. To be in rapport with someone, just focus your attention on them entirely and let your body get in tune with their movements, vocal tone, rate of speech, size and number of gestures—basically everything about them. In essence, listen with not only your ears but also your eyes. That sense of resonance will create the subconscious feeling, "I like this person because they are just like me."

Some people may have an inherently sophisticated ability to read body language. Their mirror systems may be more active and they are therefore more naturally empathetic. But if you don't trust your body to do the work for you, you can consciously mirror some things, such as gestures, for example. If the person you've just met uses his hands a lot, be sure you do the same. Don't mimic the exact movements; rather, if he makes large gestures, increase the size of your gestures. (However, never go too far, as big gestures are seen as flamboyant and over the top.) Ditto for mirroring smaller movements.

Mirroring your conversational partner helps to establish rapport quickly.

Tread lightly, though: The last thing you want to do is make someone feel like you're mimicking them. We all hated that as kids, when our annoying sibling would repeat every movement we made until we screamed, "Mo-om, he's copying!"

As humans, we want to surround ourselves with people who remind us of ourselves, other people we've known, and experiences we've had in the past. We're most comfortable when we're back in that emotional hall of mirrors that we experienced with our parents. When I see those familiar qualities in you, I think, "Wow, this person is awesome. And look, she's just like me. I must be awesome too." We boost our self-esteem by surrounding ourselves with people who are like us, because their mere presence gives us proof that we're good people.

The first-impression bottom line: the more familiar you seem to the other person, the more quickly you build rapport with him, the better impression you will leave, and the more solid footing you'll be on the next time you meet. Simple as that.

Now you have all the tools to perfect your first impression. I recommend that you systematically go through each facet detailed in this chapter, initially focusing on the areas that have given you trouble in the past. Try to use your new posture, handshake, smile, or other new body language gesture or expression every day, making that change part of your interactions with everyone—your spouse, friends, colleagues, even the bus driver and the toll taker. You'll find, after three weeks, that what felt awkward at the beginning has now become a part of your daily routine—a habit. You'll feel more confident about meeting new people, and you'll notice their reactions to you change as well. These actions and reactions will trigger a physiological response in your body, further reinforcing the good feeling that comes from establishing rapport with an ever-widening circle of people. And soon enough, you'll no longer need to practice—these body language moves will become second nature.

You have a very clear idea of all the different channels of nonverbal cues. We studied the signals shown on the face, the body, the use of space and touch, and the voice. We've seen how all of these signals come into play in a first impression. Now, let's learn about how you can read other people's secret signals to see what they're *really* thinking and feeling.

CHAPTER 7

Reading Their Secret Signals

You can observe a lot just by watching.

—Yogi Berra

Who is the best at spotting liars? Surprisingly, it's not the professionals who talk to liars all day—cops, judges, polygraphers. The best human lie detectors are a group of men and women who don't actually talk to many suspects at all—instead, they watch them.

Secret Service agents, the stone-faced heavies who surround the president and spend whole days scanning crowds for possible threats, are far better than average at detecting deception. In a study by Paul Ekman and Maureen O'Sullivan, Secret Service agents were found to be exceptionally good at identifying liars—over half of them could spot a liar with 70 to 100 percent accuracy, whereas less than a quarter of federal polygraphers had the same accuracy rate. In fact, the study found that all of the participants, aside from the Secret Service agents, had a deception detection rate equal to chance. A later study found CIA agents to be similarly skilled, with a 70 percent accuracy rate versus 51 percent for law enforcement officers.

What makes Secret Service and CIA agents so good at spotting liars is likely another case of nature *via* nurture. Their inherent talents for body language detection probably brought them to the job to begin with, and then years of conscious study of nonverbal communication made these agents masters of detection. And while you may never get top-secret clearance or international espionage training, you can still learn to detect deception, seduction, and manipulation in others by using the same basic principles: Watch and learn.

Now you are going to discover a few new techniques to help you read other people's secret signals. Surprisingly, the first things you need to look for are the signals they send when they're *not* lying.

Finding Their Normal Baseline

You know by now that only the rookie body language reader would say, "Oh, he's touching his nose—he must be lying." No one individual gesture is directly linked to deceit. It's only when you start to see clusters of gestures—two or three—that you can become more certain of their meaning. But perhaps the best way to judge a person's body language is to start with a study of her patterns to get them down cold. You have to "norm" her.

When you "norm" or "baseline" someone, you detect her deceit signals by first detecting her truth signals. Norming works on the same principle as standard lie detector tests: Once you're hooked up to the polygraph machine, the polygrapher asks a few straightforward, fact-based questions—"Is your name Colonel Mustard?"—just to get a baseline read on your physical signals. Then, he'll ask the question that he suspects will provoke an untruthful answer—"Did you kill Mr. Boddy in the conservatory with the candlestick?" The difference between your body's reactions to factual questions and your body's reaction to the provocative question is what tells the polygrapher whether or not you're lying.

Norming is easy to do, and it doesn't require a fancy machine. All you need is an unsuspecting target and a few simple questions. Here's how it works.

During a peaceful, nonconfrontational moment with your target, begin a conversation with a casual question that will require your target to dig into his memory banks to answer. You want the question to help him recall something factual and visual. For example:

You know what I was thinking about the other day—do you remember the name of that neighbor at our first house? The one who lived next door?

Make sure you can see his face while he answers the question. As the person answers the question, note the way his eyes move. Often people will look up and to the left when they try to recall a visual memory from their past; others will look up and to the right. Note the way your target's eyes move, and then repeat the process with a different question:

I was trying to remember—didn't they have a dog? What kind of dog was it?

Again, you ask a question that requires a definite, factual answer. Repeat this two or three more times until you feel confident that you know your target's facial pattern for answering a question with a factual answer. Then, move in for the kill.

Where were you last night?

If a person is trying to construct a lie, his eyes will typically shift in the opposite direction of what you have determined is normal. If he normally looks up and to the left, he's likely to look up and to the right if he is lying. That's because he's accessing a different part of the brain to construct a lie rather than recall factual information.

And there you have it—the target's "tell" when he's lying.

You can norm for many different signals. Blinking is a good one. Our blink rate increases when we're nervous, so you can study a person's calm, serene blink rate and then norm them to see their anxious blink rate. You can also do it with breathing—deep breaths versus shallow breaths—or skin color—pasty white versus flushed and blushing. You can see if the person goes from big gestures to no gestures, or small gestures to big sweeping movements. In every case, you study the person's body language in a "normal" context and then see where it goes when you ask a question he might not want to answer truthfully. Once you've seen the "tell"—which you should never reveal, of course—unless he consciously works to minimize that particular signal, that person will never be able to lie to you again.

Thankfully, sometimes you don't even have to work that hard to detect a lie. Many people are such obvious liars that all you have to do is spot their body language incongruence—the words they say do not match their body language. In fact, incongruence remains one of the easiest ways of detecting any kind of insincerity, even if it is unconscious. Remember, you are hardwired to pick up on these signals—you just have to trust your gut to always tell you the truth.

Now let's look at some common signals in different scenarios. You may find it helpful to read the signals in each of these situations.

Is She/He Lying to Me?

Not all lies are whoppers—some are the casual white lies that we all tell to keep society running smoothly. One study suggests that during ten-minute conversations with people we've never met before, 60 percent of us will lie at least once. Deception is one of the hardest things to detect, because no one particular sign means a person is lying, and only half the people who lie reveal their deceit in microexpressions. That's why, for deception especially, you must norm a person before you can read any of her facial or other body language signals. Once you've done that, look for some of these common signs:

Common Signals for Deceit

Dilated pupils

More pauses in conversation

More speech errors

Fewer specific details

More "allness" terms—all, always, everyone, none, nobody

Less eye contact or more eye contact, depending on the norm

Fewer body movements or more body movements

Sometimes more self-touching

Sweating

Higher-pitched voice

Shorter verbal responses

Flushed cheeks (when the conversation doesn't warrant it)

Increased blinking

Hands to mouth, covering it or wiping/rubbing it

Fingernail biting

Fake cough

Nose rub

Eye rubbing or pretending something is in the eye

Increased swallowing

Chewing of the inside of the mouth

Drying up of the mouth

What to do in response: If you suspect deceit, don't show it. Interestingly, one theory posits that liars and their victims tend to trade body language signals. Typically, the receiver of a lie can give off cues of recognition of the lie, which tips off the liar to change his nonverbal cues to become more believable. In other words, we may be helping liars to lie.

If you suspect someone is lying, continue to drill down into the details. Ask questions like, "What did you have for dinner? What time did you get home? Did they have any appetizers? How much did it cost? What did Mike have to drink?" Then double back. "What was your entrée again? I thought you said filet—was it just steak or filet?" Most liars don't think out every aspect of the lie and will trip themselves up very quickly.

You can also use what's called "statement analysis" as a complement to your study of a suspected liar's body language signals. Just like with body language, we learn a lot by putting ourselves in another's shoes. When you are listening to someone who leaves you feeling skeptical, ask yourself, "How would I answer a similar question?" Many liars will use what's called "distancing language" to hold the accusation at arm's length. They'll leave out references to actual names or details, speak in the second or third person, and often repeat the same stock phrases over and over.

When claiming his innocence in the murder of his wife, Nicole, O. J. Simpson wrote, "I loved Nicole, I could never do such a thing." That's a far cry from saying, "I did not kill Nicole."

You can use statement analysis technique in everyday language. Look for some of these tip-offs.

Junk words. For example, some people tend to pepper their conversations with the word *actually;* some never say it. If you're talking to a person who rarely says it, and then you hear them say "actually" more than four times in a five-minute conversation, there's a good chance there's some kind of deception going on.

Tense discrepancies. Are they speaking in the present, future, or past tense, and is it the appropriate tense? For example, a parent who has killed her own child and claimed the child has disappeared or has been abducted might say, "He *was* such a fun-loving boy." If she was still hopeful for his return, she would have said, "He *is* such a fun-loving boy."

Order of significance. Deceit can also be detected by listening to the order in which a person tells a story. If she recounts events, and their order makes no sense, it could be that she's trying to reorganize her own story as she tells it. Pay close attention to the things people say first, as those details are the ones she's been thinking about the most.

Answering the wrong question. People can sometimes withhold information by pretending to answer a question while totally evading it. Politicians often employ this tactic to avoid making unpopular statements or admitting they have made mistakes or contradicted themselves.

Is She/He Trying to Strong-Arm Me?

High school isn't the only place for bullies these days. A recent book, *The Corporation: The Pathological Pursuit of Profit and Power,* created a media firestorm with its assertion that the modern-day corporation allows abusive people to thrive because of a rampant ends-justify-the-means philosophy. In an economic downturn, strong-arming and manipulation often take the place of effective management.

Sometimes bullies can be extremely covert in their efforts to control you. The content of their words might be beyond reproach, but encounters with them somehow leave you with a sinking sensation in your stomach and doubt about your job security. Here are some of the signs that someone might be trying to strong-arm you.

Common Signals of Bullying

Invading your personal space

Standing over you

Tilting his head down at you

Arms folded

Superior gestures

"Dead," expressionless smile

No movement in the eyes

Jaw jutting out

Eye rolling

Smirking

Verbal jabs

Accidental bumps

What to do in response: Stand your ground. Bullies love a victim. Refuse to give in. You want to send the message, "I am not intimidated by you."

When a bully—or anyone—moves into your personal space, do not move. As a matter of fact, you might even lean toward that person to demonstrate that they will not be permitted to invade your personal space. If they smile at you, smile right back; maintain eye contact. Depending upon what you want the response to be, you can either open your arms to say, "I'm not intimidated by you, but I'm open to you," or cross your arms to say, "That's not going to happen. No way, no how." Decide which response suits your purpose best and stick to your guns. Only by presenting yourself in a confident manner will you discourage further attacks.

Does She/He Distrust Me?

Trust is a critical part of any long-term relationship, and once developed, it must be nurtured with care. Salespeople, lawyers, counselors, physicians, all need to inspire trust in their clients and patients. In fact, most professional relationships rely upon trust as the bedrock of team building. If someone doesn't trust you in a business setting, you need to work to gain that person's trust before you can hope to ask for anything in return. Here are some signs to tell if someone is inclined to distrust you.

Strangers constantly ask my husband how he is able to live with someone who takes in his every movement, word, and vocal change and analyzes it. His response is always the same. "I walk in the house and go right upstairs to bed." He's kidding, of course. Usually, he will respond with "That's never an issue because my body language always says exactly what it should say."

Common Signs of Distrust

- Head tilted to one side (usually accompanied by a squinted eye)
- Uneven smile or full smirk
- Crossed arms
- Squinted eyes with continual eye contact
- Evading eye contact (if they really don't believe you)
- Scratching neck
- Rubbing or pulling on ears
- Rubbing nose
- Either evading eye contact or continual eye contact
- Pulling on their lips

Common signals of distrust.

What to do in response: Open up your body language. Whenever you're trying to convince someone you're trustworthy, you should use positive, congruent body positions—smile openly, show your palms, and point your feet toward the person. Build credibility with them by keeping your spine tall and strong, and mirroring their body language and their words to build rapport. On the other hand, if you're trying to convince someone you're telling the truth when they think you're lying, it's best to assume open body language such as opening up your suit jacket (provided you have a shirt underneath), leaning slightly forward, and relaxing your posture with open palms and direct eye contact.

Is She/He About to Hire Me?

An interview can be such a heartbreaker, especially when you think you've nailed it and then you get a call that the company is going to "go in a different direction." Save yourself the anxiety of waiting to hear back and look for these signs during the interview to see if you've clinched the job. (Obviously, these are no guarantees, but if you *don't* see these signs, at least you won't get your hopes up!)

Common Signs You'll Likely Get the Job

Smiling when you smile

Consistently open and warm body language

Relaxed forehead

Maintaining eye contact and paying attention to what you are saying

Nodding when you are speaking

Leaning toward you

Seeming more enthusiastic midway through the interview

Offering to show you around after the interview

Walking around desk to shake your hand when leaving (no barriers)

Walking you all the way to the reception area, and lingering while you leave

What to do in response: Work to further cement rapport. Stay on your toes until the end of the interview—don't slack as soon as you see the interviewer smile or nod. Work to further establish rapport with mirroring movements and nods of your own. (One step in the Reiman Rapport Method, "Nod, Mirror, and Lead," on page 284, gives specific advice for these two core rapport-building skills.)

What happens if you *don't* see these signs—if the interviewer is distracted, paying more attention to her computer screen than your résumé? Often when an interviewer believes you're not the right candidate, she'll stop nodding as an unconscious way of discouraging you from speaking. If you feel you've lost the interviewer's attention, you might want to do a single, isolated, slightly flamboyant movement—perhaps a sweeping arm gesture that's not over the top, but large enough to redirect her attention. Perhaps you say, "Oh, did I show you this?" and hand the interviewer a copy of your portfolio or an article, anything to recapture her interest for a moment so you can flash that gorgeous smile and sell yourself again.

Is She/He About to Fire Me?

Layoffs and restructurings are a common occurrence these days. Many people can sense the harsh wood of the chopping block way before their number comes up; others might be completely stunned when the pink slip arrives. But managers usually have an idea of which employees they plan to let go a few weeks or even months before they actually terminate their employment. If you see these signs, take it as a possible clue for what's coming.

Common Signs of Impending Dismissal

Occasional glares

Avoiding eye contact (often seen when they don't want to let you go, but it's out of their hands)

Shaking head back and forth when you speak

Ignoring you, continuing to work while disregarding your presence

Standing over you and questioning what you are doing

Crossed arms and body tilted back during discussions with you

Doesn't raise head when you enter their office

Boss's secretary doesn't make small talk with you anymore

Stops sending e-mails

Stops small talk or any extraneous conversation

What to do in response: Emphasize the positive. Negative people are toxic to teams. Often when managers are told they need to make choices about the people on their staffs, they move to dismiss the most negative person, even if he is very talented at his job. If you suspect this might be you, keep in mind that you're not gone yet, and you might still be able to salvage your job.

If you're honest with yourself and recognize that your attitude might be the issue, you have to make a choice—you can take the package and go, or you can choose to fight back. If you choose the latter, kill them with kindness—grin at everyone, open doors for people, refuse to gossip, take it as a fresh start. Think: Mirror, nod, smile, open body posture. You might just change their minds about you.

Is She/He Going to Attack Me?

Nature is not kind to victims—several species of animals are known to isolate the weak from the herd before they close in for the kill. Indeed, predators don't always choose their victims randomly. Certain characteristics make some people more likely to be attacked than others. How can you avoid becoming a victim? Check out these signs of aggression that might lead to attack.

Common Signs of Intent to Attack

- "Stalker stare"
- Very close within your intimate or personal zone
- Fist clenched
- Smile on mouth but not in eyes, or a deep scowl of anger
- Finger pointing or jabbing
- Tongue sticking out
- Sarcasm
- High-pitched voice or low-pitched growl

When you see these signals of imminent attack, steer clear.

What to do in response: Walk with a mission. One recent study found that the more a woman lifts her feet and the slower she walks, the easier to attack she is considered to be. The women least vulnerable to attack have a vigorous, energetic walk, a long stride, widely swinging arms, a fast pace, and a few more pounds than the women who are likely to become victims. All the same characteristics define males who are most vulnerable to attack, except that weight plays an even bigger role—the more pounds he packs, the less likely he'll be attacked. Women in bare feet or heels are also more likely to be attacked than those wearing flat shoes; those wearing skirts are more likely to be attacked than those in pants.

These tips might help before the attacker spots you, but what if you're already in his sights, as with an episode of road rage or if the attacker has a weapon? Then your best bet is to adopt body language that is similar to, or slightly more submissive than, the attacker's, which will allow them to relate to you on some level. Make sure that when you speak, you are calm and even-tempered to avoid angering them further. Of course, let them take the wallet or the bag! Let them scream at you! If I crash into somebody's car by accident, and the woman gets out with bulbous eyeballs, ready to explode, the best thing to do is to defer to her anger and try to calm the situation. When someone is that irrational and already has you in her sights, the only way to neutralize that anger is to acknowledge it and try to diffuse it.

Is She Trying to Seduce Me?

For women, one of the most baffling mysteries in the world is why men don't understand their signals –often there's nothing secret about them! I can't tell you how many times I've heard from women, "I'm trying to flirt, but they just don't get it!" Guys, if you really pay attention, you'll see the ladies are giving you *plenty* of information—you just have to keep your eyes open.

Common Signals of Female Sexual Interest

Looking at you a second longer than you feel is appropriate

Looking at you, then down, then back at you one or two more times

Touching or fondling her neck or necklaces

Licking her lips

- Dangling shoe from toe
- Glancing at you over her shoulder
- Rubbing the top of her glass while looking at you
- Enjoying her food and licking her fingers
- Pushing her shoulders back and thrusting her breasts in your direction
- Fixing/tossing her hair
- Smoothing out her clothes
- Tilting her head to one side, baring her throat to you
- Exposing her palms and wrists to you
- Moving in closer when you whisper
- Crossing and uncrossing her legs
- Touching you . . . anywhere
- Gazing at your mouth
- Tilting her head down and looking up at you with big eyes (sometimes with a sideways glance)

When you see several signs like hers, you can be sure a woman is interested in you.

What to do in response: Get a clue! With this many signals, you'd have to be blind not to pick up on a couple. To make sure you're not just seeing things, try this: After you have made initial eye contact with a woman you are attracted to, keep your eyes on her a few seconds after she looks away. If you notice her start to fidget, become jittery, adjust or smooth out her clothes, fix/pat/primp her hair, and then quickly look up at you a second time, feel free to make your move—she is into you.

Is He Trying to Seduce Me?

Most men are very forthright with their attraction. Often a guy will be blatant, exploring your most erogenous parts with his eyes—and he *wants* you to know he's doing it. (He's already done it once before, probably without your knowledge.) When he is attracted to you, you'll notice a smile usually accompanying a quick fifth-of-a-second eyebrow flash—and then likely a few more of these signals as well:

Common Signals of Male Sexual Interest

- Gazing at you for a few seconds longer than you feel appropriate
- Preening himself—adjusting his socks, fixing his tie, smoothing his clothes
- Passing hands through his hair
- Touching his throat
- Stroking his chin
- Broadening chest
- Placing his hands on his hips
- Looping his thumb in his front pocket and pointing his fingers toward his genitals
- Looking at your eyes, then down to your mouth, then back up to your eyes
- Pointing his entire body toward you, especially his feet
- Raising his eyebrows at you
- Touching you on the hand, arm, or shoulder (more respectful areas to touch)
- Touching you anywhere

When you see several signs like his, you can be sure a man is interested in you.

What to do in response: Make sure he *sees* your response. The funny thing is, men might send out some obvious signals, but after that, their body language fluency hits the skids a little bit. For the most part, because men don't see body language signals as quickly as women do, they might stare and smile for a while before they get the hint that you're interested, too. If you're truly attracted, pile on the signals—if the first two don't reach him, try several more. Trust me, he just needs a bit more help than you do.

Is She/He Cheating on Me?

Few things are more tragic than a well-founded suspicion of infidelity. Either your suspicion proves true, and your relationship could be over, or your close connection has withered to the degree that you think infidelity is likely. In either case, you owe it to yourself to find out. Here are a few signs you might see when your spouse has drifted—he or she may not have strayed yet, but it's looking possible. Of course, if these signs were part of your original relationship, you need not worry; if they are new, further investigation is needed.

Common Signals of Infidelity or Waning Love

Shoulder hug instead of full frontal hug

Forward lean hug instead of lower body touching

Patting on shoulder during hugs

Avoiding eye contact

Less touching

Microexpression sneering

Pitch rising when answering questions about infidelity

Body orientation away from you, especially the feet

Less head-to-head contact/snuggling

Shifting eyes when asked whereabouts

Staring directly in eyes when asked whereabouts (overcompensating based on belief that liars can't look others in the face)

Angered when asked whereabouts

Blinking more rapidly when asked whereabouts

What to do in response: Use your norming technique and find out for sure. You likely know your spouse extremely well and already have a baseline for his or her behavior. But if your suspicions are gathering steam, you owe it to yourself to use a systematic approach to remove any doubts. Review the norming technique on pages 242–244 and apply it as soon as possible.

If you want to salvage your relationship, try this technique. A whole line of research suggests that if you want to make your marriage work, one of the best things to do is to gaze into each other's eyes for a few minutes at a time. If you can persuade your partner, try this for three minutes at a time, twice a day. It will be tough in the beginning, but it will get easier over time. Another technique for improving your relationship is to include prolonged kissing—ten to twenty seconds or longer—at least twice a day, perhaps as a morning good-bye and a nighttime good night. Do this often enough, and you'll likely find that it fulfills many needs. These techniques are not only great as a last-ditch effort to save a dwindling marriage, but can also improve the intimacy and strengthen the bonds of any romantic relationship.

Is She/He Really My Friend?

Your relationships with friends are entirely dictated by the quality of your interactions. You're not blood relatives; you're not bound by a marriage license. You are entirely in control of whether or not these people are in your life. Yet we often retain friendships that don't make us happy simply because we can't figure out any "good reason" why we shouldn't be friends. As always, you should trust your golden gut, and know that you're not beholden to remain friends with anyone who doesn't consistently show these signals.

Common Signals of Respect and Friendship

Warm, inviting smiles (not smirks or smiles of contempt)

Chest and feet pointing toward you during conversation

Listening to you without interrupting

Using appropriate turn-taking gestures

Sharing conversation equally

Showing genuine happiness for your successes

Not diverting attention back to self

Strong eye contact without needing to look away

Leaning toward you when you speak

Mirroring your movements

Nodding when you speak

Tilting head when you speak

Offering compassion when needed

What to do in response: If they don't rejuvenate you, consider walking away. When you have a good connection with a friend, both of you are apt to keep your rapport strong with lots of mirroring and positive smiles. But if you're having your doubts, ask yourself, After time with them, do I feel rejuvenated, or do I feel depleted? Energized, or spent? Sometimes people look good on paper and say all the right things, but we just don't feel settled with them. Chances are they've been sending you incongruent body language signals for a while now. Incongruent signals could be a sign your friend is depressed, but it might also be a sign your friend is lying to you, doesn't trust you, feels ambivalent about you, or otherwise feels a rift that just can't be repaired. If you feel it, too, give both of you a break. Life is too short. Trust your gut. You don't have to stay in a relationship that drains you.

Now that you've learned about the secret signals others use, let's take a look at how you can use *your* secret signals to get what you want out of every encounter with other people.

CHAPTER 8

Using Your Own Secret Signals

A stale article, if you dip it in a good, warm, sunny smile, will go off better than a fresh one that you've scowled upon.

—Nathaniel Hawthorne

Learning just one nonverbal move could make a huge difference in your social life. Just ask "Gina," one of the women who attended a body language seminar I did recently.

Gina was a beautiful woman, very put-together and energetic—but she couldn't get a date. Every week she'd go with her girlfriends to a local club to salsa dance. Her girlfriends would be on the dance floor all night. Gina would be the one at the table, guarding the drinks.

I first noticed Gina at the seminar, frantically taking notes as if she were preparing for the Harvard entrance exam. I got a call from her two days later. "You changed my life," she said. "Guys are flocking to me!" She told me how she had tried out my basic flirting technique the night before and had received more numbers in one night than she had in the six months prior.

Gina's one new move is a great example of how a single secret signal can help you connect with others. The trick is to know which signals to use in what situations to get the results you're looking for.

In the last chapter, you learned how to interpret the secret signals of others. Now it's time to learn how to transmit some of your own. In this chapter, I'll share the flirt technique I shared with Gina, as well as dozens of other ways to make your secret signals work for you.

Find Their "WIIFM"— "What's In It for Me?"

In the deepest recesses of our hearts, we're all toddlers. We want the raise, the promotion, the new car, the girl or boy—and we want them *now.* But because we're adults, we know that life is also about give-and-take. We're more likely to get what we need when we help others get what they need. In the parlance of Steven Covey, that's a win-win—the ideal outcome of any human interaction.

The key to using your secret signals to your own ends is to begin with empathy. Imagine yourself in the other person's place and think, "What's in it for me?" That great database of emotions and experiences, your mirror system, will help you recall a time when you felt similar to the other person. You'll clearly see their motivation and, with it, your path to success. Let's take a look at how you can ascertain their all-important WIIFM, use your secret signals, and get what you want in any situation. Instead of your two inner toddlers battling it out in a test of wills, first give his inner toddler a nice little hug—*then* you can steal his candy (just kidding!).

How to Seem Trustworthy (or "How to Be a Good Liar")

Listen, everybody lies. We learned in the prior chapter that 60 percent of us will lie during our first ten-minute conversation with a stranger. Another study found that the most popular middle and high school students are also the best liars. But despite the fact that everyone lies, human beings have what researchers call a "truth bias"—we are all preprogrammed to expect honesty from others. We can detect truth accurately 67 percent of the time, but a lie only 44 percent of the time.

Con men routinely exploit this truth bias, but your own social lies need not be that devious. When you use your secret signals to seem more trustworthy, you're simply helping people believe what they want to believe. (Yeah, that's it.)

Best Signs of Trustworthiness

Palms-up gestures

Eye contact

Uncrossed arms

Feet flat on floor

Posture tall and straight

Smiles, but not too many

Feet pointed toward target

Nodding when making positive points

Shaking head when making negative points

Occasional submissive shrugs

How to use the signals: Practice, practice, practice. What turns truth manipulation into *great* truth manipulation is practice. Think of yourself as an actor practicing your lines. You want to say those words so many times that they'll be flowing from your lips without any speech disturbances or any effort on your part. You can even practice when to look at a person to drive home a point and when to look away to indicate regret or remorse. While you're practicing your lines, remember your target's WIIFM and anticipate any questions they may have—that will allow you to craft your responses accordingly.

How you'll see it's working: They'll give off signs of rapport. You'll see them smile, nod, and mirror your body language back to you. If you see any smirks, nose scratches, or other signs of distrust (see

"Does She/He Distrust Me?" on page 248), you need to work harder. Add in more of the signals from the list above, breathe deeply to manage your anxiety, and hope for the best!

How to Motivate Others (or "How to Manipulate Others")

A good manager is nothing more than a benevolent manipulator. Sometimes we all need to persuade others to do our bidding. Whether you need your assistant to stay late on a Friday night, you're angling for a promotion, or you want your kid to finally clean up his room, the basic body language tools are the same.

Best Signals for Persuasion

Faster speech

Varied pitch

Open body posture

Open palms

Steady eye contact

Smiles (involving eye crinkle)

Mirror body language

For emotional request, line up with right eye

For intellectual request, line up with left eye

For a woman:

Stand face-to-face

Stand close, on the outer edge of the personal zone (approximately three feet)

For a man:

Stand at a 90-degree angle

Stand close, on the outer edge of the personal zone (approximately three to four feet)

How to use the signals: Gently but firmly. You want to convey that you're in control but that you care about how she feels. Remember the WIIFM and use that as your entryway into the discussion. For example, a staff member wants to feel indispensable to you, but she also wants to be in control of her own time. Go into her cubicle and ask, "Have a minute?" Take a moment to establish rapport. If she has a visitor's chair, sit in it and put your hands on her desk in a friendly way. Lean a bit closer than you normally would. Look her right in the eye, hunch your shoulders a bit, turn your palms up. Then ask for her help. After you've said your piece, stop talking but maintain eye contact.

The object is to motivate, not strong-arm. You'll know if you've strong-armed someone if their posture becomes submissive—avoiding eye contact, slumping shoulders, turning away from you. You don't want to see these signals—if you do, make immediate subtle efforts to rebuild rapport.

How you'll see it's working: Genuine smiles and look of pride. When you motivate someone well, you might see their pupils dilate. They'll probably nod and act like it's their idea. "It needs to be done tonight? No problem. You can count on me."

His Signals/Her Signals

Conversational Stops and Starts

One study found that men tend to interrupt more to offer statements, while women interrupt more with questions. Another study found that men also tend to break silences more often than women.

How to Negotiate Effectively

As a buyer, you have all the leverage. Truly. But you give up that leverage as soon as you start to provide any information about yourself. Some salespeople are extremely fluent in nonverbal communication and can read a lot about you within the first thirty seconds. From the moment you stepped into the showroom, he's been gauging your age, your sex, how you walk, what you look like, your clothes, what you look at, what your eyes linger on the longest, how you stand, how you smile. He's picking you apart, piece by piece, to determine your level of seriousness, what type of buyer you are, how to approach you, and how to manipulate you to get the very highest price out of you. Stay on your toes and only reveal the cues you want to reveal.

Best Signals for Retaining Negotiating Power

Closed posture

Crossed arms

A look of indifference

Closed lips

Body angled away

Subtle head shakes

How to use the signals: Be a "tough customer." Remember, he's been eyeing you since you walked in. Your body language should constantly say, "You need to do better." Disclose no details about yourself—and certainly not your degree of interest or size of budget—for as long as possible. You're here to buy a car, not make a friend. The longer you can remain aloof, the harder he's going to work to entice you. If you start all chummy, it's going to feel incredibly awkward to play hard-to-get when you talk pricing.

As he gets closer to the price you're looking for, very gradually open up your posture. Instead of crossing your arms, maybe grab your opposite arm with one hand. Instead of furrowing your brow, use a more neutral face. Don't go from scowls to grins, though—he might feel played and immediately stop playing.

When dealing with a person who is not skilled at hiding his body language signals, you have a great opportunity to norm for a "tell" on pricing. You'll be able to determine the person's bargaining threshold pretty clearly. Ask a few factual questions—"What's the list price?" "What's the standard miles per gallon?" "What's the name of this color?" Once you have seen his reactions to these kinds of questions, you'll know what his norm looks like. Then you can move in and begin to negotiate. If you name a price that he says is unlikely, but he's started to deviate from his norm, there's a good bet you're in a comfortable price range and his protests are merely to protect his margin. Stick to your guns and you should get the price you want.

How you'll see it's working: Extra efforts to warm you up. Sometimes when you're in the middle of a deal, you see body language that's so telling that you can just name your price. If he asks you tons of questions, offers extra information you didn't ask for, searches your face for clues, laughs too hard at your lame jokes—you have him. Here are some other body language signals that indicate you have complete control of the bargaining situation:

This person's signals tell you you're about to get a really good deal.

- Covering the mouth with the hand
- Fidgeting
- Biting lip
- Hand on chest or neck
- Darting eyes
- Flushed skin
- Pacing
- Perspiring

Picking at lip

Rubbing nose

Fast, shallow breathing

Openness to negotiate is one thing—but desperation is something else entirely. He's working overtime to soften you up. Politely wait him out, and you'll eventually get your price or something close to it.

How to Close the Deal

You developed rapport with your prospect. Explained the product, all the features, how it will change her life. Now it's time to close the deal. But is she ready? Before you blow all your hard work, let's take a look at what signals will tell you she's about to become a satisfied customer.

Best Signals That You Have a Deal

Change in overall body language

Smile

Enhanced eye contact

Nodding

Open palms

Forward lean

Direct body orientation

Pupil dilation

Blushing

Shallow breathing

Straightening of posture

Eye twinkle

How to use the signals: Ask at the right moment. To be able to read your client at the critical moment of closing, you have to norm her first. (See "Finding Their Normal Baseline," on page 242). Use that information to watch her body language as you end your pitch—whatever signals she sends next indicates her answer. If you see "no" gestures—folded arms, tapping, hands over the mouth, eye squinting—don't end your pitch yet. Once she verbally says no, it's tough to turn it around, so try a different tack. If she takes a sip of a drink, cleans her glasses, or strokes her chin, those are "maybe" signals—keep additional convincing points ready so you can capitalize on her indecision. If you see the "yes" signs on the list above, go for it—she's yours.

How you'll see it's working: A sudden change in body language. Look for deviations from the norm, the transitions or shifts as people make up their minds. You want to be able to detect if somebody suddenly gets excited or nervous. When the time comes to ask her for the sale, your norm will be able to tell you if her body language is changing because she's thinking, "No way do I want this," or, "Oh, boy, I'm going to say yes, but I want to try to negotiate a better price."

How to Build a United Team

Some managers think the best way to inspire better performance is to create a sense of competition among the ranks. Often this practice leads to rampant backstabbing and other corporate blood sports. While I agree that a spirited sales contest or design competition can stir up creative juices, the healthiest, most loyal teams have an abiding sense of esprit de corps. Try a few of these signals to start building a united, mutually supportive team among your employees.

Best Signals to Create Unity

Democratic seating (round table is best)

Equal eye contact with entire team

Smiles

No smirks or private glances to individuals

Allowing appropriate turn-taking

Direct body orientation to team member who is speaking

Energetic vocal tone

Small but vigorous gestures

How to use the signals: Uniformly. When you're the leader of a team, either as a supervisor or a project leader, you need to make certain that you offer the same opportunity to all of your team members. Create lots of opportunities for fun group gatherings—department getaways, seminars, lunches, and so on. Allow each and every member of your team the chance to make contributions, both to conversations and to projects. You want the team members to support one another and work together. You set the tone—moderate the group with open body posture so others will mirror that stance with one another. Take care to make eye contact with everyone and ensure everyone gets a chance to speak. The guiding question becomes, "What's in it for *us*?" and you should start every meeting by answering that question for the team.

How you'll see it's working: Group rapport. Group rapport is most evident when everyone has the same look on his face, the same degree of energy, and even laughs at the same time. You might encourage rapport by starting the meeting with something engaging, like a group "shout out" or having everyone pound on the table or stomp their feet at once—something lively will not only lighten the mood but also get them actively mirroring one another. Once everyone is in tune with one another and rapport begins, it can continue to have powerful effects long after the meeting ends.

How to Seduce Him

Body language, at its core, is the language of seduction. Just like our primate ancestors, we too have a strong desire to propagate the species—or at least to practice doing so. Using body language to seduce a lover, whether in a nightclub or a breakfast nook, can be one of life's greatest pleasures, so have fun with it.

Best Signals for Seducing Him

For a complete list, see "Common Signals of Female Sexual Interest" on pages 253–254.

How to use the signals: Try the flirt technique. Remember Gina, the salsa-dancing woman who revolutionized her love life with one technique? Here's an expanded version of the flirt technique that I offered to Gina—I guarantee you'll get similar results, too.

When you get to a party or a bar, any room with people milling around, pause at the entranceway and allow people to glance your way. Take this moment to let your eyes sweep the room, taking in as many faces as possible until you see the guy you potentially want to speak to.

For the next few minutes, just join the crowd and mill about the room yourself. Then, intentionally walk toward him. Once you know his eyes are pointed in your direction, let him get a look at you while you toss your hair back—preening while exposing your neck at the same time.

Continue past him and accidentally brush him as you coyly say, "Oh, excuse me." Tilt your head slightly downward, tucking your chin; look him directly in the eye while smiling and maintaining eye contact, and continue to very slowly walk by, briefly glancing over your shoulder to make eye contact once again. Then smile, look down, and look up at his eyes again. Casually walk away, moving to a point in the room where you can still make eye contact with him and continue to glance in his direction as often as you feel comfortable doing so. If you notice *he* has noticed and is smiling, force yourself to hold his gaze until he makes his move—and he will. If he has not yet noticed

Five Strategies for . . .

A Great Presentation

Polished presentation skills are a must in today's corporate environment. Not surprisingly, research shows that audiences rate nonverbal style as equally important to the content of a presentation itself. Don't let your career stagnate due to lackluster presentations—use these strategies to make your next one shine.

Keep yourself loose. Take ten very slow deep breaths right before you walk into the room—they'll allow you to relax and also lower the pitch of your voice. Walk onto the stage with power and purpose. While standing, keep your weight balanced symmetrically on both legs, or sit with your feet flat on the floor. Push your shoulders down and keep them relaxed; when many speakers get nervous, their shoulders lift from the tension, and they wind up looking like they have no necks. Don't fidget, and don't hold anything in your hands. If you are using PowerPoint and need a clicker, either make sure you don't play with it or put it down until you are ready to change screens.

Make contact with individuals. Don't stand behind a podium (unless you have to). Let them see your legs—when you cover them up, people subconsciously feel a barrier between you and them. Move your eyes around the room, settling on individual faces. Make eye contact, smile, hold eye contact, finish a thought, and then look to the next person. If you're speaking to a large group, try to hit several people in every row until you can't focus on faces anymore—then bring your gaze back to the front rows again.

Start with a story, end with a bang. Don't start with "Welcome, thanks for joining me" if you can avoid it—boring! Every presentation has a story lurking inside—maybe it's simply the "aha!" moment when a new product was invented, or a funny joke that the CEO played on one of his executives, or a personal story that relates to the presentation. Tell the story at a fast pace to infect people with your energy. People will remember how you start your presentation and how you end it—they won't remember the middle. For the most part, they won't remember anything but perhaps the first and last three minutes. Make 'em good.

Keep moving. Be energized, quick; move around a lot at the beginning of your talk to keep people on their toes. Use your hands to help you articulate your point. Powerful gestures will create movement that stimulates and attracts the audience's eye. Think contained and thoughtful, not sloppy or overly dramatic.

Recapture those who stray. If you see someone averting their gaze, try to focus on them and recapture their interest.

And Three Things Not to Do

Don't tell a joke if you're not a trained comedian—if it falls flat, you'll never get them back.

Don't make a pratfall on the way in—people will lose respect for you and think you're a clown. Don't try to be Dick Van Dyke.

Don't ask for questions from audiences unless you are specifically asked to offer a Q&A session. If you don't know an answer, whatever knowledge or inspiration you've shared in the spectacular talk you're just given could be replaced by doubt about your credibility.

your advances, you now have an option to move yourself closer to him and continue the flirting process.

If you're already at the party and you're in visual range, position yourself with your back to him, about ten to thirty feet away. Look over your shoulder. Make eye contact, smile, look down a couple seconds, look back up and smile again, and then turn your head. Repeat several times if necessary. Men are not as quick as women when picking up body language cues.

That's it! So simple, so effective.

How you'll see it's working: He keeps moving closer to you. And once he makes his move, let him keep making it. Men automatically assume you are flirting with them if you stand too close because they are not good at discerning the difference between friendly behavior and flirting. So the choice is yours. You can either keep your distance and force him to lean in to you, or you can slowly move into his personal space. The thrill of the chase applies even within that very close personal space.

How to Seduce Her

Here's a big secret, guys: women like to be heard. You don't need to pull some crazy pickup line off the Internet—most women will be pleasantly surprised if you just make eye contact, tilt your head and nod when they talk, and actually show some comprehension of the words coming out of their mouths.

Best Signals for Seducing Her

For a complete list, see "Common Signals of Male Sexual Interest" on page 255.

How to use the signals: Sparingly. Believe me, no woman wants to see you touching your chest, licking your lips, running your fingers through your hair, and staring—all at the same time. (She might even think you're a predator.) Remember, women are good at detecting whatever signal you give off. Less is more. If you just focus on making eye contact, and *then watch her response,* she'll take care of letting you know if she's interested.

How you'll see it's working: Pay attention! As I said in the last chapter, the biggest mistake men make in the seduction arena is they don't pay close enough attention to women's signals. If you're interested, keep watching her for those signals. But *never* go into a woman's personal space uninvited unless you are a master manipulator and ladykiller, or you are willing to face the consequences.

Let's say you notice the girl at the bookstore and your heart skips a beat. You can't keep your eyes off her, and your thoughts are wandering to what-ifs. Now's your time to make a move.

If she hasn't noticed you yet, walk over to the section of books she is looking at and look for a title of interest. Stand tall with your body weight equally distributed on both legs while squaring your shoulders (remember, women love dominant men who take up space), attempt to make eye contact, and point your body and feet in the direction of your love interest.

If she hasn't caught your eye yet, subtly pretend you are interested in the book directly in front of her. Smile and politely ask her to shift over so you can reach across her. As you do so, grab the book and perhaps lightly brush up against her, giving you the opportunity to begin a quick conversation with an "Excuse me," perhaps while running your fingers over your lower lip (giving the impression that you are deeply interested in the book and perhaps something else). Remember, both men and women love to feel like you find them fascinating, so maintain eye contact, smile, and nod to encourage continued conversation.

How to Approach a Group

I can't tell you how many of my clients have come to me for help with this one. While many people feel a bit uneasy in a group setting, others have much more anxiety about mixing and mingling. Don't fret—learning certain key signals can help smooth your path.

Best Signals It Is OK to Enter into a Group

The group has three or more people

Uncrossed arms

Eyes scanning the crowd

Open body position

Open palms

Any feet, legs, trunk, or chest pointed away from center of group

How to use the signals: Don't approach a closed group. Many times my clients will say, "I always feel like I'm getting the brush-off at parties." But I have to wonder if they're not reading the group's signals correctly. If all the members of a group are standing with their feet and bodies pointed toward one another, the group is closed, and you're not invited. Don't even attempt to break into a closed group. That's when you experience those painful moments—"Hey, guys, nice party!"—when everyone just turns their heads to you, not their bodies, and stares. Awkward!

How you'll see it's working: Look for an entranceway. If you see at least one person's feet poking out away from the group, that's an entranceway. Take a moment to become aware of your body—elongate your neck, pull back your shoulders, take a deep breath. Then approach the person whose body language is most welcoming. She'll likely invite you right into the group. Allow the other person to start the conversation, even if it's just, "Hey, what's up?" If you launch headlong into a new topic without having a feel for what they've been talking about, you risk being rejected again.

How to Make and Keep True Friends

The best way to make a true friend is to start with some good raw material. You'll likely be doing a lot of mirroring during your time together, so surround yourself with positive people. Moods are contagious—stay clear of negative and draining people.

Best Signals for Building Rapport with Friends

Open body posture

Open palms

Genuine smiles

Making strong eye contact without needing to look away

Feet pointed in their direction

Leaning toward them when you speak

Mirroring movements

Reflecting facial gestures

Nodding

Tilting head

Focused listening, without interruption

Using appropriate turn-taking gestures

Sharing conversation equally

Showing genuine happiness for their successes

Not diverting attention back to yourself

How to use the signals: Listen twice as much as you speak. When you're first getting to know someone, you can achieve several things by listening: (1) you gather a lot of information about her, to decide whether you'd actually like to be her friend; (2) you mirror her facial experiences, which is flattering and bound to endear you to her; and (3) you help her to talk through her problems, which feels very therapeutic for her, reinforcing the good feeling. Make sure to do some talking, though—you don't want to set up a one-way dynamic that will make you feel resentful or make her feel the pressure to keep the conversation going.

How you'll see it's working: When you feel good being around them. As I mentioned in chapter 7, the best indication of a true friend is how you feel when you leave him. Start by picking the people you'd most like to emulate, and then do just that! Benjamin Disraeli said it best: "The greatest good you can do for another is not just to share your riches, but to reveal to him his own."

How to Parent Better

I know how often parents hear, "You are your children's most important model." This is true—research has proven that the body language kids see in their homes will be the body language they use with their friends, teachers, lovers, and future families, for the rest of their lives. If you want them to have strong and healthy relationships, give them lots of positive emotions to mirror and help them label their own emotions, so they can learn how to communicate their thoughts and feelings with honesty and without shame.

Best Signals for Parenting

Open body posture

Uncrossed arms

Open palms

No scowls, smirks, or other sarcastic expressions

Hugs (at least four or more a day)

Showing genuine excitement about your child's accomplishments

Showing delight in your child's physical appearance (no matter what color her hair)

Focused listening without interruption

Mirroring emotions and facial gestures without negating them

Genuine smiles

Feet pointed in your child's direction

Using appropriate turn-taking gestures

Sharing conversation equally

Making strong eye contact

Leaning toward your child when you speak

Mirroring movements

Nodding

Tilting head

Physically getting down to your child's level (on your knees) when speaking to her

How to use the signals: To tune in and understand. You always want your body language to be open whenever you're dealing with a crisis with the child. Whether it's the girl that was left standing at the door with no date or the five-year-old that had an accident in her pants, drop the parent stance—arms crossed, leaning on one leg, that skeptical eyebrow. The kid just thinks, "I'm in trouble *and* I'm being judged."

Beginning with the emotional house of mirrors in their babyhood, your kids need to be seen, heard, and reflected. Don't squash their natural nonverbal expressions with statements like, "Stop crying," or "Wipe that smile off your face." Don't negate their feelings by saying, "That didn't hurt!" or "Come on, cheer up!" This is how we make kids into nonverbal idiots—we don't allow them to accurately label their own feelings, so they become confused and lose their innate ability to express themselves or to read other people.

Instead, get down to their level, look them in the eye, and say things like, "It looks like you're upset—what happened? Do you want to talk about it?" And then, just listen to whatever emotion they're experiencing before you think about what comes next. Make it safe for them to feel their feelings instead of suppressing them with a "stiff upper lip" or a cookie that "makes it feel better."

How you'll see it's working: Your kids are empathetic with others. In the long run, and even in the short run, you'll see that empathy reflected back to you all through your house. First you'll see it in your toddler who tenderly cares for her dolls or pets his dog gently. Then you'll see it in your kindergartener who takes turns and shares well with others. And, perhaps even more gratifying, you'll see it with your older child, who shows tenderness for a special needs kid, or shows his respect with good table manners (which you modeled), or even takes on a larger social cause, because he feels empathy for others' plights. All possible because instead of minimizing his emotions or negating his nonverbal signals, you simply mirrored him back to himself. I think that's pretty cool stuff.

CHAPTER 9

Become a Master Communicator: The Reiman Rapport Method

Sometimes your joy is the source of your smile,
but sometimes your smile can be the source of your joy.
—Thich Nhat Hanh

Many people think social success is about having a great personality or being "the life of the party." Although the ability to entertain other people can be very useful, it doesn't always build rapport. But open, warm, empathetic body language works every time you use it.

You now know how body language can impact every area of your life. You know that the content of spoken words makes up less than 10 percent of the impact of your entire message. You know that all of your individual signals—your posture, walk, smell, smile, and dozens of other body language cues—speak much louder than those words.

But did you know that, out of all of the tens of thousands of possible signals you can send in any interaction, just a small handful could make the difference between fumbling that critical deal or actually getting the "yes," or between parting ways forever with a wonderful person or falling hopelessly in love? It's true.

I've developed a system that will help you build congruent, welcoming, universally pleasing body language, in any situation, with any individual. I call this ten-point system the Reiman Rapport Method. This system will work on anyone from your baby or your lover to your soon-to-be best friend or your prospective boss. Some of these techniques might be familiar to you, some might be new. The trick is to combine them into one powerful system that you can apply to every interaction.

Over the years, I've taught elements of this system to scores of people. I've consistently found that any time two human beings are in a room together, using these ten key signals will bring them closer and keep them "in sync," often for life. Doesn't that sound useful?

I usually recommend that you take at least one week, and ideally three weeks, to master each step of the Reiman Rapport Method before you add on the next. Taking your time like this will make these changes permanent habits, which is what you're striving for. Practice several times a day—at least three to five. Develop these skills, make each one an instinctive habit, and you may never have to think about your body language again—you'll automatically be sending out the right signals. You'll have become a true Master Communicator.

1. Relax Your Face

Throughout the book, we've learned how our mirror systems make moods extremely contagious. Just seeing and sensing other people's anxiety makes us nervous; as a result, we tend to avoid insecure people because we find them unsettling. To put people at ease and start to build rapport, your primary mood should be one of confident relaxation. And a smooth forehead is one of the main ways your face tells other people you are relaxed.

Before you head into a meeting or a party, take a moment to focus on your face. Your face sets the tone for your body, so use the following technique to smooth and relax your face. You can think of this skill as both a way to communicate confident body language and as an "off" switch for your own anxiety.

Take a nice slow, deep breath and allow the breath to release fully and completely. Relax your scalp and send that relaxation down into the forehead; feel the forehead smoothing out softly and completely. Allow relaxation to move down toward your eyelids, sending that relaxation sweeping across your cheeks and down into your mouth. Make sure your teeth aren't clenched together and relax your chin and jaw—your entire face relaxes, and you feel good. Follow up with the following mantra: "Scalp, forehead, eyelids, cheeks, mouth, jaw."

2. Create Clear Symmetry in Your Body

Once your face is relaxed, the next step in creating rapport is to align your body in a balanced symmetry that conveys attractiveness, health, and a confident calm. As we discussed in the first impressions chapter, when you first meet someone, it is especially important to keep your body straight and tall, with your weight balanced equally on both feet, your arms at your sides. Visualize the vertebrae of your spine as a stack of dice, one on top of another. Elongate your neck, drop your shoulders, and draw in your belly button. Lift your chin, but make sure not to lift it so far that your nose is positioned at a snooty angle. Instead, strive to keep your chin parallel to the floor—that will convey confidence and steadiness. Keep your body posture open—crossing your arms or legs throws off the symmetry and makes you appear closed off. Finally, always make sure your feet are symmetrical with your upper body in that they point to the person with whom you're speaking.

This body language signal indicates powerful interest, and in itself will make the other person feel heard and valued.

3. Flash Your Social Smile

A good smile shows you're confident, in control, and feel good about yourself; it's one of your most versatile body language tools. Studies have shown that people will unconsciously return a smile when one is offered, touching off a biochemical cascade of pleasurable feelings inside both of you.

We'd all love to have reasons to flash genuine smiles all day long, but you'll need a forced or "social" smile in other settings, so you may as well have one prepared for that purpose. Social smiles, when they look phony, can be off-putting. That's why you have to craft your social smile as carefully as you would put together your résumé—it's equally, if not more, important to your career and your earning potential.

Start by looking in the mirror, which can be hard because often we're so self-conscious about smiling. Make your widest, cheesiest grin and see how that looks. Then work smaller until you find a "size" of smile that feels comfortable and is not strained. Make sure you smile broadly enough to mimic some characteristics of the genuine smile, such as a crinkle in your crow's-feet and a slight lift in your cheeks, but not so broadly that it exposes your gums. Smile with your eyes—you'll feel your eyes close slightly when you get it right. Make tweaks to diminish any nostril flaring or to compensate for any imbalances in your facial features. (For example, when I smile a genuine smile, one of my eyes looks bigger than the other. So I've worked on minimizing this trait in my social smile.)

Once you have a social smile you like, practice it as often as you can. Smile on and off for five minutes, at least three or four times a day, both in the bathroom mirror or while you're driving or at your desk at work. (Some people even hang a mirror next to their phone so they can practice it at their desk. If you smile while talking on the phone, people will hear that in your voice. It's a bonus!)

If you practice this as often as I suggest, you'll likely enjoy a side benefit of feeling more positive. Simply activating the muscles in your face that are used for smiling has been associated with improved mood. Practice often, and your muscles will become so "used to" this smile, you'll automatically use it in all social situations.

4. Perfect Your Handshake

We first talked about the one perfect handshake in chapter 4, "The Languages of Space and Touch" (see "Touch Signal: The Handshake" on pages 162–165). Did you work on that yet? The handshake will serve you well in every social and business situation, but you need to be sure you're making the right moves.

As a reminder:

Go toward the person you are greeting, lean slightly forward, look him in the eye, extend your right hand horizontally, and simultaneously introduce yourself. (Step in, reach forward, hands meet: "Hi, Tonya Reiman, nice to meet you," as the hand pumps up and down two or three times.) Always make sure the handshake is done with the right hand, never *the left. If you are carrying items in your right hand, shift them to the left. The only exception would be a broken or missing arm.*

Be sure to offer your full palm and have it meet theirs entirely. Your grip should feel easy and comfortable, the same pressure as if you were trying to hold hands with them. This grip suggests self-confidence and enthusiasm. All parts of your body should be pointed toward the person. Try to align your right eye with his or her right eye.

If you keep your thumb pointing straight up, you'll ensure a neutral handshake. Your elbow should be slightly bent. If your elbow is straight, you might be too far away from the person. Don't just shake the wrist or the fingers, but the entire arm. To finish, open your hand wide and re-

lease the entire hand at the same time. The whole handshake should not last more than two to three seconds.

Practice this handshake with a close friend several times a day for three weeks, or until you have it down. When you're greeting a stranger or an associate, always extend your hand first. You'll unconsciously be seen as the person who's in control of the situation, a person who is confident, warm, and welcoming.

5. Nod, Mirror, and Lead

Every human has a basic need to feel heard and be seen. This hunger to see ourselves reflected back to us begins during infancy, when we enter an emotional house of mirrors with our parents. When we receive this same kind of warm attention and reflection as an adult, we bond deeply with the other person. We become a team that is more likely to seek a solution that provides benefits for both of us, whether that would be an agreement to be best friends, or set up a lunch date, or just sign a contract.

You can very quickly tap in to another's innate desire to be heard and acknowledged by simply nodding. Close attention is such a rarity in today's world that any kind of focused listening can feel like a balm to your soul. A nod tells the other person, literally, "I hear you," and the muscular movement itself also predisposes your brain to feel positive about the other person. That feeling will be evident in your microexpressions, which the speaker will "hear," feel even more appreciated, and thereby experience more enhanced rapport!

To allow the nod to help bolster rapport, try to nod two to three times at least every 30 to 45 seconds while the other person is talking. Slow down, focus on their words, and try not to think about how you'll respond until it's your turn to speak. It's better that you respond with a bit of a pregnant pause to collect your thoughts than it is to be visibly thinking of your response instead of listening. (Side note: Make it a personal rule to *never* interrupt. Any interruption, even if it is to agree with someone, basically says, "My thoughts are more important than your thoughts.")

Similar to the nod is the body language mirror—when you mirror someone's actions and emotions back to them, they will feel affirmed. At the start of the conversation, take note of their body posture—where are their feet pointed? What do they do with their hands? Wait a few minutes, and then subtly mirror their body with similar, but not identical, movements. If someone takes a drink of water, you don't have to take a drink of water—if you pick up a fork, you're still mirroring enough to build rapport. Also, try to mirror the speed of their speech—a slow talker gets very thrown by a fast talker, and vice versa.

Bear in mind that, just as when you unconsciously adopt a bit of a southern drawl when you speak with someone from Alabama, your body will sometimes naturally start to mirror someone else—if you relax, stay open to their body language, and let it guide yours. But once you've mastered basic mirroring, you can move onto advanced mirroring skills, such as matching breathing and even blink rate. (See sidebar "The Mirror Master," on page 286.)

The last aspect of this technique is to lead, which you'll do to determine if rapport has truly been established. After several minutes of mirroring, you will attempt to lead. Lead by making a movement that is different from what your conversational partner is doing—if you both have your arms folded, you will unfold yours and place them on the arms of your chair, for example. If they follow you, you are in rapport. If not, keep trying—you'll get there.

6. Use Strong, Contained Hand Gestures

Hand gestures have a great impact on our interpretation of spoken ideas. Studies have found that people remember verbal messages much more clearly when they are accompanied by hand gestures. If

The Mirror Master

Advanced Rapport Techniques

Once you've developed the ability to mirror someone else's body movements, gestures, and speech, you can move on to two more advanced mirroring techniques that work even more covertly to build rapport.

To mirror breathing: Use the first few minutes of the encounter to get a read on his breathing patterns. (Rapid breathing at the start might be due to nerves—if you mirrored that, he would never calm down!) Subtly glance at his torso to diagnose a chest or belly breather. Then just match his style. You don't have to inhale every time he inhales, but if he's taking short, shallow chest breaths, do that. If he's taking long belly breaths, do that. You will eventually sync with each other.

To mirror blinking: If you're such a master that all the other mirroring techniques have become second nature, you can try to mirror blinking. Just as with breathing, take the first few minutes to get a sense of how often he blinks and then match his rate. He'll unconsciously read your blinking as a reflection of his own state of mind. Fair warning: Matching the blink rate is very difficult and can easily backfire. Do not attempt unless you are truly a Master Communicator!

you tend to keep your hands in your lap when you speak, you're in danger of fading into the wallpaper! You need to develop a set of gestures that feels comfortable for you, so you give your verbal messages more power.

As with the other skills in the Reiman Rapport Method, practice is key. Every day, take a few paragraphs of text from the newspaper or the Internet and do an interpretative reading of it, as if you were standing in front of a small group. Experiment with different styles of hand gestures to find out what feels most comfortable for you. You want your hand gestures to feel natural but polished, just like your social smile.

Keep your hands open and your palms exposed. Use gestures to punctuate your points, and keep your hands within an imaginary box that stretches from hipline to chin and shoulder to shoulder. (Of course, a few inches past the shoulders on either side is still seen as professional, but don't go far beyond that.) Don't let your gestures fly above your chin on a regular basis—they would be seen as erratic and flamboyant. In fact, don't overdo it in general—overgesticulators are seen as silly, scatterbrained, and unprofessional. On the other hand, people who use contained gestures that match their speech patterns convey energy, original ideas, and fluent thinking.

There may be moments during a sales call when you want to make an authoritative gesture, such as when you're trying to stress your expertise. For example, when you're making your best pitch about why your product makes an important difference in someone's life, it's OK to use the palm-down gesture, which says, "I'm the expert on this part of the discussion." Then you could flip your palms over to turn the discussion over to them, to indicate that you're open to everything. Gestures that match your words help to underscore your message and make you seem that much more trustworthy.

7. Vary Your Vocal Pitch

Many factors affect paralanguage, the messages other than speech that we send with our voice, such as loudness, rate, tone, nasality, and many other qualities. One in particular—your pitch—has a great impact on how others view you. Voices with lower pitch are universally preferred over shrill, high-pitched voices because high pitch is associated with anxiety. When we're under stress, all of our muscles contract, including our vocal cords. On the other hand, while a low pitch is usually associated with confidence, a consistently low-pitched monotone voice will make you sound low-energy and depressed. That's part of the reason why men and women who *vary* their pitch are thought of as more dynamic and extroverted. Try some of these tips to help you vary your vocal pitch to keep your listener interested and your conversation lively.

First, use a digital recorder to tape a few of your daily gesture-practice readings. Note the normal pitch variation in your voice—do you need to work on this? Then when you sing along to the radio, raise and lower your voice by an octave above and below your natural voice, to help you develop greater range.

When we're nervous, many of us breathe shallowly into our chest, but the voice originates in the diaphragm, not the chest. To access the diaphragm fully, allow your belly button to expand on the inhale, contract on the exhale. Before you enter a meeting, take five deep, slow belly breaths. Continue breathing from the belly during the meeting, and try to pace yourself so you retain control over your voice.

8. Respect Their Personal Space

Staking out territory is one of our most basic instincts. We all have a fundamental need to control our own little environment, the personal bubble that extends two to three feet away from our body. Unless you're interacting with a dear friend, lover, or family member, take extreme caution in "penetrating" this bubble. When we're approached in an intimate way, especially in North America and Northern Europe, where personal zones of space are larger than in countries farther south, we can feel threatened or manipulated on a primal level. When you reach out to touch a recent acquaintance on the arm, if that person is what I call a "mush"—a touchy-feely person, like me—he won't mind a bit. (In fact, he'll probably do it to you first.) But the people who mind will *really* mind—and if you've already made the first move and entered their personal space, you may have just blown all of your prior efforts to develop rapport.

Bottom line, wait for the other person's signal—a touch on the arm, an approach from them—before you enter his personal space. And once he's sent you that signal, use that permission wisely. For example, you might want to touch the person immediately before you make a key point to help it stick. Look him in the eyes, state your point, and simultaneously use your pointer finger and middle finger to touch his forearm. And then smoothly withdraw your hand—don't let it linger for more than two or three seconds.

Just a touch or two the first time you meet is plenty. If you establish rapport in other ways, you'll have time enough for hugs further down the road.

9. Anchor Good Feelings

Let's say you've spent a few minutes accumulating "yes" hits. Or maybe you've already had a few positive experiences with someone, and you're ready to solidify your relationship with her. You might be ready to cement that rapport with what's called an "anchor."

An anchor is a mental association that links one strong emotional memory with another object, gesture, touch, smell, or sound. (Think of the music in the shower scene in *Psycho*—that's a big anchor of fear for a lot of people!) Your objective is to link a positive emotion within your friend to something about yourself—a word you say, a touch on the forearm, a gesture you make. Then any time you make the same movement or say the same word, the anchor is triggered again, and positive associations about you will flood back. Here's how it can work:

Let's say you're talking to a friend, and she recalls a moment of intense joy—the moment when she first held her newborn baby, for example. You ask her to recall the memory in as much vivid detail as possible, really digging into the specifics of the evening—you want her to come as close to reexperiencing that moment as possible. Just as she is at the emotional peak of her recollection, you can create an anchor by touching her on the forearm or shoulder or saying something somewhat louder than normal: "*Wow,* that's amazing!" Once the anchor is created, you'll be able to trigger that emotion again and again, simply by repeating that same initial statement or touch. That doesn't mean you should sit there and pat her constantly, but it does mean that when you want to make a real point, that's when touch will be most effective.

Anchoring works best when the person you are trying to bond with is in the moment of extreme joy, not just recollecting it. Those experiences do not happen often with acquaintances, but they (hopefully) happen all the time with friends and family. Use that moment when your child finishes a big project or wins a trophy to anchor his feelings of pride and accomplishment with a warm hug, a thumbs-up, or a kiss on the forehead.

Anchors are often the product of spontaneous moments of shared laughter. My daughter and I both get grossed out quite easily, and in the past my husband has humorously tormented me over meals by saying things such as "Oink oink" when we eat ham or "Mooooo" when we eat hamburgers, silly stuff that gives him pleasure. One day while we were eating steak, my husband murmured something softly under his breath, and in the loudest possible voice my son, Christian, said, "Dad, why did you just say 'charred animal flesh'?" My husband let out a howl so loud the entire family cracked up, I mean hysterical belly laughing over three simple words. Now, a couple of years later, no matter where we are, who we are with, or what we are doing, if any of us says the words "charred animal flesh," we all laugh. Why? Because those three silly words became anchored to a specific experience the entire family shared. It became a private joke that no one else understood (until now), and that anchor now arouses a specific emotion in our family members—happiness.

Do you want to anchor confidence in your child? I use this in my hypnosis practice with adults and children all the time. Follow the above steps of eliciting a story from your child or by being in the moment. . . . When your child is at the peak moment in the experience or memory of the experience, have them put their thumb and forefinger together and say a word that resonates with them. For example, your child is on the baseball team, but lacks confidence in his ability to hit the ball. Either bring him to a moment when he hit the ball or let him imagine he is hitting the ball by running through a visualization of him at a game, walking up to the plate, picking up his bat, adjusting his hat, practicing his swing before the pitcher actually throws the ball, and then *whack* . . . he smacks the ball out of the park, getting a home run. When he is right in the midst of feeling the thrill of that home run, immediately have him put his thumb and forefinger together while repeating the phrase "home run" to himself several times. Do this over and over again, as often as possible. Eventually, with some practice, each time he goes up to the plate and puts his thumb and forefinger together as he murmurs "home run" to himself, he will have the confidence to crack the ball out of the park. This works for everything from studying for exams to meeting new kids.

I often anchor feelings of disgust in cigarettes for clients who come to me wanting to quit smoking. It is as simple as allowing them to reach a hypnotic state and then offering them the anchor/suggestion that each and every time they think about smoking, they will think the words *horrible, disgusting,* and *dirty.* This is a very effective way to push someone away from a cigarette. Of course, with a habit, there is a little more to it than this, but this is the basic premise.

Anchoring is just one of the many reasons I recommend that everyone touch their friends and relatives more. Not only are we a touch-starved nation, we're missing out on so many opportunities to create positive, adaptive anchors that we can use again and again to reinforce positive emotions and warm connections.

10. Create a Plan of Action (POA)

Throughout the book, we've talked about many of the ways the mirror system plays a huge role in communication. We've seen how the mirror neuron (the Swiss Army knife of body language) helps us imitate, understand, and anticipate the actions, feelings, and motivations of others. In this final rapport-building skill, we'll again draw on the mirror neuron to help us with one of the things it does best—recalling past feelings to help us create new ones. This final rapport-building technique taps the mirror system to combine all of the first nine Reiman Rapport Method signals into one useful tool that will help you master any anticipated event or encounter.

In the same way that the mirror neuron helps the pianist perfect her Bach concerto or the basketball player ace his jump shot, the mirror neuron can also help us practice every body language aspect of an anticipated event. The Plan of Action is like a step-by-step recipe for a positive experience you want to happen in the future. You'll use the POA to "fake it till you make it," rehearse an encounter so many times that your brain and body feel like you've already experienced it. Let's see how this works.

Let's say you're going to a group interview, which you absolutely dread. To prepare you POA, you'll first do research. You'll drive to the office and scope out the entrance; call the switchboard for the proper pronunciation of the name of everyone you will be meeting; do a Google search to learn more about each individual's background. (It goes without saying that you'll also do all of the prep work in chapter 6, "Mastering First Impressions," from whitening your teeth to shining your shoes!)

Taking all this information into account, you'll script out some responses to the interviewers' anticipated questions. And then, you'll create your POA, which might go something like this:

I'm walking through the door, smiling. My arms and legs are in sync. I introduce myself and ask to be announced. I remain standing with my weight equally placed on both legs, my briefcase in one hand. I look at a sample of the company literature while I wait. I see the interviewer striding down the hall. I meet her eyes, smile, and move toward her. She extends her hand, and I say my name as I shake it. . . .

. . . When they ask me to talk about my last job, I say, "What a great question. I'd love to talk about that. I had a wonderful experience at Acme Corporation. Perhaps I could talk specifically about the accomplishments I had at Acme that have prepared me to succeed in growing your business at Beeswax Company. One of the things I'm most proud of . . ."

. . . When we come to the end of the interview, I stand up and smoothly button up my suit jacket. I smile and, if appropriate, move toward the person closest to me to begin my good-byes. I look into the first person's eyes, extend my hand, shake, and say, "It was so nice to meet you" and say his or her name. Then I move to the next person, and say, "Thanks again for having me" and I say his or her name. I extend my hand to each person in turn, repeating their names. I say good-bye to the group and stride confidently and purposefully to the exit, say good-bye to the receptionist, and walk directly to my car.

You'll recite the entire sequence of the POA out loud to yourself, picturing the events clearly in your mind. Repeat the full sequence at least four or five times a day during the week leading up to the anticipated event. By the time you get to the interview, you'll feel right at home.

I've used the example of a job interview here, but you can do a POA for any encounter—when you want to make the best impression at a party, ask someone out, campaign for a raise, anything. Even after hundreds of speaking engagements, I still do this. I'll arrive at the venue an hour early, go into the speaking hall, stand on the stage, and scream out into the room, "Hello, everybody! I'm Tonya Reiman!" By visualizing myself in that setting in front of the crowd, I make that room my own.

You can also use this technique to help you enforce any body language skill or situation you might struggle with. For example, you could create a generic first-impressions POA—"walk in sync, chin up high, nice natural smile, making eye contact"—that you can draw on every time you enter a room.

Or, if you were having trouble with an intimidating bully of a boss, your POA could be something like this:

> *When my boss comes into my office, I do not allow her to stand over me in my personal space. As soon as she comes through the doorway, I stand up and move to greet her. If she suggests that we sit, I take a seat and angle myself toward the door. If she makes a move into my personal space, I hold my ground. If she makes a negative remark, I do not respond defensively and do not break eye contact. I return her gaze calmly, with my shoulders down and my forehead relaxed.*

You might not get many opportunities to try these scenarios out in real time, but you can practice them as many times as you want in your head. When you visualize a scenario over and over again, you trick your brain into believing that the event has already happened. When the big day finally happens, it will feel like old hat, and the real event will flow much easier.

A POA allows you to "prime" yourself to react in ways that you've predetermined will serve your purpose. Instead of falling back on instinctive reactions or habits that don't serve you, you'll be in control. No matter what body language gets thrown at you, you will remember your POA, and you will be able to respond accordingly.

I've chosen the POA as the capstone for the Reiman Rapport Method, because I've seen how it can transform people's use of body language into a tool not only for building rapport but also for creating amazing positive transformation in their own lives. People who had previously been crippled by social anxiety have used the POA to come out of their shells and build supportive networks of friends. Others who had stagnated in their careers used the POA to catapult themselves into the next level of excellence. Whenever I work with a new client on their POA, I recall that expression: "If you can see it, you can achieve it." If you can visualize becoming a Master Communicator, you can most certainly become one, too. Come visit me at www.BodyLanguageUniversity.com to share your story.

Appendix: Frequently Asked Questions

Q: I always seem to talk too fast and interrupt others when I'm in conversation. I think I do it because I'm trying to get my point across, and I'm afraid I won't get the chance. Do you have any tips for me?

The most useful tip in all situations is to be self-aware. You already know you have this tendency, which is a huge step in the right direction. Talking over others shows a tremendous lack of respect and can get you into trouble in all of your relationships. But armed with this knowledge and enough careful attention, you can prevent this tendency.

First, practice speaking in slow sentences while you are alone. Once a day, read aloud and at a slow speed a short paragraph of text from the newspaper, a magazine, or a book. Fully articulate each word and rest for a beat between sentences. As with so many aspects of body language, this practice will train you and help your body remember the feeling of speaking more slowly, so you can tap this feeling the next time you're conversing.

Also, before you're about to start a conversation—either before you pick up the phone, or before you head into a meeting or a party—take three minutes to do some deep breathing to help you relax, slow your heart rate, and neutralize any anxiety or impatience. Create a mental phrase you can use to remind yourself to speak slowly and let the other person finish his thoughts before you interrupt. Try something like, "Patient, calm, attentive."

Finally, really listen to what the other person is saying. Force yourself to hear each word and allow him to continue talking without using your voice to interrupt. If the other person goes on for a while, you can use nonverbal signals to indicate you're ready to speak—such as shifting slightly in your chair, or breaking eye contact more often—but don't allow yourself to break in verbally. You might even pinch yourself gently on the palm when you get the urge to interrupt—that can disrupt the compulsion and help you to refocus on the give-and-take of the conversation.

Q: I'm interested in a guy at work, but every time I go to speak to him he backs away from me. What can I do to see if he likes me?

First, I would never recommend dating someone at work. Secondly, if you want to maintain even a decent working relationship, I would suggest keeping some distance between him and yourself. Whenever I hear someone is backing away from another person, I automatically assume he feels that the other person has entered into his personal space, which is a definite no-no. Most people experience a visceral reaction to protect themselves when their personal space is breached. To be safe, just steer clear until he approaches you.

Q: Every time I have all the attention in the room on me (when I have to make a speech, for example), I am always so nervous. To make matters worse, I feel like everybody notices my nervousness! How can I hide that? What should I do—or not do—to act more confident in front of people?

You have no idea how common this problem is. Very few people are extremely confident in situations in which all eyes are upon them. Luckily, there are a few quick techniques you can employ to feel and appear more confident. All of these movements look very powerful to the outside observer, but these movements also cause biochemical changes in your body that tell your brain that you *are* more confident. Try this:

1. Pull your shoulders back and down, feel your shoulder blades lower, and elongate your neck.

2. Push your chest slightly forward, just the amount it would rise in a deep breath.
3. Pull your stomach in lightly, sending your navel toward your back—just enough to support your back, but not enough to make you feel breathless.
4. Maintain eye contact with your audience, shifting your gaze around the room until you feel you've visually connected with nearly every person in the room.
5. Don't hide behind a podium—your audience might get the impression you are hiding from them. If given a choice, do not use a podium.
6. Keep your hands visible to the audience.
7. Use economical gestures to punctuate points, but do not overgesticulate (too much gesturing conveys nervousness).
8. Stand straight up with your legs steady and your weight equally balanced on each leg.
9. Always smile—a smile screams confidence and will always make you feel better, in any situation.
10. Consider using a self-hypnosis CD to help you increase self-confidence. It really works!

Q: What are some of the most common body language flaws you have witnessed?

Here are just a few common ones; a full list would be much, much longer!

Getting into others' personal space

"Closing" body language due to nervousness—crossing arms or legs, or pointing body and/or feet away from the conversation

Slumping onto a large chair instead of sitting up straight

Not enough eye contact, or sometimes too much eye contact—what I call the "stalker stare"

Looking angry, which is sometimes also caused by nervousness and not having a "ready and relaxed face" (people need to learn how to relax the entire face, but especially the lips)

Adjusting clothes during the interview, or perhaps a woman adjusting her panty hose

Q: What does it mean when someone constantly shifts and moves around?

Shifting from one foot to another usually indicates a high level of anxiety. This could mean someone is lying to you, or it could mean she is just plain nervous. The same conclusions can be drawn when someone crosses and then uncrosses legs, or crosses the left over the right and then changes to right over left. Sure, that person's legs could be tired from staying in one position. Or, she could be worried that her spouse has found a questionable e-mail on his computer, and still be unsure as to what the outcome will be. Either way, be aware that when other people are watching you, they will perceive this type of shifting as uneasiness, which will often lead them to question your capabilities as well as their trust in your competence. In every situation, you are always best served by using smooth, steady movements and keeping your body posture balanced on both sides.

(One exception: Any parent could tell you that if you see this type of movement in a preschooler, it's likely that you're viewing an emerging bathroom emergency!)

Q: I'm curious if you are familiar with what some experts describe as the unconscious hello.

An unconscious hello is typically a way of responding to or initiating a "hello" with your face and/or head as well as your body. Typically these hellos are unintentional ways of breaking the ice, but with just a bit of practice on your part, the habit of remaining open to and initiating the unconscious hello can become a fantastic, very versatile networking tool that works in any setting.

To me, the unconscious hello could be simply the nod of a head, a smile, eye contact, turning your body toward someone, or even opening your arms or legs in the direction of someone who sees you. You're basically saying, "I acknowledge you," to the other person, which opens the door to further communication, be it verbal or just more exchanged glances or smiles. When you share an unconscious hello, it's almost as if you've met that person without having to invest the time to introduce yourself!

If you think about your office or neighborhood, you probably can picture several people whom you "know" but with whom you've never actually had a conversation. It's likely that you two "met" with an initial unconscious hello, which then turned into a standard nonverbal greeting (a wave or a more deliberate nod) in subsequent encounters. Consciously developing this habit will help you vastly expand your circle of acquaintances and can turn you into one of those people of whom others say, "Seems like a really good person."

Q. Are recruiters aware of a candidate's body language?

Yes. Some recruiters pick it up unconsciously, and others study it consciously. I have taught classes to managers on how to look for specific signs during interviews. The astute ones who are aware of the significance of body language will usually be looking for specific movements that indicate confidence, such as direct eye contact, obvious interest, high energy level, courteousness, and honest signals such as open palms and uncrossed arms. The ones who do not consciously pick up these signals will just get a "feel" for a candidate. This is why interviewees have to realize that important hiring decisions are sometimes made within the first few minutes.

Q: I am a researcher for a major company. On occasion we scientists are asked to present our work to the division. Usually all the high-level directors are there, along with other management types, including the vice president. I wish I didn't have to, but I must ask—why will the VP not keep his fingers out of his nose? Is he feeling bored and

showing his disrespect for our research, or is this just a very bad habit that he can't break?
It's hard to give you an answer on this because I do not have access to any accompanying gestures. However, I will tell you that most often nose pickers are simply in the habit of picking their nose. Nose picking does tend to occur most often when someone is bored, and to demonstrate that they are not intimidated by social norms. But for some, it becomes a compulsive habit that they cannot break.

If I were you, in the absence of other proof, I would take it as a positive sign. Perhaps he is so absorbed in the presentation that he's not even aware of what he's doing. Or, maybe he is a nervous nose picker, and your intellectual prowess intimidates him! Regardless, you cannot change his behavior and you certainly can't call attention to it, so you'd be better off to create an explanation that plays in your favor and move on. Better to have him pick his nose than pick apart your research!

Q: Is it true that men who put their thumbs in their belt loops are more prone to be perverts?
The infamous thumbs-in-belt gesture is rather forward. However, it is not an intentional sign of aggression. Typically a man will use this to emphasize the area he feels is significant for a woman to notice; it allows him to demonstrate what he believes to be his dominant status. It is not, however, directly related to sexual deviance, just sexuality in general.

Q: I have a problem. In general, people take an immediate dislike to me before I have even spoken. I can sense the atmosphere. Please don't say it's my imagination. I often think maybe I give off bad vibrations, and they detect it.
I won't say it's your imagination, but I will say that it's something you can change. I'm sure that if you're picking up on this kind of

reaction, you're likely mirroring that rejected feeling back to other people, and that exchange alone is going to perpetuate the cycle even more. So let's start at the beginning. Even if your original premise were true—that you give off "bad vibes"—you can change this. "Bad vibes" are usually just the combination of unintentionally negative body language signals. Perhaps the natural set of your face is a scowl. When you enter a room, you might not be thinking about anything negative, but because the relaxed position of your face gives off a negative signal, people presume that you are not friendly. Take a few minutes every day to practice shifting your face into an open, gentle smile. Simply tip the corners of your mouth up instead of down—not fake or blindingly toothy, just relaxed and pleasant. Look at yourself in the mirror as you do it—what does your face feel like? Try to memorize that feeling and make it a habit to consciously duplicate this social smile every time you enter any room containing other people. That could be all you need to do to turn things around.

Once you've practiced and perfected your social smile, go back and review chapter 6, "Mastering First Impressions." When meeting people for the first time, everything from the tone of your voice to the eye contact you make and the way you hold your body will make the difference between your making the cut as a "yes" or being discarded as a "no." Go through that chapter and tackle one facet a week, practicing it the way you did your new social smile, until you build an unbeatable first impression.

One more thing: Because you've encountered this kind of reception in the past, you may be unconsciously expecting to be rejected every time you enter a similar situation. That's a psychological barrier that you'll have to force yourself to knock down. Create a personal mantra that you can tap in this situation, something like, "Confident, open, happy." Repeat it to yourself as you practice your smile, so you can draw on it as a reminder every time you flash your new social smile.

Q: What kind of an impact does chewing gum have on a first impression?

Overall, chewing gum indicates anxiety and frustration. Does that mean everyone who chews gum is anxious and frustrated? No, but it does mean that they might be perceived that way.

When you chew gum, you're basically saying, "I have extra energy that I don't know what to do with—I chew gum to help me control myself." These days, stars like Britney Spears, Drew Barrymore, and Tom Cruise constantly chew gum in front of the cameras. And research by Professor Andrew Scholey from the Northumbria University in the U.K. found that chewing gum might actually help you think more quickly by increasing the levels of oxygen and glucose available to the brain. But most would agree that whether you chomp with an open mouth or gently nibble, there's no way to chew gum and look relaxed or smart (or even sexy) at the same time.

Bottom line: If you're concerned about your breath, use breath strips, suck on a small mint, or give your mouth a quick rinse before meeting others. If you have come to depend on the act of chewing gum to stem anxiety, it's no longer a fun treat—it's a crutch. By all means, enjoy it discreetly or when you're alone to help you concentrate, but to project the best image to others, skip the gum.

Q: I am a poker player. Do you have any pointers on body language that would help tell me when a person is bluffing? I am sometimes able to get a read on other players by being observant and using my experience, but I am always looking for new tells.

In chapter 7, "Reading Their Secret Signals," you learned how to norm people. Use that technique at the beginning of a game so you can determine how the other players typically react to a winning hand versus a losing hand. Find their norms and begin to look for the cues that indicate deception, discomfort, and uneasiness. Keep in mind that when we know we are being watched, we become self-aware. The body recognizes that it can be read easily, so movements often become jerky and strained in an attempt to keep all the secrets inside. Look for signals that demonstrate incongruence, such as hands and arms being perfectly still, but legs and toes jazzing and tapping. Watch for the easy things to detect, such as changes in breathing patterns. Is she breathing shallowly because she is excited about her hand, or does she normally breathe shallowly? Has his swallowing increased, demonstrating that he is feeling anxious about something? Is she touching her face more than usual, a sign that might indicate she is holding back information? Are there any beads of sweat on her forehead, indicating anxiety? Have you noticed that he is blinking much more rapidly than earlier, or perhaps suddenly attempting not to blink at all? Watch players when they first pick up their hands; do you notice any fleeting expressions of glee or anger crossing their faces? Are their pupils dilating due to the excitement of a good hand? Where do they look immediately after they look at their cards—do they look at you with a smile, or do they look toward the exit, unconsciously indicating their wish for escape? Can you see them physically writhing under the pressure of a bad hand? Finally, do they subconsciously lick their lips in anticipation of a big pot? There are many, many cues, but these are just a few to look out for when playing cards.

A poker player friend of mine swears by Paul Ekman's *Unmasking the Face.* When his landmark work on universal facial expressions was revealed in the mid-twentieth century, it was a watershed moment in our field. Ekman also created a system that allows for the detection and categorization of countless fleeting expressions of human emotion. Once learned, this system—called the Facial Action Coding System (FACS)—reveals another world of people's hidden thoughts, and can be very helpful in a number of situations.

Q: Can your body language be too aggressive?

The cardinal rule in body language is never to disregard the feelings of your listener. Few people enjoy being bullied; no interaction benefits when one party feels unfairly overpowered by another. Your goal is always to establish rapport first. Then, and only then, can you attempt to sway your listener with *assertive*, not aggressive, body language.

When you use aggressive body language, you're telling the other person that you are superior and that yours is the only opinion that matters. When you use assertive body language, you acknowledge the worthiness of both parties' points of view while you remain confident about your right to support your own argument.

Once you have established rapport, you can easily lead someone into the following body stances to ensure a relaxed yet productive conversation:

1. While the other person sums up his position, practice good listening to understand his position fully and gather information to which you can directly respond in your rebuttal. (As a general rule, ensure that no matter who you are speaking with, they always feel heard and respected.)

2. Maintain eye contact, a relaxed face, and balanced, vertical posture; don't lean forward or otherwise enter the other person's personal space any farther than you had during your initial approach.

3. When you start to speak, never be forceful or overly loud; in fact, keep your voice low and steady, without a trace of strain.

4. Begin to make your point by first acknowledging the validity of the other person's thoughts on the matter (or at least his feelings about them) with open expressions, such as "I can see your point." Then say, "Here's my thinking," and state your case. During the meat of your argument,

steadily hold his gaze and, especially as you make your most salient points, touch him briefly on the hand or forearm. End with a genuine smile if appropriate. This kind of assertive communication will get you much further than trying to overpower someone with consciously aggressive body language. Don't forget that when most animals, especially humans, are cornered, they will fight back.

Q: What is the difference between manipulation and your methods of building rapport?

Very little, actually.

Q: What's a "halo effect"?

The halo effect is the generally positive feeling we develop toward someone or something based on an unrelated, irrelevant attribute or feature. For example, multiple studies have shown that most people believe individuals who wear eyeglasses are more intelligent than those who do not—but in reality, are eyeglasses really a sign of anything other than bad vision? Another example: I might decide that a particular brand of handbag is higher quality or worth more than an equally priced item simply because I saw a picture of a celebrity who was photographed carrying that particular handbag into the grocery store.

The halo effect exists everywhere you look. Judges give lighter sentences to more attractive defendants; tall men are perceived as more powerful than shorter men; women with smaller breasts and brown hair are perceived as smarter than women with larger breasts and blond hair. The halo effect is the engine of the advertising industry—it creates associations that tap in to our primal desire to mirror higher-status associates and have them mirror us. (If I buy this bag, I'll be more like [fill in your favorite movie star here]—and then she'll be more "like me.") In our consumer culture, the examples of the halo effect go on and on.

Q: My friend told me that if a person crosses his arms he is being unconsciously defensive—do you agree?

My professional opinion is . . . maybe. Perhaps the individual is just cold. Perhaps this is a comfortable stance for him, and it is just a habit. However, you can never use one signal—such as arm crossing—as the sole basis for determining someone's feelings. You must always look for clusters of signals and postures.

To determine if a person is truly defensive, start off by taking in the context of the situation. Is there another reason he is folding his arms? Is it cold in the room? (If the person is a woman, she might be trying to cover her stiffened nipples.) Is he mirroring the body language of someone else? Once you have ruled out these questions, look for other defensive signals: Is his chin down? Is he leaning back instead of standing up straight or leaning forward? Are his eyes "slitlike"? Does he appear overly rigid in his stance? Is he standing with his legs crossed as well as his arms? All of these signals together could almost certainly indicate defensiveness, but one of them in isolation could have a completely innocuous explanation.

Linking signals together is the only way you can get an accurate read on an individual's state of mind.

Q: What body language signs can I look for that love may be fading? I am getting a sinking feeling that my husband is cheating on me, but I don't know how to confirm it. Can I do that with body language?

The only way to confirm adultery with any degree of certainty is to have it on camera or video. However, short of hiring a private investigator, there are a few signs you can look for.

- Does he willingly hug you anymore? When he hugs you, is he pulling away, or is he giving you a full frontal hug?
- When you're talking, does he maintain eye contact with you? Is he able to look you in the eye and tell you that he loves you? That's a very big

sign of intimacy, and one of the first to go when someone feels guilty or is looking to leave a relationship.

- Are you in sync with him? Do you both sit or stand the same way while talking?

All these subtle cues can tell a story, but one of the biggest indicators of cheating is a change in appearance. If you notice your husband is suddenly taking much greater care of his appearance—for example, wearing cologne when he never wore it before—that would be legitimate cause for concern.

Try this: In the general course of conversation, ask him a few questions to which he'll readily know the answer, such as, "How was work today?" "Did that presentation go OK?" "What day is John's birthday again?" Let him answer at length, without interruption. After he's finished answering, in exactly the same tone of voice, say, "I noticed you started wearing cologne again. Why?" If he has nothing to hide, he'll be flattered that you noticed and probably smile or make a joke. If he's trying to conceal something, he will most likely be slightly startled, stumble over his response, or even get angry. In any case, you'll be able to sense a difference in the tone of the conversation from the first three questions, and that will give you your answer.

Q: My department at work includes people from several cultures: American, Vietnamese, Indian, Filipino, Irish, and Belgian. I sometimes have a hard time reading some of my colleagues, and I suspect the same is true for them. How can we handle this?

Lucky you! The opportunity to work with people of different cultures is rich with possibility, but I can understand that it can cause some confusion.

While many aspects of body language are culturally based—such as the use of interpersonal space and touch, and the use of certain gestures—many expressions of emotion—namely surprise, fear, anger, sadness, disgust, happiness, and contempt—are universal. Every human on earth has them, from the most remote villages to the most urbane city centers. While it might seem quite basic, acknowledging this elemental fact can profoundly affect your openness to and dealings with people from other cultures.

Unfortunately, the corporate culture in the United States rarely encourages raw expressions of emotion, so it's highly unlikely that you'll ever see true fear, disgust, or even happiness at work. And once we step away from those universals, cultural differences can sometimes come between us.

If all of the colleagues are peers—in other words, all on the same status rung at work—you might consider setting up opportunities to get together outside of work so you can get to know each other better. Away from the grind, with inhibitions down, people are more likely to share the details about their families and personal lives that will help you round out your pictures of them.

Studies show that the more contact an individual has with other cultures, the more open and less biased they become toward all cultures. In this case, the more you and your colleagues interact outside of work, the more likely you all will be to recognize each other as individuals and not representations of your cultures. And the closer you become as individuals, the better able you'll be to read their body language signals. You may even be able to start to distinguish which signals are cultural and which are individual—but, in my opinion, you'll never gain an honest understanding of the difference without first getting to know them as people.

Q: What does hypnosis feel like?

I get this question on almost a daily basis from clients. Most people believe that once hypnotized, they will enter into some zombie land, during which time the hypnotist will have complete and utter control over them. This is not the case. Hypnosis is a natural state that most of us enter into almost every day. Hypnosis can be used to create positive habits as well as alter negative habits. Hypnosis can help with everything from weight loss to fear of public speaking, from smoking to sleeping problems. The majority of the population is hypnotizable on some level; naturally, some individuals will go deeper into a trance than others. However, most change can occur at light levels.

Generally, hypnosis will start off with some progressive body relaxation to induce a calm, enjoyable state. Still, there are times when hypnosis is frustrating and tedious. One of the most interesting sessions I had was when a young lady came into my office because she could not remember the events of a specific night. Her fear was that she had been drugged and raped. Using a method known as hypnotic regression, we reexperienced the evening in question over and over, each time making the picture more complete, until breakthrough. Luckily, she came back to the room remembering the entire evening, and realizing nothing had happened. The session was emotional and utterly exhausting, but when she left she was brimming with relief.

One of the best ways for people to easily relate to hypnosis is to remember a time when they were driving from one place to another while in deep thought. Suddenly, they were at their destination with little or no memory of arriving there. During this "highway hypnosis," the mind gets divided between the task at hand—driving—and the deep thoughts the individual is contemplating—in other words, your subconscious mind is on autopilot as your conscious mind thinks about what happened at work or home today, or what you are going to cook for dinner. In this situation, a light hypnosis occurs naturally and is not dangerous. (Please never listen to a hypnotic CD in the car, as an intentionally induced trance could take you deeper and be dangerous while driving.)

If you have experienced this highway hypnosis phenomenon, you have actually experienced hypnosis. Usually, hypnosis will feel like a nice state of relaxation, perhaps that state between wakefulness and twilight sleep. First-time hypnotees usually return to the waking state and suggest they were not "under," only to be shocked to acknowledge the length of time that has passed. (Time distortion is a big telltale sign of hypnosis.) In general, think of hypnosis as a journey of relaxation.

Q: I'm fascinated by body language. How can I keep learning more?

Wonderful! I'm glad you share my fascination with this exciting field. Come visit me at www.BodyLanguageUniversity.com to learn more about all areas of nonverbal communication.

References

Aboyoun, D., and J. Dabbs. "Hess Pupil Dilation Findings: Sex or Novelty?" *Social Behavior and Personality* 26, no. 4 (1998).

Ali Aryan, H. "Tooth-Whitening Industry Opens Wide with Myriad Procedures and Products." *San Diego Union-Tribune,* March 15, 2005.

Allott, R. "Imitation in Language and Speech: Roles and Functional Base." In *Proceedings of the AISB Second International Symposium on Imitation in Animals and Artifacts*. Aberystwyth: University of Wales, 2003.

Arnold, C. "An Examination of the Role of Listening in Judgments of Communication Competence in Co-Workers." *Journal of Business Communication* 32, no. 2 (1995).

Asselta, C. "A Case Study of Two Computer Methods Used to Simulate Fires in Industrial Facilities." Washington, D.C.: Department of Energy, 1997. http://handle.dtic.mil/100.2/ADA341986.

Azar, B. "How Mimicry Begat Culture." *APA Monitor on Psychology* 36, no. 9 (2005).

Bailenson, J., J. Blascovich, A. Beall, and J. Loomis. "Equilibrium Theory Revisited: Mutual Gaze and Personal Space in Virtual Environments." *Presence* 10, no. 6 (2001).

Bear, M., B. Connors, and M. Paradiso. *Neuroscience: Exploring the Brain*. 2d. ed. Philadelphia: Lippincott, Williams & Wilkins, 2000.

Borenstein, E., and E. Ruppin. "The Evolution of Imitation and Mirror Neurons in Adaptive Agents." *Cognitive Systems Research* 6, no. 3 (2005).

Bos, E., A. Bouhys, E. Geerts, T. van Os, and J. Ormel. "Stressful Life Events as a Link between Problems in Nonverbal Communication and Recurrence of Depression." *Journal of Affective Disorders* 97, nos. 1–3 (2007).

Boucher, G. "May the Best, or Tallest, Man Win." *Los Angeles Times,* October 30, 2000.

Bowen, E., and J. Montepare. "Nonverbal Behavior in a Global Context: A Time for Dialogue." *Journal of Nonverbal Behavior* 31, no. 3 (2007).

Bowen, E., and S. Nowicki. "The Nonverbal Decoding Ability of Children Exposed to Family Violence or Maltreatment: Prospective Evidence from a British Cohort." *Journal of Nonverbal Behavior* 31, no. 3 (2007).

Briñol, P., and R. Petty. "Overt Head Movements and Persuasion: A Self-

Validation Analysis." *Journal of Personality and Social Psychology* 84, no. 6 (2003).

Bulwer, J. *Chirologia and Chironomia*. Carbondale: Southern Illinois University Press, 1974.

Burgoon, J., D. Buller, and W. Woodall. *Nonverbal Communication*. New York: Harper & Row, 1989.

Burgoon, J., L. Stern, and L. Dillman. *Interpersonal Adaptation*. New York: Cambridge University Press, 1995.

Calrton Abrams, D. "The Making of a Modern Dad: It Takes a Lot More than Testosterone to Make a Father Out of a Man." *Psychology Today*, May 24, 2005, psychologytoday.com/articles/pto-20020301=000025.html.

Canary, D., and K. Dindia, eds. *Sex Differences and Similarities in Communication*. Mahwah, N.J.: Lawrence Erlbaum Associates, 1998.

Case, A., and C. Paxson. "Stature and Status: Height, Ability, and Labor Market Outcomes." NBER Working Papers 12466, National Bureau of Economic Research, 2006.

Chaplin, W., J. Phillips, J. Brown, N. Clanton, and J. Stein. "Handshaking, Gender, Personality, and First Impressions." *Journal of Personality and Social Psychology* 79, no. 1 (2000).

Chattopadhyay, A., D. Dahl, R. Ritchie, and K. Shahin. "Hearing Voices: The Impact of Announcer Speech Characteristics on Consumer Response to Broadcast Advertising." *Journal of Consumer Psychology* 13, no. 3 (2003).

Chipman, K., and E. Hampson. "A Female Advantage in the Serial Production of Non-Representational Learned Gestures." *Neuropsychologia* 44, no. 12 (2006).

Coan, J., H. Schaefer, and R. Davidson. "Lending a Hand: Social Regulation of the Neural Response to Threat." *Psychological Science* 17, no. 12 (2006).

Cook-Euell, V. "Size—The Other Diversity." *Mosaics: SHRM Focuses on Workplace Diversity* 10, no. 3 (2004).

Cornwell, J. "The Face of Things to Come." *Sunday Times* (London), December 11, 2005.

Dapretto, M., M. Davies, J. Pfeifer, A. Scott, M. Sigman, S. Bookheimer, and M. Iacoboni. "Understanding Emotions in Others: Mirror Neuron Dysfunction in Children with Autism Spectrum Disorders." *Nature Neuroscience*, no. 9 (2006).

Darwin, C. *The Expression of the Emotions in Man and Animals*. Edited by Paul Ekman. 3d ed. New York: Oxford University Press, 1998.

Davenport, C. "Strength in Numbers: Clubs for Tall People." *Washington Post*, June 27, 2000.

Davis M., K. Markus, and S. Walters. "Judging the Credibility of Criminal Suspect Statements: Does Mode of Presentation Matter?" *Journal of Nonverbal Behavior* 30, no. 4 (2006).

de Waal, F. *Our Inner Ape*. New York: Riverhead/Penguin, 2005.

Dellinger, K., and C. Williams. "Makeup at Work: Negotiating Appearance Rules in the Workplace." *Gender and Society* 11, no. 2 (1997).

Diego, M. A., et. al. "Aggressive Adolescents Benefit from Massage Therapy." *Adolescence* 37 (2002).

Dimberg, U., M. Thunberg, and K. Elmehed. "Unconscious Facial Reactions to Emotional Facial Expressions." *Psychological Science* 11, no. 1 (2000).

Dimitrius, J., and M. Mazzarella. *Reading People*. New York: Random House, 1998.

Druckman, D., R. Rozelle, and J. Baxter. *Nonverbal Communication*. Calif.: Beverly Hills, (1982).

Ekman, P. *Emotions Revealed*. 2d ed. New York: Henry Holt, 2007.

______. "A Few Can Catch a Liar." *Psychological Science* 10, no. 3 (1999).

Ekman, P., and W. Friesen. *Unmasking the Face: A Guide to Recognizing Emotions from Facial Expressions*. Cambridge: Malor Books, 2003.

Ekman, P., and M. O'Sullivan. "Who Can Catch a Liar?" *American Psychologist* 46, no. 9 (1991).

Estrada C., S. Patel, G. Talente, and S. Kraemer. "The 10-Minute Oral Presentation: What Should I Focus On?" *American Journal of the Medical Sciences* 329, no. 6 (2005).

"Facial Analysis." Department of Otolaryngology, University of Texas Medical Branch, Galveston, 1997. http://www.utmb.edu/otoref/grnds/facial 2.html.

Feldman, R., J. Tomasian, and E. Coats. "Nonverbal Deception Abilities and Adolescents' Social Competence: Adolescents with Higher Social Skills are Better Liars." *Journal of Nonverbal Behavior* 23, no. 4 (1999).

Feldman, R. S., J. A. Forrest, and B. R. Happ. "Self-Presentation and Verbal Deception: Do Self-Presenters Lie More?" *Basic and Applied Social Psychology* 24, no. 2 (2002).

Field, T. "American Adolescents Touch Each Other Less and Are More Aggressive Toward Their Peers as Compared with French Adolescents." *Adolescence* 34, no. 136 (1999).

Field, T., N. Grizzle, F. Scafidi, and S. Schanberg. "Massage and Relaxation Therapies' Effects on Depressed Adolescent Mothers." *Adolescence* 31 (1996).

Finzi, E., and E. Wasserman. "Treatment of Depression with Botulinum Toxin A: A Case Series." *Dermatological Surgery* 32, no. 5 (2006).

Fisman, R., S. Iyengar, E. Kamenica, and I. Simonson. "Gender Differences in Mate Selection: Evidence from a Speed Dating Experiment." *Quarterly Journal of Economics* 121, no. 2 (2006).

Foreman, J. "A Conversation with Paul Ekman: The 43 Facial Muscles that Reveal Even the Most Fleeting Emotions." *New York Times*, August 5, 2003.

Franken, S. "Read My Mood: In Business World, Much of What's Said and Heard is Never Spoken." *Pittsburgh Post-Gazette*, March 11, 2001.

Gallese, V. "Intentional Attunement: A Neurophysiological Perspective on Social Cognition and Its Disruption in Autism." *Brain Research* 1079, no. 1 (2006).

———. "Intentional Attunement: The Mirror Neuron System and Its Role in Interpersonal Relations." *Interdisciplines*, 2007, www.interdisciplines.org/mirror/papers/1.

Geen, T., and L. Tassinary. "The Mechanization of Emotional Expression in John Bulwer's 'Pathomyotomia' (1649)." *American Journal of Psychology* 115, no. 2 (2002).

Givens, D. *The Nonverbal Dictionary of Gestures, Signs, and Body Language Cues*. Spokane, Wash.: Center for Nonverbal Studies Press, 2006.

Gladwell, M. *Blink*. New York: Little, Brown, 2005.

———. "What the Dog Saw." *New Yorker*, May 22, 2006.

Glasgow, G. "A Semantic Index of Vocal Pitch." *Speech Monographs* 19 (1952).

Goldberg, C. "We Feel Your Pain . . . and Your Happiness, Too: The Human Brain's Source of Empathy May Also Play a Role in Autism." *Boston Globe*, December 12, 2005.

Goldin-Meadow, S., Wagner. "How our hands help us learn," *Trends in Cognitive Science*, Vol. 9, No. 5 (2005).

Goleman, D. *Emotional Intelligence*. New York: Bantam, 1995.

———. *Social Intelligence*. New York: Bantam, 2006.

Goodman, W. *The Invisible Woman: Confronting Weight Predjudice in America*. Carlsbad, Calif.: Gurze Books, 1995.

Gopnik, A., A. Meltzoff, and P. Kuhl. *The Scientist in the Crib*. New York: Morrow, 1999.

Goren-Inbar, N., et al. "Evidence of Hominid Control of Fire at Gesher Benot Ya'acov, Israel." *Science* 304 (2004).

Gortmaker, S., A. Must, J. Perrin, A. Sobol, and W. Dietz. "Social and Economic Consequences of Overweight in Adolescence and Young Adulthood." *New England Journal of Medicine* 329, no. 14 (1993).

Grandin, T., and C. Johnson. *Animals in Translation*. New York: Scribner, 2005.

Gunns, R., L. Johnston, and S. Hudson. "Victim Selection and Kinematics: A Point-Light Investigation of Vulnerability to Attack." *Journal of Nonverbal Behavior* 26, no. 3 (2002).

Hall, J. *Nonverbal Sex Difference*. Baltimore: Johns Hopkins University Press, 1984.

Hernandez-Reif, M., T. Field, and H. Theakston. "Multiple Sclerosis Patients Benefit from Massage Therapy." *Journal of Bodywork and Movement Therapies* 2 (1998).

Hirsch, A., and C. Wolf. "Practical Methods for Detecting Mendacity: A Case Study." *Journal of the American Academy of Psychiatry Law* 29, no. 4 (2001).

Hogan, K. *The Science of Influence*. Hoboken, New Jersey: Wiley, 2005.

"How to Spot a Liar." *Time*, August 28, 2006.

Iacoboni, M., I. Molnar-Szakacs, V. Gallese, G. Buccino, J. Mazziotta, et al. "Grasping the Intentions of Others with One's Own Mirror Neuron System." *PLoS Biology* 3, no. 3 (2005).

"Imaging Study Provides Further Clues about Autism." Press release, University of California, Los Angeles, April 30, 2007.

Indersmitten, T., and R. Gur. "Emotion Processing in Chimeric Faces: Hemispheric Asymmetries in Expression and Recognition of Emotions." *Journal of Neuroscience* 23, no. 9 (2003).

Jabbi, M., M. Swart, and C. Keysers. "Empathy for Positive and Negative Emotions in the Gustatory Cortex." *Neuroimage* 34, no. 4 (2007).

Judge, T., and D. Cable. "The Effect of Physical Height on Workplace Success and Income: Preliminary Test of a Theoretical Model." *Journal of Applied Psychology* 89, no. 3 (2004).

Jung, V., R. Short, N. Letourneau, and D. Andrews. "Interventions with Depressed Mothers and Their Infants: Modifying Interactive Behaviours?" *Journal of Affective Disorders* 98, no. 3 (2007).

Keysers, C., and V. Gazzola. "Towards a Unifying Neural Theory of Social Cognition." *Progress in Brain Research* 156 (2006).

Kimbrough Oller, D., U. Griebel, and K. Plunkett, eds. "Laughter Beyond Our Grasp: What Mirror Neurons Can, and Cannot, Do for Language

Evolution." *Evolution of Communication Systems: A Comparative Approach*. The Vienna Series in Theoretical Biology. Cambridge, Mass.: MIT Press, 2002.

Kita, S. "Pointing: A Foundational Building Block." In *Pointing*. Mahwah, N.J.: Lawrence Erlbaum, 2003.

Knapp, M. L., and J. A. Hall. *Nonverbal Communication in Human Interaction*. 5th ed. Forth Worth, Tex.: Harcourt Brace Jovanovich, 2002.

Knöfler, T., and M. Imhof. "Does Sexual Orientation Have an Impact on Nonverbal Behavior in Interpersonal Communication?" *Journal of Nonverbal Behavior* 31, no. 3 (2007).

Krumhuber, E., A. Manstead, and A. Kappas. "Temporal Aspects of Facial Displays in Person and Expression Perception: The Effects of Smile Dynamics, Head-tilt, and Gender." *Journal of Nonverbal Behavior* 31, no. 1 (2007).

Kuczynski, A. "New York Drops Its Game Face." *New York Times*, September 16, 2001.

Kyle, D., I. Heike, and M. Mahler. "The Effects of Hair Color and Cosmetic Use on Perceptions of a Female's Ability." *Psychology of Women Quarterly* 20, no. 3 (1996).

LaBarbera, P., and J. MacLachlan. "Time Compressed Speech in Radio Advertising." *Journal of Marketing* 16 (1979).

Lahav, A., E. Saltzman, and G. Schlaug. "Action Representation of Sound: Audiomotor Recognition Network While Listening to Newly Acquired Actions." *Journal of Neuroscience* 27, no. 2 (2007).

Leathers, D. G. *Successful Nonverbal Communication: Principles and Applications*. 3d ed. Needham Heights, Mass.: Allyn and Bacon, 1997.

Legato, M. *Why Men Never Remember and Women Never Forget*. Emmaus, Pa.: Rodale, 2005.

Levine, J., and J. Larkworthy. *Smile! The Ultimate Guide to Achieving Smile Beauty*. New York: Warner Wellness Central, 2006.

Lomax, C. "Proxemics in Public: Space Violations as a Function of Dyad Composition." Paper presented at the meeting of the Southeastern Psychological Association, New Orleans, 1994.

Lykken, D. "Happiness: The Nature and Nurture of Joy and Contentment." *Journal of Happiness Studies* 2, no. 3 (2001).

Mangan, K. "Horse Sense or Nonsense? Critics Decry What They Consider the 'Softening' of Medical Education." *Chronicle of Higher Education*, July 5, 2002.

McClish, M. *I Know You Are Lying*. Winterville, N.C.: Policeemployment .com, 2001.

McCroskey, J. "The Role of Culture in a Communibiological Approach to Communication." Presentation to Pacific and Asian Communication Association, 2000.

McCroskey, J., T. Young, and V. Richmond. "A Simulation Methodology for Proxemic Research." *Sign Language Studies*, no. 17 (1977).

McKay, M., M. Davis, and P. Fanning. *Messages: The Communication Skills Book*. 2d ed. Oakland, Calif.: New Harbinger, 1995.

McNeill, D. *Gesture and Thought*. Chicago: University of Chicago Press, 2005.

______. *The Face*. Boston: Little, Brown, 1998.

McNeill, D., B. Bertenthál, J. Cole, and S. Gallagher. "Gesture-First, but No Gestures? Commentary on Michael A. Arbib." *Behavioral and Brain Sciences* 28 (2005).

Meltzoff, A. "Like Me: A Foundation for Social Cognition." *Developmental Science* 10, no. 1 (2007).

Morris, D. *Body Talk*. New York: Crown, 1994.

Morris, D., P. Collett, P. Marsh, and M. O'Shaughnessy. *Gestures*. New York: Stein and Day, 1979.

Morris, D. *Manwatching*. New York: Harry N. Abrams, 1977.

Mullen, B., et al. "Newscasters' Facial Expressions and Voting Behavior of Viewers: Can a Smile Elect a President?" *Journal of Personality and Social Psychology* 51, no. 2 (1986).

Mulvaney, B. "Gender Differences in Communication: An Intercultural Experience." Department of Communication, Florida Atlantic University, Boca Raton, 1994.

Murphy S., and R. Zajonc. "Affect, Cognition, and Awareness: Affective Priming with Optimal and Suboptimal Stimulus Exposures." *Journal of Personality and Social Psychology* 64, no. 5 (1993).

"Muscle Movements: Research into Tiny Muscle Movements Proves Useful in Anti-Terror Investigations." *Patient Care Law Weekly*, June 4, 2006.

Nazareno, A. "Body Language Can Send Crucial, Lasting Signals about You." *San Antonio Express-News*, July 3, 2004.

O'Sullivan, M. "The Fundamental Attribution Error in Detecting Deception: The Boy-Who-Cried-Wolf Effect." *Personality and Social Psychology Bulletin* 29, no. 10 (2003).

Ogilvie, M., and P. Kristensen-Bach. "Why Women Wear Lipstick: Preliminary Findings." *Marketing Update: News from the Australian Marketing Institute* (Edith Cowan University) 2002.

Patterson, M., Y. Iizuka, M. Tubbs, J. Ansel, M. Tsutsumi, and J. Anson. "Passing Encounters East and West: Comparing Japanese and American Pedestrian Interactions." *Journal of Nonverbal Behavior* 31, no. 3 (2007).

Persico, N., A. Postlewaite, and D. Silverman. "The Effect of Adolescent Experience on Labor Market Outcomes: The Case of Height." *Journal of Political Economy* 112, no. 5 (2004).

Pischedda, A., and A. Chippindale. "Intralocus Sexual Conflict Diminishes the Benefits of Sexual Selection." *PLoS Biology* 4, no. 11 (2006).

"Psychoanalysis: In Search of Its Soul." *Time*, March 7, 1969.

Richardson, H. "Kangaroo Care: Why Does It Work?" *Midwifery Today*, no. 44 (1997).

Ridley, M. *Nature Via Nurture: Genes, Experience, and What Makes Us Human*. New York: HarperCollins, 2003.

Roe, D., and K. Eickwort. "Relationships between Obesity and Associated Health Factors with Unemployment among Low Income Women." *Journal of the American Medical Women's Association* 31 (1976).

Schwartz, J. "Obesity Affects Economic, Social Status; Women Fare Worse." *Washington Post*, September 30, 1993.

Shibley Hyde, J. "The Gender Similarities Hypothesis." *American Psychologist* 60, no. 6 (2005).

Singh, D. "Adaptive Significance of Female Physical Attractiveness: Role of Waist-to-Hip Ratio." *Journal of Personality and Social Psychology* 65, no. 2 (1993).

Sprenger, M. *Learning and Memory: The Brain in Action.* Alexandria, Va.: Association for Education and Curriculum Development, 1999.

Tombs, S., and I. Silverman. "Pupillometry." *Evolution and Human Behavior* 25, no. 4 (2004).

Toth, E. "Does Your Voice Make them Scream?" *Chronicle of Higher Education*, July 14, 2003.

van Boven, S. "In the Blink of an Eye." *Newsweek*, October 21, 1996.

Voros, S. "Weight Discrimination Runs Rampant in Hiring." Career Journal, *Wall Street Journal Online*, http://careerjournal.com/myc/climbingladder/20000905=voros.html.

Vrij, A., K. Edward, K. Roberts, and R. Bull. "Detecting Deceit via Analysis of Verbal and Nonverbal Behavior." *Journal of Nonverbal Behavior* 24, no. 4 (2000).

Walker, R. "A Whiter Shade of Pale." *Scotland on Sunday*, April 8, 2007.

Warren, J., D. Sauter, F. Eisner, J. Wiland, M. Dresner, R. Wise, S. Rosen, and S. Scott. "Positive Emotions Preferentially Engage an Auditory-Motor 'Mirror' System." *Journal of Neuroscience* 26, no. 50 (2006).

Wilkinson L., A. Scholey, and K. Wesnes. "Chewing Gum Selectively Improves Aspects of Memory in Healthy Volunteers." *Appetite*, no. 38 (2002).

Willis, J., and A. Todoroy. "First Impressions: Making Up Your Mind After a 100-Ms Exposure to a Face." *Psychological Science* 17, no. 7 (2006).

Winkielman, P., J. Halberstadt, T. Fazendeiro, and S. Catty. "Prototypes Are Attractive Because They Are Easy on the Mind." *Psychological Science* 17, no. 9 (2006).

Wrench, J., M. Corrigan, J. McCroskey, and N. Punyanunt-Carter. "Religious Fundamentalism and Intercultural Communication: The Relationships among Ethnocentrism, Intercultural Communication Apprehension, Religious Fundamentalism, Homonegativity, and Tolerance for Religious Disagreements." *Journal of Intercultural Communication Research* 35, no. 1 (2006).

Yamamoto, K., and N. Suzuki. "The Effects of Social Interaction and Personal Relationships on Facial Expressions." *Journal of Nonverbal Behavior* 30, no. 4 (2006).

Yin Loke, K. "Consequences of Childhood and Adolescent Obesity." *Asia Pacific Journal of Clinical Nutrition* 11, no. 3 (2002).

Photo Credits

Page 26: *left:* Photo by Joel Sartore/National Geographic/Getty Images; *center*: Photo by Christopher Furlong/Getty Images; *right:* Photo by Express newspapers/Getty Images

Page 34: Courtesy of author

Page 45: Photo by Mark Mainz/Getty Images

Page 46: Photo by Hulton Archive/Getty Images

Page 47: Photo by Paul J. Richards/AFP/Getty Images

Page 48: Photo by Peter Beavis/Taxi/Getty Images

Page 48: Photo by George Marks/Retrofile/Getty Images

Page 49: Photo by Spencer Platt/Getty Images

Page 50: Photo by Manny Ceneta/Getty Images

Page 60: Photo by Hussein Anwar/Sipa

Page 63: ©NBC/Courtesy: Everett Collection

Page 64: *left:* Photo by Silver Screen Collection/Hulton Archive/Getty Images; *right:* Photo by Hulton Archive/Getty Images

Page 74: Photo by Mark Wilson/Getty Images

Page 82: Photo by Giulio Marcocchi/Reportage Getty Images

Page 105: Photo by Vince Bucci/Getty Images

Page 126: Courtesy of Bill O'Reilly

Page 130: Photo by Robert Giroux/AFP/Getty Images

Page 132: Courtesy of the author

Page 134: Photo by Carlos Alvarez/Getty Images

Page 162: Courtesy of Bill O'Reilly

Index

Page numbers in *italics* refer to illustrations.